DOGMA ➤ *Volume 1: God in Revelation*

A PROJECT OF JOHN XXIII INSTITUTE
Saint Xavier College, Chicago
Under the theological supervision of T. Patrick Burke

DOGMA
by Michael Schmaus

1 *God in Revelation*

SHEED AND WARD : NEW YORK

© Sheed and Ward, Inc., 1968

Library of Congress Catalog Card Number 68-26033

Nihil Obstat, Leo J. Steady, Ph.D., S.T.D., Censor Librorum; Imprimatur, +Robert F. Joyce, Bishop of Burlington; August 2, 1968. The Nihil Obstat and Imprimatur are official declarations that a book or pamphlet is considered to be free of doctrinal or moral error. No implication is contained therein that those who have granted the Nihil Obstat and the Imprimatur agree with the contents, opinions or statements expressed.

Manufactured in the United States of America

Foreword

The present work was written over a period of more than a year at the John XXIII Institute, Saint Xavier College, Chicago. I would like to express my heartfelt gratitude to the college and its entire faculty, especially the President, Sister Mary Olivia, R.S.M., and the Dean, Sister Mary Silveria, R.S.M., and the Director of the Institute, Miss Claudette Dwyer. I am also indebted to the translators, who have worked with knowledge and dedication to get the German text into a form more adapted to American ways of thought.

Particular thanks must go to Dr. Patrick Burke. He provided valuable stimulus for the work and made many useful suggestions; and he has undertaken the final revision of the American edition. He has gone to exceptional pains with it and has brought valued understanding to it.

To avoid any misunderstanding, I would like to stress that this work is not at all a summary or revision of my older German text (*Katholische Dogmatik*), but a completely new treatment of theology based on the developments which have taken place as a result of the Second Vatican Council.

MICHAEL SCHMAUS

Contents

Preface

This volume and the ones which will follow it are intended as an attempt to present and interpret the faith of the Catholic Church in a fashion intelligible to modern man. This aim is based on a presupposition: that the mind of modern man works with different concepts, images, and attitudes—with another understanding of being and a different feeling for life—from that which characterized earlier ages. As a result, certain ideas which formerly were self-evident and seemed important and significant are now either inaccessible or hardly accessible to the contemporary mind: they seem obsolete and outworn, remote from life and from the world. If we do not advert to this transformation, neither our preaching nor our theology will be effective where they must be effective if they are to have any point—namely, with modern man. Taking the situation of the times into account does not mean subordinating the Christian faith to the wishes and demands of the present. It simply means presenting the faith within those horizons and perspectives in which our age is running its course.

God's word, which we make our own through faith, is always expressed in a particular form at a particular time, although its inner core never changes. It is not bound up with any one idea of the world or any specific cultural situation: salvation through Christ has been promised to all men, whatever their understanding of the world or their type of culture. Modern man, like the

men of all other ages, is meant to discover through experience
that the Christian faith does not deprive him of any of the reality
of life. Not only does it not burden or repress him—although
certain elements of the faith may seem like a burden to him—but,
on the contrary, his life is deepened, expanded, and purified by
it. Faith opens new vistas, guarantees an absolute meaning to
life and endows it with a new dynamism. Thus the purpose of
this work is to liberate the reader from any distrust and discom-
fort he might feel in the face of Christianity, to make it possible
for him to approach it with openness and joy. It must be made
clear that faith is not a diversion for expelling boredom, not
something for those who attach their hopes to the hereafter
because they do not know what to do with their lives on earth.

This undertaking implies that nothing of the old faith shall be
eliminated, nor anything added; it shall be presented unabridged
and unfalsified. It is of special importance that the faith should
be presented not only as a phenomenon of a distant past with
simple cultural and social structures, but as a phenomenon which
is a power in the present and full of promise for the future. Only
such a presentation can evoke and clarify the questions for
which, consciously or unconsciously, modern man demands an
answer. The work is also intended to help contemporary man to
reach a clearer and more profound understanding of himself,
and to show him the fact of salvation which God has revealed
and the path to it. At the same time an attempt will be made to
discover solutions for the basic problems that beset him. The aim
of the work thus corresponds to the spirit of the Second Vatican
Council and of Popes John XXIII and Paul VI, for the statements of the council and of the popes urge repeatedly that the
Church shall be presented to modern man in a way that is accessible to him. The procedure presupposes, of course, the
distinction between what is changeable and what is unchangeable
—one which is by no means simple to make. It requires a deep
insight into the nature of the faith.

The point of these considerations is not to claim that the
following work is the only way to pursue the study of theology.
The faith is certainly a unity, and a unique unity, because there

is only one God and one Christ. But there are many theologies, as is shown by the variety of theological schools and the diversity of viewpoints among the greatest teachers of theology. The author of this work would be guilty of conceit if he considered his kind of theology as the only correct one. Others see other things and in a different way. Only a variety of theological melodies can result in theological harmony.

The following attempt is being undertaken on the basis of the present state of theological research and especially on the basis of present exegesis. In this field of knowledge, as in theology as a whole, there are still many open questions, and some problems will probably always resist solution. Unclarified questions will be mentioned as such in this work; they will not, we hope, be answered precipitately or with excessive confidence. This would contradict the absolute truthfulness and intellectual honesty which is rightly demanded by the Church and by theology itself.

It is anticipated that the principal readers of the work will be priests and students of theology. By students of theology I understand both those who are preparing for the priesthood and those who as laymen aspire to a theological education. But the work is also intended to serve the interests of broader circles. It would give the author special satisfaction if the book should prove to be of any use to teachers of theology in the performance of their difficult task according to the needs of our time. In all the statements made, it will be the author's aim to keep in mind non-Catholic Christians and non-Christians. In the spirit of the ecumenical movement, the book is intended to be of service to that form of encounter which is dialogue. This is true even of those parts of the text where that intention may not be obvious Readers familiar with the problems in the area will realize from our formulations that a dialogue is being carried on here with Protestant theology and with atheist humanism. There can be no question of sterile polemics or apologetics; rather, it is a question of elaborating what is problematic and what is common ground and indicating what separates. Indeed we must make it clear from the outset that in our time the lines of demarcation are no longer as distinct as they formerly appeared; in fact, they not infrequently become blurred, though they have not disappeared.

The scope of the work necessitates the elimination of certain material which would be worth treating but which would increase the size of the volumes without being indispensable for the understanding of the faith. The treatment of other questions, unfortunately, must be condensed to so few words that we run the risk that the significance of what is said may be overlooked.

The work departs from the usual arrangement of textbooks of dogmatic theology. Customarily these are organized in the following way: after a short introduction to the concept of dogmatic theology, there follows a presentation of God as One and as Three in One, analysis of the doctrine of creation, interpretation of Christ and his work (frequently ecclesiology is treated here), the doctrine of grace, the doctrine of the sacraments, and finally the doctrine of the last things. (No doubt there are always differences in detail.)

This arrangement presupposes a definite view of theology: a theology of concept or of essence. It asks and states, or tries to state, what God is, what Jesus Christ is, what man is, what grace is, what the sacraments are, and so on. This method has its origin in the way of thinking which took root in the West through Greek philosophy. It may be termed ontological thinking. The question of action or function is certainly posed, but it is secondary in importance. This theology serves a legitimate and important concern. Its greatest representative is Thomas Aquinas. It has produced great achievements. It is concerned with truth in the first place; in the second, with man. It looks not for the place of truth in life, but for truth itself.

There is another type of theology which may be called realistic or existential. Its first question concerns action or function. It interprets divine truth primarily not in its being but in its relationship to man. Naturally it does not by-pass the question of truth, but its main concern is to investigate it and to describe its place in life. This theology is closely related to the way in which Sacred Scripture itself bears witness to divine revelation. Its great representatives are Augustine, Bonaventure, Newman.

This second kind of theology requires a different plan of treatment—namely, one which focuses its attention on man as the receiver of divine revelation. Divine revelation and human faith will be presented here primarily as the saving encounter between God and man. God reveals himself in history as man's helper and savior, even as his Salvation itself; and it is in this gift of himself that he addresses man as a free being and opens to him an "absolute future." The doctrine of the Savior—that is, of Jesus who is the Christ—flows from this conception of the Word of God. We study the actions and the teachings of Christ; finally we investigate his being, which makes his teachings and actions intelligible. The study of the nature of Christ implicitly contains the doctrine of the Trinity. In such a framework the revelation concerning God and creation is treated as preparation for the Christ-event. The section on Christology gives rise to the question about the way in which each human generation encounters Christ until the end of time. This is the question of the Church as the community of salvation which lives through Christ. Finally, after a discussion of the problem of the individual person (Theological Anthropology) the work ends with a brief treatment of man's absolute future.

The reader will not find any separate formal treatment of the sacraments. They are treated either in the sections on ecclesiology or in theological anthropology, according to the roles they play in human life. The Eucharist appears as the central event and reality in the life of the Church. Baptism and Confirmation are explained as signs of divine acceptance, effective of salvation. Holy Orders is understood as a differentiating symbol of salvation within the people of God. The sacrament of Penance is discussed here as the sacramental sign of the ongoing self-reformation and renewal of the Church; later it is treated under another aspect in the section on theological anthropology. The Sacrament of Matrimony is understood as that encounter with Christ within the Church in which two people of different sexes give themselves to each other in order to achieve unity and guarantee the biological existence of the world and the church. The Anointing of the Sick is explained in Theological Anthropology as that sign of salvation through which those who believe in Christ enter into a special communion with the crucified Lord. All the sacraments are looked upon as articulations and actualizations of the one fundamental, universal sacrament, which is the Church. Problems concerning the "sacraments in general" will be treated in the section entitled "The Church as Fundamental Sacrament."

The material therefore organizes itself conveniently into six parts: I, God in Revelation; II, God and Creation; III, Jesus Christ; IV, The Church; V, Christian Anthropology; VI, The Ultimate Realities. Certain questions merely alluded to in "God in Revelation" are given more detailed treatment in one of the later sections.

The names of those theologians whose works benefited this book in a special way are listed in the bibliography.

DOGMA ➤ *Volume 1: God in Revelation*

I

Theology
for the Contemporary World
and the Possibilities
of Divine Self-Revelation

1

Theology
for the Contemporary World
and the Possibilities
of Divine Self-Revelation

◄ 1

Theology for Modern Man

MODERN MAN

Divine revelation as proclaimed in the Church is a salvific dialogue between God and humanity, the offer of salvation made by a free God to a free man. This dialogue of salvation aims at the divinization of man and indeed of the entire creation. All the substantive statements in this work have as their object the manifestation of that revelation, in which all things particular, individual, and isolated are gathered up into one final, conclusive unity.

Therefore, we must first make several statements about modern man. Let us emphasize from the outset that modern man as such—that is, a being who embodies in himself all the characteristics of modern life—does not exist. Nevertheless it is possible to speak of modern man in the sense that men today have in common an intellectual horizon which is peculiar to our time, a horizon within which they live out their lives, pursue their goals, and develop their conceptual expressions.

It is possible to list the following characteristics of modern men:

(1) The movement towards the union of all men and all nations in the oneness of the human community. This includes the notions of a common destiny and mutual responsibility.

(2) Dedication to the world in its secularity. This means that the world is demythologized and denumenized. It is understood

5

solely in terms of itself, and no longer in terms of God. The world is nothing but world, with no extramundane background. It is filled exclusively with itself (J. Metz).

(3) The creative transformation of the world and of man himself. Modern man regards the world not as a complete and finished reality, but as material given to him to transform and to rebuild. Science and technology furnish the means for this process. Since the world is being brought more and more under man's domination, it is becoming a hominized world. For the sake of clarity, let us observe that the term hominization means something quite different from humanization. Hominization implies that the world is a creation of man. The man who relies on science and technology is convinced that only now, after billions of years of evolution, is the world leaving its nursery and coming of age, aided by the findings of physics, astrophysics, biology, and other branches of science. The world self is creating itself. The human ego is enthralled by the future.

(4) It is of special significance that man hopes he can make himself also the object of his creative transformation. He aspires to the formation of a new man, a superman, for whom suffering, death, and disaster are eliminated, or at least lose their sting. Medicine, depth psychology, and chemistry open up hitherto unimagined vistas of the future. From such a point of view, man as he is today looks like a first rough draft of the true, authentic man to come. The man of the present exists as the hope of himself. Automatization, cybernetics, and sociology feed man's expectations of a general situation to come in which all men will be able to live in freedom and happiness, where evil in all its forms will be abolished. According to this view man as an individual and as a member of the community is only on his way to himself within the universe as a whole. The world is not, as classical physics saw it, a finished network of causes and effects; rather it is open-ended, moving forwards towards its true existence.

(5) Certain virtues are proper to man as he tries to realize such a future; namely, a spirit of enterprise, inventiveness, initiative, courage, tolerance, altruism, fellowship, and the willingness for sacrifice. These are active virtues. Secular man actively takes a

risk in thrusting himself forward into the universe, and in certain circumstances he is quite willing to sacrifice his life for another person, to give up his personal present in favor of the greater future.

(6) Weariness, irritation, and even hostility towards God are other characteristic elements in our hominized world. God does not manifest himself; he cannot be found there. If there were a God in the world, he would simply be a hindrance to it. God does not involve himself in a world created by man. He neither speaks nor acts; he is not seen; he is not heard. Modern man, on his side, generally has no use for God. He does not need him. Indeed, it often seems as if he had no capacity for God. The dictum of Augustine that man's heart is restless until it finds rest in God, Pascal's observation that man transcends himself infinitely—these seem to have no meaning now, or at best a very limited validity. If God did exist in our hominized world, it would be as an enemy of man and his freedom, one to be fought against. The humanism to which our hominized world aspires will therefore be a God-free, even a Godless, humanism, and as such inimical to God.

Ideas like these are not making their initial appearance in our time; they have a long history. Nineteenth-century philosophies like those of Feuerbach and Marx still have an explosive power in our day, and for such thinkers God is but an obstacle in the individual and social life of man; he is at best superfluous.

In their fully developed form these attitudes have no place in the life of a believer, but as a challenge or a temptation they play a part even in his life. Theology therefore must take note of these currents of thought not only for the sake of nonbelievers but also to assist the believer. On the other hand, of course, it is not always easy to determine who the nonbeliever, the atheist, really is. Is it simply the man who calls himself an atheist and considers himself to be one? Can we be certain that a man who calls himself a believer is not in reality an atheist? Or are attitudes the decisive factor—the love of one's neighbor, the readiness to help and to sacrifice? That is, is the criterion not a mere matter of formulas, but rather one of existential behavior? May we not say that the true atheist is only that man who never places himself unconditionally at the disposal of another person, who refuses in principle to give concrete expression to the love of his neighbor? Conversely, is not the believer the man who is ready to help his fellow-man unconditionally, even to the point of sacrificing his own life? We cannot overlook the fact that all earthly love is an expression of the love of God.

THE CHURCH AND MODERN MAN

Modern atheistic or anti-theistic humanism has many roots. The Church has often been held responsible for the contemporary phenomenon of secularization. It has been reproached for the fact that the world was not taken seriously and not enough scope was given to science and human knowledge. Such a reproach is not completely unjustified. It is true that Thomas Aquinas affirmed the autonomy of secular disciplines, but his thesis had no immediate effect. At the beginning of the modern era, with the case of Galileo, the gap between the Church and the sciences became fatefully obvious. Since that time tension between the two has grown, with the Church moving farther and farther from the world, and the sciences farther and farther from the Church. In the nineteenth century new problems of a social, political, and cultural nature were added to those presented by the sciences. A summary of the severe criticism which the Church in its turn leveled against certain phenomena of the modern period is contained in the 1864 *Syllabus* of Pope Pius IX. These strictures can be understood in the light of the historical situation of that time, for the genuine progressive advances of the era were so closely bound up with anti-ecclesiastical forms that their real nature was obscured. This is true in particular of human freedom—to mention but one example. Since the situation has changed essentially, there is no reason now for the Church to uphold the condemnations of that era. For the cultural, moral, and political values which are particularly close to the heart of modern man have in the meantime been liberated from their anti-ecclesiastical matrix and are now clearly seen in their own inherent significance. We shall return to this point in more detail later. But it must be admitted that the tension between the Church and the world was aggravated for a long time by the *Syllabus*.

Furthermore, men of the modern era have tended to reproach the Church for its one-sided cultivation of the so-called passive virtues such as humility and obedience. Corresponding with this was an exaggerated stress on the afterlife. God was experienced not as a mystery in the world but as a being above and beyond the world; his immanence was overshadowed by his transcendence. Not infrequently this was linked with the notion of a God localized somewhere outside the world—an idea which was not sufficiently criticized in preaching. Heaven understood in this transcendent way was seen as man's goal; the world was viewed only as a stage on which the actors prepared for eternal life, as a springboard to heaven. The world's own values were recognized either insufficiently or not at all. The relative autonomy of a dynamic world never emerged from such conceptions and provided no challenge to human powers.

Preaching of this kind is certainly understandable, because the question of eternal salvation is the Church's primary concern. Such sermons were even, in the beginning, considered indispensable if men were gradually to be freed from their attachment to this world and if the eschatological life, which differs so radically from earthly life, were to be allowed to penetrate more deeply and powerfully into human consciousness. But this kind of proclamation was bound to seem one-sided and incomplete as soon as it had accomplished what it set out to do. What was neglected in this view was that salvation is attained not beyond or outside the pattern of this world but in and through it.

For a long time now preaching in the Church has been dominated, or at least menaced, by a spiritualism which made it seem as if man were only soul. Witness the widely used formula: Save your soul. But in reality, salvation was promised to the whole human being, not to his soul alone, and it was promised not only to the individual man but to all mankind, even to the whole of creation. This situation has been responsible for the undervaluation of that which is truly human, and particularly of human freedom. The proclamation of Christ always involves the reality of God and man's encounter with him. But it is precisely through this encounter that man is intended to find himself and to become truly a human being. The contention of Feuerbach, in the last century, that through his worship of God man weakened and repudiated his own nature was a disastrous error, although in the light of the general situation it was an understandable one. In reality, by his surrender to God man is not alienated from his true self, but, as we shall shortly see in greater detail, is led to himself. The same criticism applies, from a collective aspect, to the thesis which Karl Marx formulated regarding society.

Despite these and other factors which make modern man's attitudes understandable, though not acceptable, two crucial questions arise from the sphere of Christian faith to confront the radical hopes and strivings of modern man. First, is there not a necessary contradiction between the Christian faith and the modern conception of the world, so that one excludes the other? Secondly, will not such radically future-oriented efforts bring about a reduction of what is human instead of a genuine humanity? This latter question is all the more serious, of course, since the Christian faith maintains that its own role is to open for man the path to a mature and full humanity.

In answer to the first question, there is, in fact, no necessary opposition between Christianity and the modern world. One need not choose in a radical either-or; one can be both modern and Christian at the same time. Christian faith does not annul anything contained in science and technology, human education and culture, man's structuring of his world and his hope for the future. In fact it would not be meaningless to discuss whether the real aims of Marxism are irreconcilably opposed to Christianity— whether, on the contrary, they might not be actualized as a social and economic order within Christianity as an all-encompassing whole. The faith therefore constitutes no barrier either for science or for the formation of the world order. If it has been one occasionally in the past—e.g., in the Galileo case and in regard to the theory of evolution—the Second Vatican Council has formally acknowledged and deplored the error. This council adopted a completely revised attitude towards human values.

The Church, it is true, offers no concrete proposals for the structuring of the future within the world, makes no pronouncements concerning the right form of culture or politics or social order. However, in the Pastoral Constitution on the Church in the Modern World she obliges her members to assume full responsibility for the achievement of a right world-order; that is to say, for the humanization of all earthly structures. Through her proclamation of the gospel she tries to make people able and ready to assume such responsibility in the world. She particularly praises the attitudes close to the heart of modern man—freedom, a sense of responsibility, initiative, involvement. Amazing as it may seem, the ideals of the French Revolution—freedom, equality, fraternity —once criticized by the Church, are now the object of her teaching. This becomes understandable when we realize that those ideals have been liberated from earlier anti-ecclesiastical entanglements and that the Church is developing a new understanding of herself. When the Church praises these ideals as Christian virtues, she is not taking over something alien to her but is developing something that is part of her very being.

Christianity, it is true, looks beyond earthly hopes for the future, seeing through them to an absolute future—namely, to God's immediate communication of himself to human society and its individual members, and so to the divinization of men. This absolute future transcends even the most revolutionary earthly hopes for the future. It reveals these hopes, even in the loftiest and most intense desires and images to which they give rise, as only penultimate values. This does not mean that the absolute future negates the value of the hopes which arise from within the confines of this world, but that it revolutionizes all that is human. Only thus does it enable it to become so fully itself. Hence a meaning is given even to earthly values which cannot be arrived at from their significance in themselves. In the light of the absolute future they are seen as ways and means to the absolute. Furthermore, they will not simply vanish in that absolute future, but will remain, preserved in new forms. Thus the earth and the building up of our world have not only historical but eternal significance. In comparison with Christian expectations for the future, that hope of the future which is exclusively immanent and limited to this world is seen to be short-sighted, however high and strong it may be. Moved by this anticipation man will undertake innumerable laborious, and extremely successful, steps towards transcendence in a horizontal direction, steps which encounter obstacles and never achieve their final goal. The individual thereby transcends himself with respect to society and also to the world of matter. But he neglects the inexpressible mystery which embraces and pervades the entire world and human society. He does not question enough. He is not radical enough. In this dimension Christianity does not mean an end to revolution, but that mankind shall radically transform itself.

Concerning the second question, there are serious misgivings that such extreme confidence in science and technology may leave no room for genuine human values like friendship, love, joy. These are no mere gestures expressive of manipulable nerve impulses but have their own intrinsic meaning, despite the fact that they can be externalized only through the medium of physiological processes. Anthropology can never be reduced to physiology or biochemistry. If someone produces sounds on the piano and asks a scientist—let us say a physicist—to analyze them, he will get a precise result which can be represented in mathematical and physical formulas. However, it is obvious that the process is not exhaustively described by mathematical or physical formulas. The central fact has been omitted; namely, the melody, which is beyond the reach of mathematical and physical, or chemical and physiological, methods. And yet the melody is the true reality, having an immanent meaning which can be reached only through spiritual understanding. This meaning lies at once within and beyond physical processes. It cannot be actualized without those processes, but it is something more and something different from them.

Human personality is a mystery which is revealed in love and friendship. An examination of man exclusively by mathematical and physical, or chemical and biological, methods must necessarily leave out of consideration his unique mystery—a mystery that is not exhausted by processes accessible to the natural sciences. To assume that it is would be to make man exclusively dynamic and active and to destroy what is specifically human in him. Where mere utility prevails, meaningfulness perishes. The human element in man is corroded and even destroyed.

There is a further objection. The effort to bring about an entirely new future in the creative transformation of our world and of the individual person will need an indefinite length of time. But the individual lives here and now, and his life is short. He cannot extend it into the hoped-for future. He is therefore expected to sacrifice his present to the future, and this is true not merely of one person or another: where violence is used to create the future, innumerable individuals are sacrificed on the altar of this humanistic hope. A future humanization of the world is bought at the price of anti-humanism in the present.

Moreover, the mere lengthening of the life span which many expect from medicine and biochemistry would mean not a liberation but a burden unless it involved an intensification of life hitherto unknown to us, not only with respect to its external course but in its inner, fulfilled vitality. Naturally this could not be restricted to the biological sphere, but would have to include the dimensions of the mind—cognition, will, and feeling, as well. How is this to take place? On the other hand, the ascent which is hoped for towards the absolute, the infinite and inexpressible mystery, requires that the human spirit shall be functioning at the point of its utmost intensity; yet this very intensity is rejected or outlawed through the rejection of religious faith. And if man is frequently unaware of the intensity of spirit activated in religious faith, this stems from his lack of readiness for self-transcendence —that is, it is a consequence of sin, which is in its essence the assertion of self against reality. These considerations make certain statements of Nietzsche comprehensible—that the man in whom God is "dead" is the small man; or that "in the world in which God has died the same things recur in eternal, deadly monotony." From the indefinite lengthening of human life, whether individually or collectively, nothing very much can be gained.

In the present situation the believer in Christ may be disturbed both for the sake of Christianity and for the sake of man. To the extent that he is concerned for Christianity, he may take comfort from the fact that it is guaranteed by an irrevocable promise, and it can fulfill a representative salvific function even though the number of its adherents may be reduced to a few.

On the other hand, as far as man is concerned, the believer in Christ is convinced that true humanity can be found only in the radical self-transcendence of man and in God's unconditional gift of himself. Therefore he fears for the future of true humanity, genuine humanism.

THEOLOGY IN THE MODERN WORLD

If theology is to do justice to the present situation it must take account of the secular viewpoints described above. It must do that, however, not simply from opportunism, but because it is the task of theology to reach man in whatever historical situation he may be. We pointed out above that theology must be anthropological in orientation. Such an anthropological theology will be concerned with man in community, and in the totality of his being; it will be existential, dynamic, and eschatological. A theology that is communal and total in this sense teaches that the Christian faith aims at the perfection of the whole man, not only his soul, and of mankind as a whole. Its message is addressed to the individual, but insofar as he is a member of the community. Christianity does not conceive of the individual as isolated but as the member of a community, who comes to the possession of his unique and indelible individuality through his membership. He attains his own individual ego only as a member of the whole, which is moving towards a destiny that is an inexpressible mystery, and he is called to participate in the life of that mystery.

As far as the existential element is concerned, the Christian faith, as man's response to divine revelation, must be shown to have genuine meaning for him, and therefore power to bring him fulfillment. With regard to its dynamic character, revelation is to be presented both in its own history and in the history of its effects—that is, in its character as act. Otherwise we would have merely a description of static essences. But the principal stress in this work will be placed on the eschatological. All particular statements are to be understood in the light of the eschatological point of view; thus it will be shown that God has destined man for an absolute future. This future will consist in the unveiled self-communication of God and in the divinization of creation which this brings about. It will not be static but dynamic, insofar as God's self-communication will be steadily intensified. Whatever saving work God has accomplished and is accomplishing in history through his dialogue with man serves the future and has its meaning in the future. This future is the reason for the past. Thus God stands before man calling and promising.

Christianity, therefore, is a way forward, not backward. Whenever faith looks backward—that is, to the saving act of God in the past which serves the future—it does so in order to strive towards the future all the more courageously and hopefully, supported by the foundation laid in the past. The past guarantees that man is not chasing after utopia or a mere ideology when he strives towards the absolute future—that is, the direct encounter with the self-communicating mystery which we call God. What is decisive is the "whither," not the "whence." But the "whence" guarantees the "whither." The existential and the eschatological viewpoints do not exclude questions concerning essence. The ontological aspect of reality cannot be omitted from Catholic theology; a theology that eliminated it would be stunted. However, ontological considerations must be given their proper place—they serve the existential and eschatological. The latter are clarified and interpreted by the ontological, which in turn receives its meaning from the eschatological. Salvation comes not through metaphysics but through history. Yet for history the question of being is indispensable. Although in the Scriptures the functional aspect, the actions of God and of Christ, stands in the foreground, the ontological question, the question of being, forces itself on the mind. The human mind, because of its structure, asks the question: Who is the God that grants us salvation? The question also has an objective meaning, in that God presents himself in his actions. Only one who denies the reality of God's action and considers it a mere construct of the imagination can consider the ontological question meaningless.

How can we explain that salvation comes to us through history and from the future, and that we can thus grasp it in freedom? This question leads to the concept of revelation. Revelation will be treated of firstly insofar as it is possible, then as it is actual and historical.

Readings

Burke, Patrick (ed.). *The Word in History.* New York, Sheed and Ward, 1966.

Rahner, Karl. "Thoughts on the Possibility of Belief Today" in *Theological Investigations,* V. Baltimore, Helicon, 1966.

◄ 2

The Possibility and Extent
of the Saving Dialogue
between God and Man:
The Transcendental
Explanation of Revelation

THE AIMS OF MODERNISM

We must first give consideration to a problem which has been smoldering since the days of Modernism. The Modernism of the beginning of our century was thought of at the time as a collection of disastrous heresies developing out of the modern philosophy and the critical, historical investigation of Sacred Scripture in the eighteenth and nineteenth centuries. Schleiermacher, with his theology of inner experience, was the father of Modernism, which was condemned in its material statements, and rightly so. But its dynamic concern was then neither acknowledged nor resolved. According to Modernism any religious faith is a form of expression of the inner religious emotion in man. The Christian faith is the expression of these religious feelings, ideas, and representations which prevailed in Jesus. According to this opinion, those who believe in Christ participate in Christ's religious life. Since, however, inner experiences change continually with the passage of time, so too dogmas are subject to continuous change in their forms of expression. However unhappy the substance of these opinions may be, they express a genuine problem; namely, the question whether Christian revelation represents for man something purely external, something which alienates him from his true essence, or whether it has a true source in his inner life.

This question arises particularly with regard to the authoritative communication of revelation by the Church. If we grant that revelation only comes to man from the outside, it seems as if it must remain something external to human nature and hence a violation of man's inmost being. But if we regard Christianity as something in accordance with human nature, and even arising from its depths, then it seems to lose itself in subjectivism, to be without objective validity. In this way both the divine origin of revelation and its promulgation by the Church are brought into question and even denied. The problem, therefore, is one of the relation between immanence and transcendence. Can what is transcendent become immanent in such a way that it does not lose its transcendental character? Can, on the other hand, immanence be so ordered to transcendence that it does not lose its character of immanence? Can one live thus in the other? Can transcendence create immanence, an inner religious life? Can the latter be born of transcendance and nourished by it?

We find related problems, differently structured, in the present-day theologies of Rudolf Bultmann, Harvey Cox, Paul Tillich, Dietrich Bonhoeffer, John A. T. Robinson, Fritz Buri. These theologians, despite their differences, agree in seeing the religious element exclusively in the encounter of man with man, or in love for the neighbor—that is, its movement is completely in a horizontal direction. For them, theology is pure anthropology—not in that sweeping sense in which Ludwig Feuerbach in his time declared that theology is physiology, but nevertheless in the sense that they conceive man as without conscious movement towards

God. While Feuerbach declared explicitly that man is God for man, the claim of these contemporary theologians is that God can be found only in man; and that he is worshipped in man, even if he does not become explicitly an object of consciousness.[1]

MAN'S RECEPTIVENESS FOR GOD

It may be helpful for the analysis of the problem if we begin with an examination of the relationship of the individual to the individual, to the community, and to nature. By his very essence man has a relationship to his fellow-man. Human existence is essentially coexistence, a fact that expresses itself perhaps most clearly in human speech. The articulateness of man is a manifestation of and a witness to the truly human. Man cannot conceive of or understand himself without bringing into his self-consciousness other persons and the material world. They are constitutive elements of his self-consciousness. In opening himself to another individual, he opens himself at the same time to the community and the material world. Owing to his corporeality man can perfect his existence in no other way than in this self-transcending movement outward towards the world. Nor is it left to his pleasure whether he does so or not. Self-transcendence is contained in his self-affirmation and forms one element of its complex realization. These relationships become even more evident when we see man in the act of being or becoming a personality, and from the aspect of the future. Personality means that man possesses himself, that he is himself in openness towards the other. A person is essentially one who is open for the other person. To close oneself off means in its last extreme to destroy oneself.

The human person cannot be understood apart from the act of becoming. He assumes his true form at any time only by going out of himself towards the other. If man remains by himself, he will not develop into what he can and should become. He succeeds in becoming himself only by forsaking himself. He who preserves his life will lose it. Only he who surrenders it will gain it. Such dialectic statements become comprehensible when we realize that the encounter awakens, releases, and actualizes potentialities within us. Without the call of the other, such qualities would slumber on in the depths of the self, never to be raised above the realm of mere potentiality. We cannot know beforehand what a human being is capable of. Again and again we are surprised at the powers which sleep in ourselves, unconscious and unknown, and which emerge only at the hour when they are summoned forth. Then we may come to believe that we no longer know ourselves. In such situations it becomes apparent how profound a transformation can be effected by an encounter. Yet this process does not alienate us from our own ego. On the contrary, only in this way does our ego attain its fulfillment and its genuine being.

The process of becoming carries man towards a goal. That goal is, in the last analysis, man-being-himself, authentic existence; or, in scriptural terms, the whole and integral existence which begins with the resurrection and the divinization of man. Man cannot reach this goal unless he steadily transcends himself towards his fellow-man and through him towards the material world.

Such reflections offer us the key for understanding man's encounter with God, as it occurs in divine revelation. The special character of this encounter derives from the fact that God is not a "Thou" like the human "thou": he is the creator of man, and man is a creature. Being a creature implies two things: man's dependence on God, and his existence in his own right. Here an antinomy opens up which cannot be satisfactorily resolved. At the very root of human existence, therefore, we find a mystery. In the relation of man to God these two opposing elements are both present.

If we say God created man, this only states the fact of the matter, not the modality. It does not exclude the fact that man made his appearance in the stream of evolution only after billions of years, that he appears in a definite world situation, by an event in which matter transcended itself in one essential leap under God's creative influence, and that in this newly structured matter spirit arose as a formative principle through God's creative power. We should not consider God's creation of man as a single act of time. It is rather a continuous happening. Man continues to exist by being continuously created by God. God, in a perpetual creative act, releases him into his existence and his freedom.

Man is distinguished from other creatures by the fact that, in the matter which is a constitutive element of his being, spirit has "opened its eyes." From this hour, creation in the form of man can reflect on itself and on its origin—i.e., on God. Within history this process reaches its climax in Jesus Christ. For in him matter transcends itself not only into spirit, so that the two form one being, but beyond the created spirit into God, so that God is the subsisting ground of the man Jesus Christ (Karl Rahner).

Man's origin from God's creative will and his inherent relation to God find their psychological expression in his implicit awareness of God. The proofs for the existence of God may be understood as a reflection on this implicit awareness and its rational explication. In this implicit awareness man's ontological relationship to God forces itself into the sphere of consciousness. This makes the fact comprehensible that, as Carl Gustav Jung notes, the idea of an all-powerful being is to be found everywhere. In Jung's terminology it is an archetype. To remain emotionally healthy man must not suppress the images of the divine which occupy his conscious or unconscious mind. Jung assures us that no patient can be truly cured until he attains a religious attitude. Such an attitude means that the man is open to God. Thus for Jung turning to God is not a sign of infantile helplessness or weakness in the face of a powerful destiny, not a man-made opium for the restless soul, but the expression of human nature. The decisive anthropological question here is whether or not man necessarily has a relationship to the infinite. Such observations lead to the conclusion that God's turning to man does not mean alienation or oppression but liberation for what is truly human, the unchaining of his fettered potentialities.

This again becomes evident from another point of view. When God creates, he necessarily represents himself. In creating he goes out beyond himself, and yet at the same time remains with himself. The result of his creative activity is an analogous realization of himself. We say of man that God has sketched his own likeness in him. In Scripture man is called God's "image" in that he is called to participate in freedom in God's activity as Ruler. A similar process takes place in human language. In our words we go out of ourselves, moving towards the other. We express ourselves and "come to appearance," even when we do not speak about our-

selves but about objects different from us. We do this more fully
when in our words we disclose ourself, that is to say, our inner being. When we talk about objects we can be our own listeners. But
when we enter into self-disclosure, we cannot be detached specta-
tors.

Because of his relationship to God established in creation, man,
in trying to understand himself, understands and must understand
himself as God's image. He therefore can and does see God in
himself as in a mirror. Bonaventure analyzes this state of affairs
with a characteristic nuance when he declares that man is closest
to being God's image when he is active, and above all, when he
turns to God in believing and loving. With this explanation Bonaventure makes God's image in man a dynamic one. In such an
understanding of himself man can experience God. The image of
God is not a fixed state, but a perpetual becoming. It is living in a
process of formation. The creature is on the way to forming the
image of God.

God-consciousness appears here as an element of human self-
consciousness. If it is missing from human self-consciousness, then
man's understanding of himself does not reach the depths of his
being.

Consciousness of God is an element of our consciousness and understanding of ourselves. Consciousness of the world is also an
element of our experience of ourselves. But these two do not take
place alongside one another. It is rather a matter of one single
movement of consciousness. When a man, driven by his nature,
transcends himself towards mankind and the material world, he
encounters the divine Thou, unless he prematurely stops the movement. He cannot be conscious of God without being conscious of
his fellow-creatures. He cannot be conscious of his fellow-creatures
without being in some way aware of the creator.

THE NATURAL EXPERIENCE OF GOD AS
THE STARTING-POINT FOR
"SUPERNATURAL" REVELATION

Man's experience of himself, which because of man's nature contains in itself the experience and awareness of God, is the starting-

point for that divine self-communication which theology usually calls "supernatural" revelation. What is meant by "supernatural" will be explained later. As a result of the bond with God and the divine established through man's being an image of and having a relation to God, there is in man a certain correspondence to God which is a point of departure for the divine self-communication. Thus through the act of divine self-communication man is not invaded by an alien power, but rather taken into the confidence of a familiar reality. His experience of God enables him to hear God's call. God's word to him is not unintelligible—"double-Dutch." Understanding is even possible when God's call conveys more things—and other things—than he can comprehend conceptually through reflection. Since man belongs to God, God's call can always reach and influence him. God's word can always take root in his soul. Thus he is led beyond his natural experience of God because of the character of transcendence which renders him open to God. In other words, his origin gives man a positive capacity for what is supernatural in the strict sense of the word, a capacity inherent in his nature. By his nature he possesses a "supernatural existential" (Karl Rahner). He is capable of a dialogue with God, even though in such a dialogue communications are made to him which, since they cannot arise out of his own human nature and are thus not mere actualizations of his own inner possibilities, may present him with the unexpected, and even with demands which seem excessive, because they lead him beyond all his ordinary experience. After all, it is not astonishing if man is led by God beyond his immanent possibilities. For the inexpressible mystery which God is, which makes contact with man in the process of revelation, is something wholly other than man. Assuredly it is, to use one of Tillich's expressions, that which is deepest, innermost in man; but it is this in such a way that it also transcends man. It is in man's transcendent depths, in his own inner self, that he transcends himself. Since it is other than man, this mystery says other things than man can say or even expect; but even in that way, inevitably, it becomes the very inner self of man. God starts from the experience of God which is naturally immanent in man, and actualizes this beyond its own status into a new dimension of existence and into a new religious state of consciousness. In this process

God does not overwhelm man in a way that would endanger or annihilate his freedom. Rather, in addressing man's a priori experience of God, he accomplishes his self-communication as an offer which man can accept or reject in full freedom.

We must add another observation here. As we have just said, God changes the condition of man's consciousness by his self-revelation to the human spirit. To be sure, the process of self-revelation does not mean only a touching of the human mind externally; there is likewise an "inner illumination," to use an expression familiar in theology. The divine self-revelation is thus connected with the illumination of human consciousness through grace. Naturally this does not mean an increase of human gifts. Such an idea would be fantastic. Rather, a new view of reality, a new horizon of understanding of being and of the self, a new perspective opens up. An analogy for the thing that happens can be found in our everyday experience, when we must and can say in regard to a certain experience: "Only then were my eyes really opened." The creative transformation of man's consciousness by God is identical with the divine act of self-revelation. The former neither precedes nor follows the latter but coincides with it. This problem will be discussed again in the next chapter.

There is one problem which we cannot pursue here with the necessary precision, although it belongs to the most important questions with reference to our subject: How can the individual man addressed by God be certain that the voice calling him from within is not his own but that of the transcendent God? Since this problem is very much the subject of a theological discipline of its own, fundamental theology, we can treat it only briefly here. Fundamental theology is concerned with the power with which God declares himself to man by communicating with him inwardly, and with the divine signs and miracles which vouch for the authenticity of the process of revelation. We shall give some attention to these matters later on. The inexpressible personal mystery which asserts its power within the man called by it announces itself with such clarity, purity, and distinctness as the mystery of God that the man touched by it cannot escape it by evasion or flight, try as he will. This is clear to us from the experience which the prophets of the Old Testament—e.g. Isaiah, Jeremiah—had of

God. The divine self-communication is destined in the first place
for the individual recipient. But he, by the divine commandment,
is turned towards the community, to whom God will give his word
with such power that the group will accept the revelation. What is
revealed is presented again to later generations by the word of
preaching. Hence the past is always being realized anew, and the
hearers are able to attain an immediate relation to the mediated
revelation.

DIVINE AND HUMAN ELEMENTS IN
GOD'S REVELATION

It is essential that man, touched by divine self-revelation, should
comprehend what comes to him as the communication of God.
Theologians have discussed the problem of whether God's self-
revelation is accomplished in externally visible phenomena or only
in acts of inner illumination. In most cases we shall probably have
to assume the second mode. In this way God acts on the human
mind and heart—that is, on the whole man with all his human
capacities. He gives man not only an inner existential impetus but
also meaningful knowledge. What man touched by God experiences in his inner self he then translates into a particular language
of words and images according to his personal peculiarities, his disposition, his world of ideas, his store of imagery, his cultural situation, his political judgment, his understanding of being. That is
how God's epiphany occurs, his advance into the world through
the medium of man. The images and ideas of which the recipient
of divine self-communication avails himself here arise not only
from his individuality but also from society—which may mean
from the mythology of the environment in which he lives. Divine
self-communication can be expressed in mythical images. This does
not mean that it ever becomes itself a myth. For myth does not consist in the use of mythical images: a myth in the strict sense of the
word is a drama.

The form or pattern of the utterance which represents a divine
revelation can be an instructive statement, a call, an admonition,
praise, a warning, a threat of punishment, or a promise. The pat-

tern of the *promise* includes in itself all other forms, just as they themselves are linked with one another.

The result of our reflection is that divine revelation is always a synthesis of divine initiative and human response. A revelation which did not evoke an answer from man would be a divine call into empty space. It would be meaningless and hence not from God. In revelation something pertaining to God is shown to man. If there were nobody to whom something was shown, the act of showing would be an empty gesture. Man's response therefore is part of God's revelation.

If every divine self-revelation finds completion only in the human answer, whether negative or positive, then every divine revelation involves an incarnation of God in human words and images, and in such words and images as are determined by the time, the culture, and even the political structures of the individual historical period to which the revelation is made. As a result, the content of the divine revelation, though unchangeable in itself, can and must be subsequently translated into other words and images. This means not only into another grammar and vocabulary but into other modes and forms of thinking. For example, the divine revelation given in the Near East, which has its own way of thinking, can be translated into European modes of thought or into the thought-forms of the culture of India or China. Divine revelation is not inextricably bound up with any one world view; any conception of the world can serve as a form to express what God has revealed of himself. No matter how closely connected the content of divine self-revelation as found in God's utterance to the recipient of that revelation may be with the particular speech-forms of the recipient, the two dimensions are still not identical and can therefore be separated from each other. Such a translation will admittedly never be perfect. Yet it will succeed to the extent that the core of meaning is found unabridged and unfalsified in its new form.

THE POSSIBILITY OF REJECTING GOD

In spite of man's comparative closeness to God, and despite the fact that the divine grace granted through God's self-revelation has touched and illuminated him and transformed his consciousness, man can and does experience God's self-revelation to him as an alienation from his own nature. Various reasons can be given for this, of which the first is the sheer otherness of God; but, most important, there is in man's attitude towards God an inexplicable recalcitrance, which is grounded in human freedom and which rises to the surface whenever he is called forth from that state of self-assertiveness which belongs to his nature and expected obediently to enter another field of existence. Let us remember that creatureliness includes two different things: a relation of dependence towards God, and existence as an independent self. It is hard to reconcile these two factors with one another. If dependence on God is absolutized and the existence of man as ego denied, we move towards pantheism. If, *vice versa,* the existence of the ego is absolutized and dependence on God negated, we move towards atheism. It is easier for thinkers to opt for one pole of these alternatives than to find a meaningful synthesis of the two. Man's freedom makes him capable of such one-sidedness, whether it be Hegel's pantheistic amalgamation or Marx's disengagement from God and autocratic revolt against him.

As a result of this man can be irritated by the form revelation takes—that is, by God's incarnation in an unimpressive human form—and, over and above that, by the manner in which God's self-revelation is proclaimed. For it is irritating when the proclamation is made with excessive authority and self-assurance, or when it does not allow the humanistic character and the humanistic goal of divine revelation to become visible.

THE TRANSMISSION OF DIVINE SELF-REVELATION

Special problems arise from the fact that God does not illumine the mind of every single individual, nor does he grant the grace of a new consciousness directly to everyone; he turns rather to one person as the representative of a group, as the deputy of many, as "a corporate personality." Such a man then is expected to hand on to his group, or even to others outside the group, what he has received. A mission of this kind is an essential component of the process in which particular divine revelations are made. This includes at the same time the challenge to others to trust such a chosen one in regard to the deepest concern of their lives, the question of salvation, and to submit to his word. This can be a blow to one's own self-concept. Irritation may arise: Why he and not I? For confidence in such a recipient of revelation seems impossible without some form of submission to his word, which he proclaims to be God's word.

Yet, although the movement in a man's inner self is initiated by the word of another, this need not mean that the ego thus addressed is overpowered. This is true because all human existence is in essence, and not just in practice, coexistence; and therefore every individual can unfold and develop his own human nature only by receiving the other into his consciousness and his life. This process is experienced more profoundly in human love. The reception of the beloved "thou" is felt and experienced not as an overpowering but as a fulfillment of the ego.

In the case of divine self-revelation, we must add that the listener or recipient is enriched and brought to a higher level of existence not just by participating in the life and the self-consciousness of another person which is objectified in the word, but by the action of God himself. Assuredly it is he who has shaped and developed the consciousness which takes concrete form in the word of the speaker; thus God himself addresses the individual. But he nevertheless chooses man as a medium. God approaches man through man, and it remains his secret whom he selects as the way to the other. He chooses this way, however, because of the co-humanity of individual men. This resembles the highest form of human encounter in love. It is the inexpressible mystery of God's love which, by means of the direct recipient of revelation, desires to plunge itself into the hearts of others. Where, in the Old Testament, the divine message is summarized, love is proclaimed as the nucleus of the whole divine utterance.

The unity of the human group which already existed before the act of divine self-revelation is then deepened and vitalized by the word of revelation which the person moved by God addresses to the others. Divine self-revelation has a socializing power. Man is intended to experience and to exercise, in the dimension of religion, the solidarity and fraternity which binds him by his nature. In religion as in other realms of human existence man is not expected to live simply alongside his fellow-men like a monad. Solidarity in religion does not build a wall between God and the individual which might prevent direct contact. Every individual as a member of the group exists in an immediate relationship to God. It is more exact to say as a member *of* the group, not as *with* the group, because in that way the individual stands out more clearly in his individuality (Karl Rahner).

THE HISTORICAL CHARACTER OF DIVINE REVELATION

Closely bound up with the communal dimension of religion is the historical character of God's self-revelation. The fact that revelation occurs in history not only opens up a new set of problems but can even wreck religious faith. For it raises the question whether the almighty and omnipresent God, in the universality of his actions, really stepped out of his inaccessibility at one particular hour only within history; whether he really revealed to man the way to himself in one particular place only in the entire cosmos, and then only through one particular individual who had been chosen by him. Is such a thing in any way possible? If, however, it did happen, did it not happen then only for those men closely connected in time and space with that point in the vast co-ordinate system of history? To speak more concretely, Is the divine revelation proclaimed by Christianity intended perhaps only for the western world or for even just a part of it, while the experience of God that Buddhism expresses is more relevant for far-eastern man?

If, however, the revelation God made of himself at a particular time and in a particular place is to have universal significance, we must then ask how men separated from the event in space and time by perhaps thousands or hundreds of thousands of years are to share in this revelation. Does not man's inherent self-esteem suffer a blow when he hears that his relationship to God and his consequent salvation was decided in an obscure corner of the vast universe? Practically speaking, the question assumes the following form in the Christian sphere: Can a savior come from Nazareth, a small village in a country of little historical significance? Can the redeemer come from a group of lower-class people? Can we in our modern complicated world find support today from events that occurred in such simple economic and social structures?

Here too, a more exact analysis may prove illuminating. We will move the discussion forward by first asking what is meant by the word "historical." The term as used here includes the following three elements: an action takes place in freedom; this action is significant for the future and thus makes for continuity; and finally, its significance pertains to the larger community. The present-day theology of demythologization distinguishes between the two German terms, "historisch" and "geschichtlich." This distinction, difficult to render in English, serves to clarify the significance of past events. An event is "historisch" if it took place once in the course of human development, but now belongs to the past and has no further bearing either on individual or collective existence. An event is "geschichtlich," on the other hand, if it took place once in the past but still continues to make itself felt even to the present day, moving and determining human life.

Man is by nature historically oriented. As being and becoming, he is largely determined at any given moment by his collective and individual past, as he reaches out from his present into the future. Nobody can, so to speak, start his life at zero. Man can never raise himself up off the ground of history into a history-free realm. From the beginning he is born into a historical situation with definite political and cultural, scientific and religious, societal and technological elements. These affect and determine him throughout his life, putting their stamp on his acts of freedom. He is certainly not totally predestined by his environment as by a pre-established power. Yet because of his historical situation he is not capable of making every possible decision, but only of making certain provisional plans. "There is a time for everything." On the other hand, every man participates in shaping the future.

The future is not something that merely moves towards man; it is rather created and formed by his cooperation. Only the conviction that one could live his life outside this world could bring one to attempt to escape the historical course of life. Such an acosmic, unworldly stance or expectation can only be a mirage, an illusion.

This becomes even clearer if we look for a moment at far-eastern religious ideas. Here it is the ideal of the religious man to withdraw from the world into the mystery of the divine. In spite of all philosophical and religious contradictions it is a commonplace of Indian thought that the world is without beginning and end. The world evolves from a simple undeveloped state into the manifold of external phenomena and withdraws again into itself, in periodic alternation. The original ground from which it comes is the divine, which is understood as an impersonal being. All phenomena of the visible world, therefore, are incarnations of the divine, and no one thing is preferable to the other. Indian thought revels in dizzying numerical calculations indicating the duration of various periods of history. In mighty periodic rhythms the course of events repeats itself incessantly without beginning or end, an eternal motion in an eternal cycle. And this motion contains within itself its own meaning. The human soul is drawn into this cycle. Borne by a kind of ethereal body, it migrates after death into another creature, a god, a man of higher or lower rank, an animal, or a plant. From this belief grows the feeling of solidarity with all living creatures. What determines the manner of reincarnation is the karma, the sum total of bad and good deeds at the end of life. The karma imprints itself in the ethereal body and leads it to a corresponding new existence. Only when no karma is left does the succession of lives reach its end in Nirvana. For the ordinary man this is attainable only in the far-distant future or not at all. Thus, according to a frequently recurring image, man resembles a shipwrecked person in a little boat on the storm-whipped ocean, searching for a safe harbor. He knows that such a harbor exists, but not where it is nor how to get there; he does not know whether the direction chosen is bringing him nearer to the harbor or taking him farther away. But that is not considered a calamity, for the motion itself is salvation, even though it never reaches a goal.

Classical Greek thought also lacks any fully developed notion of the historical nature of man, although this deficiency is not as obvious as in Indian thought. Greek thinkers concentrate their attention not on growth and decline but on the timeless universal. This is true both for the idealistic and the materialistic systems of Greek philosophy. According to Greek philosophical teaching, the truly human life is attained when man elevates himself to the sphere of timeless being. He finds the meaning of his existence not in individual history but in immersion in the universal. If we look for a symbol of this way of thinking it would again have to be the circle, whose line returns again and again upon itself. (That there are other interpretations of circle symbolism—as, for example, in the writings of Bonaventure—is a fact we shall not develop further here.)

In the face of these ahistorical world views, it is all the more significant that, as our present-day experience shows, they cannot be sustained for any length of time, and that the thrust towards historicity is felt even within them. Since human existence is in its essence bound up with the world, this is not to be wondered at but to be expected. Thus, for instance, modern Buddhism is to a high degree concerned with history. Such an interest in history is simply an expression of man's involvement in time, of his being and becoming.

Therefore God, if he calls man at all, calls him as he exists in a particular historical situation. No man exists apart from such a condition. No matter whether we define man with Aristotle as *animal rationale* or with modern thinkers as *homo faber* or according to theological tradition as *animal amans* or *orans* or *se transcendens,* man never actualizes these sides of his nature outside history. He always is what he is as stamped by history. God can call him only as a person marked with a particular historical character and as a member of a group. In this process the individual as constituted by and situated in history can at any given moment become God's port of entry into humanity. The word of revelation is addressed to all through the one individual, and the word must then spread and penetrate everywhere. The moment the word goes forth is at one definite date in history. But its goal is the entire earth, even the cosmos. Atomic physics and the technology developed from it offer us today an example of this expansion and explosive power in an entirely different field. It is important to remember that God himself remains present in the fact that the good news he has announced is disseminating itself. He communicates himself to the whole of mankind through an individual or a human group. In this process he himself always remains the subject: the initiator. He cannot become an object.

The human group thus laid hold of by God cannot in its historical action abstract from the new consciousness that was formed by the divine mystery. This consciousness will rather be a dynamic factor in shaping the world, and thus will have a historical impact. It will play its role in creating a definite image of man, and thus will be of no little consequence for the structuring of society.

Furthermore, a generation living in a particular period of history will not take to its grave what it has salvifically experienced from the depths of divine mystery, but will hand it on to future generations, to its children and grandchildren. In that way tradition develops. The tradition is determined by the fact that each succeeding generation knows itself to be stamped and formed by what is handed on to it. It feels influenced by it in the shaping of its future, even when it discriminates and selects critically, as long as vital forces flow from the tradition.

Our survey shows that the objection raised by Theodor Lessing, "accidental historical truths can never become proofs of necessary rational truths," has no bearing on the problem of divine self-revelation, valid as his thesis may be in itself. Lessing's assertion is influenced by the ideas of the Enlightenment, according to which the human mind can accept only what can be demonstrated by reason, and reason must contest any claim that history may raise to be able to make statements of universal validity. But the formulation of the question by Lessing and the entire Enlightenment by-passes revelation entirely, since it is not a question here of the communication of universally valid truths, but rather precisely a matter of historical events. It concerns the actual concrete appearance of God in history, an event which is transmitted from one generation to the next through the medium of individual men. Augustine has this situation in mind in his work *De vera religione* when he says: "The principal object of this faith is history, and the prophecies of those arrangements made by divine providence for the salvation of the human race, which is to be transformed and newly created for eternal salvation." [2]

Having presented the various possibilities of divine self-revelation, we turn now to the actual event. We do not intend to discuss the meaning of revelation in any exhaustive way, because that is the domain of fundamental theology. Only those elements which serve the purpose of this book will be singled out for discussion.

Readings

de Lubac, Henri. *The Discovery of God.* Translated by Alexander Dru. New York, P. J. Kenedy and Sons, 1960.

Rahner, Karl. "Concerning the Relationship Between Nature and Grace" in *Theological Investigations,* I. Baltimore, Helicon, 1961.

—— "Some Implications of the Scholastic Concept of Uncreated Grace" in *Theological Investigations,* I. Baltimore, Helicon, 1961.

—— "Nature and Grace" in *Theological Investigations,* IV. Baltimore, Helicon, 1967.

Notes

[1] Cf. Karl Rahner, "Theology and Anthropology," in Patrick Burke, ed., *The Word in History* (New York: Sheed and Ward, 1966).

[2] VIII,13.

◄ II

God's Saving Approach to Man in Historical Actions and Words

◂ 3

God's Self-Revelation: Its Freedom, Its Forms, Its Summit in Jesus Christ

We begin our reflections with the statement that God seems to be silent. Whereas for some this seems to be a matter of indifference, there are many others who endure it in despair. But if God did speak once in history, then it is not a question of personal need or preference whether a man listens to him or closes his ears; it becomes, on the contrary, a solemn responsibility for each man to listen to God speaking. If he has entered in this way into nature and history, man must entrust himself to his word.

God has indeed revealed himself to his creatures and in this way has made himself accessible to us. This means that in spite of his transcendence, that hidden, inexpressible mystery which we call God has become audible and visible throughout created reality. In fact, this happens precisely through the medium of created reality.

THE FREEDOM OF GOD'S SELF-REVELATION AND OF MAN'S RESPONSE

When God acts, he does so in complete freedom. This is not, however, as many late scholastic theologians (though not Duns

Scotus) believed, an arbitrary freedom. It is rather bound to the being of God as spirit, and is the expression of this. Thus the freedom we should ascribe to God in revealing himself differs both from the neo-Platonic concept of emanations and from Engels' doctrine of the self-movement of the Spirit to its highest fulfillment. If full freedom is ascribed to God, this means that he is neither compelled by his own nature to reveal himself nor forced to it by a reality other than himself. God is subject to coercion neither from within nor from without.

If we investigate the question why God in this freedom has revealed himself, we are confronted with an insoluble mystery. We shall encounter it again when we attempt to analyze the concept of creation. First of all we should state that only within the Godhead, in the dialogue between Father and Son, can there be found a reason for God's communication of himself in creation. The adequate self-utterance of God occurs in that divine word which we customarily call God's Son. Clearly, God's happiness in his own adequate self-communication in his Son is so profound and so moving that he wishes to achieve such happiness in still another, though inadequate, way. We cannot explain this concept in greater detail at the moment, but let us describe this inadequate form of God's expression in creation as his "analogous" self-communication. Here the aim of the divine self-communication becomes visible in the dimension of creaturely life. This aim is the dialogue of God with man. God's primal intention in revealing himself is apparently concerned with this dialogue.

This, however, implies that man is capable of such dialogue, that he is divinized, therefore, without ceasing to be a creature. That God desires and loves the dialogue with man is evident from the fact that he has resumed it again and again, even though man has tried to escape it. God has never given up in history. Over and over he has spoken out anew so that the dialogue could be continued and brought nearer to its ultimate goal.

God's freedom finds its parallel in man's freedom in the assimilation of God's self-revelation. Human freedom is so profoundly radical that man, in spite of his creaturehood, can deny God an answer and can thus escape the divine partner of the dialogue.

God's word does not impose itself on man, a fact that becomes evident in a special way in John 5,32ff. Here we find the strange statement that he who accepts Jesus' testimony of revelation has attested that God is true. The acceptance of the testimony is faith, which in this case is understood as man's assent to the word of God. By this assent the believer affirms the truth of God. By his assent he puts God's truth into effect for himself.

Behind this thesis of St. John's is the idea that God grants man the freedom to attest God's truth by his assent, and to affirm to God himself that his revelation is truth and that he himself by this revelation is proved faithful and true. It also becomes abundantly clear that God, in spite of the freedom he grants to man, is very much concerned about man's response.[1]

God's revelation has many degrees, many styles, and many forms, but it is always in and through the world familiar to us that God has revealed himself, not through a distant hereafter unintelligible to us. Whoever seeks God must seek him in the world, or he will not find him. In the letter to the Hebrews the multiplicity of God's self-revelation is attested and described in the following way: "In many and various ways God spoke of old to our fathers through the prophets; but in these last days he has spoken to us through a Son, whom he appointed the heir of all things, through whom also he created the world. He reflects the glory of God and bears the very stamp of his nature, upholding the universe by his word of power. When he had made purification for sins, he sat down at the right hand of the Majesty on high." (Heb. 1,1-3, *RSV*) [2]

THE MANIFOLD FORMS OF GOD'S SELF-REVELATION

What follows will amount to an analysis of this text, for its expresses the different levels of the revelation, the continuity, and its culmination in Christ. The Second Vatican Council as well as the First addressed itself to the question of God's self-revelation in our world. According to Vatican I divine self-revelation *in* nature and *through* nature results in the fact that God can be recognized

in the world. Therefore anyone who looks not only at the surface
of the world but tries to penetrate into the depths, where it
reveals itself in its mystery, encounters that which is completely
other than the world, namely, God. (See below, p. 65.)

Within the self-revelation of God in the cosmos there is still
another mode. God has revealed himself not only through nature
but also in the course of history. The Second Vatican Council
stated, in the Dogmatic Constitution on Divine Revelation:

> In His goodness and wisdom, God chose to reveal Himself and to
> make known to us the hidden purpose of His will (cf. Eph. 1:9) by
> which through Christ the Word made flesh, man has access to the
> Father in the Holy Spirit and comes to share in the divine nature (cf.
> Eph. 2:18; 2 Pet. 1:4). Through this revelation, therefore, the invisible
> God (cf. Col. 1:15; 1 Tim. 1:17) out of the abundance of His love
> speaks to men as friends (cf. Ex. 33:11; Jn. 15:14–15) and lives among
> them (cf. Bar. 3:38), so that He may invite and take them into fellow-
> ship with Himself. This plan of revelation is realized by deeds and
> words having an inner unity: the deeds wrought by God in the history
> of salvation manifest and confirm the teaching and realities signified by
> the words, while the words proclaim the deeds and clarify the mystery
> contained in them. By this revelation then, the deepest truth about God
> and the salvation of man is made clear to us in Christ, who is the
> Mediator and at the same time the fullness of all revelation.[3]

THE GOAL OF THE DIVINE
SELF-REVELATION

If we compare this text with an analogous text of the First
Vatican Council, we are immediately struck by the difference
between them and the progress that has been made. The First
Vatican Council moves to a certain extent in the same formulations as the Second, but it cannot be denied that it puts the
stress on intellectual truth, affirmed in the act of faith, which the
council describes as an acceptance of truth on the authority of
God who is revealing. The First Vatican Council was oriented in
all its statements primarily to the outside world. It was a council
that had its origin in the motive of self-defense. The adversaries

against whom it made its statements were manifold. They had, however, one thing in common—the rejection of the divine revelation proclaimed by the Church. Vatican I was, to use a technical term, a council oriented towards fundamental theology. Vatican II, on the other hand, speaks first of all to those within. It contributes first to the Church's understanding of itself, and only then does it address itself to the outside world. In striving to understand revelation in its full sense, it tries to interpret it not only as a statement of God about himself—that is, as doctrine, as a truth about God—but also as a statement God makes *for us,* as a word or act of God by which he unveils himself to man. God addresses man and promises himself to him. The goal of this self-revelation of God is the participation of the creature in the divine life; in other words, the deification of creation. This divine aim is the ultimate basis for God's self-communication to man.

The full realization of this will occur in the future, a fact which explains why God's self-communication is always oriented towards the future. Transfiguration is its *Telos.* The First Vatican Council also mentioned these existential elements, but it did not emphasize them as much as the Second. It may not be superfluous to illustrate this from another experience in everyday life. There is a great difference between a conversation which a person has with one of his acquaintances in which he tells him interesting news items, gives him information which his conversation partner may need to make important decisions—perhaps even offers him his *curriculum vitae*—and a conversation in which he opens his heart to him in friendship or love. Only in the latter case is there really a personal exchange. All the other communication takes place on the level of the interesting or the helpful.

It is, of course, conceivable that God could have brought about the absolute future of man directly and without the long march of history; that is, that he could have granted himself to man immediately, in a vertical movement of humanity without any horizontal movement. God's reason for choosing the way through history to the absolute future is wrapped in profound mystery. We may, however, assume that God loves the dynamic and not the static, that he prefers becoming as a way to perfection. Perhaps

God's predilection for what is dynamic lies in his character as absolute action, which we shall describe later. Every revelation is another stage on the road into the absolute future.

GOD'S REVELATION OF HIMSELF IN CONCEALMENT

One may ask why God has to undertake such a tedious and protracted labor when he wishes to begin a dialogue with man. One reason is that he is personal; another, more important one, however, is that because of his transcendence he is hidden from every creature, not just in the sense that he lives behind a curtain which we cannot pull away, but also in the sense that he is completely other and therefore cannot be reached with our organs of perception. God is an ineffable mystery not only with respect to one aspect of his being, but in his total reality. Even when he does show himself to us, his mystery does not become thereby transparent—not that he wants to keep anything from us, but his very nature renders it impossible. He can grant us a glimpse into the veiled mystery which he is, but it still remains a mystery. Thus his self-revelation cannot be subjected to intramundane standards. This holds good even for its most intense realization, the revelation of God in Jesus Christ. What function miracle and prophecy may have in this process will be discussed in another chapter.

It would be a superficial conception of the mystery of God to equate it with a riddle. A riddle can be solved by intelligent and acute people, or at least it is not insoluble in principle. According to the prophet Isaiah (45,15) God is a "hidden" God. Luther's experience of this hiddenness, which he describes in the *theologia crucis* as a blessing and yet terrifying, is shared by many mystics.

On the other hand, there is certainly a deep longing in man to behold this mystery which is the transcendent core of the world. In all the endeavors of the human spirit, and in all his attempts to shape the world, man is always on the way to those transcendent depths of mystery in himself whether he knows it or not, and even when it goes against his will. The human spirit is "ordered"—to use an expression of Thomas Aquinas—to the vision of God, the inexpressible, without being able to reach this goal by means of its own strength. In the last analysis man is given a task which he cannot fulfill but which he must nevertheless master in order to reach the fullness of his own nature, and thus to come to himself. He lives in tension, since a goal is set for him without whose realization he cannot become himself, but which he is not able to realize. In this insoluble dilemma the promise comes to him that God in his mercy will grant him that for which his nature is intended.

In the Old Testament Moses asked God to show him his face (Ex.33,18-23). The request was denied because no man can see God and live (cf. Dt.5,24-27). Moses was only permitted to see "God's back." In the New Testament also, Philip uttered the same request (Jn. 14,8), and it was denied. He was allowed to hear, however, that he could see the Father he longed to see in the face of Jesus Christ. In other words, as long as man lives in history he can never behold God in his unveiled reality—so to speak, in his own shape—but only in one which is really foreign to the divine nature. Even where God shows himself intensively he can show himself only in the refraction of the creature. The direct vision of the mystery of God is the salvific gift of the future. It is precisely this vision which establishes the radical character of the future.

God's self-revelation, which occurs within human history, is ordained to his direct and immediate self-communication in the future. That is the ultimate meaning of every divine self-communication. In view of the signs of God's presence in history, men can traverse with hope, both in their individual and their collective existence, the way into the absolute future, despite their many sufferings and difficulties, efforts and labors, obstacles and setbacks.

The dialectic of divine self-revelation, according to which God shows himself only in a veiled manner and God's word can only be known in man's word, gains its utmost poignancy in Christ's crucifixion (1 Cor. 2,1-12). When the apostle Paul preached the cross of Christ, and in particular when he proclaimed the crucified as the one sent by God, to the highly cultured Greeks with their philosophy and art, he obviously suffered deeply from the burdensome thought that a man who had been executed as a criminal was supposed to be the promised savior. All his life he wrestled with this depressing fact. In his first letter to the Christian congregation at Corinth he admitted that according to the standards of philosophy and common sense it is foolishness to expect salvation from a man who has been crucified. But then immediately this position is reversed: God's wisdom fulfills itself in precisely this mode of revelation which looks like folly to men. Men are not to be captured and overpowered by human wisdom, the wisdom of this world; it is the divine wisdom, wholly other than the wisdom of the world and hidden from it, which calls for man's decision in freedom. Indeed man is only capable of such decision through the spirit of God, through the divine wisdom, which the human spirit, so sure of itself and boastful of its own strength, is incapable of grasping.

Paul finds a solution in the fact that the incomprehensible death on the cross actually became the way to life. Therefore, he proclaims the reality of Christ's resurrection with really fervent concern and most emphatic resoluteness. The texts in which Paul tries to express the solution to the scandal of Golgotha are so moving that it would be well to quote the most important sentences verbatim. They deserve to be read very carefully, thoughtfully, and slowly:

And now, my brothers, I must remind you of the gospel that I preached to you; the gospel which you received, on which you have taken your stand, and which is now bringing you salvation. Do you still hold fast the Gospel as I preached it to you? If not, your conversion was in vain. First and foremost, I handed on to you the facts which had been imparted to me: that Christ died for our sins, in accordance with the scriptures; that he was buried; that he was raised to life on the third day, according to the scriptures; and that he appeared to Cephas, and afterwards to the Twelve. Then he appeared to over five hundred of our brothers at once, most of whom are still alive, though some have died. Then he appeared to James, and afterwards to all the apostles. In the end he appeared even to me; though this birth of mine was monstrous, for I had persecuted the church of God. (1 Cor. 15,1–9, *NEB*) [4]

The denial of Christ's resurrection according to Paul could have annihilating consequences:

> Now if this is what we proclaim, that Christ was raised from the dead, how can some of you say there is no resurrection of the dead? If there be no resurrection, then Christ was not raised; and if Christ was not raised, then our gospel is null and void, and so is your faith; and we turn out to be lying witnesses for God, because we bore witness that he raised Christ to life, whereas, if the dead are not raised, he did not raise him. For if the dead are not raised, it follows that Christ was not raised; and if Christ was not raised, your faith has nothing in it and you are still in your old state of sin. It follows also that those who have died within Christ's fellowship are utterly lost. If it is for this life only that Christ has given us hope, we of all men are to be pitied. (1 Cor. 15,12–19. *NEB*)

Thereupon follows, like a kind of liberation for the reader who has been strained to the utmost, the renewed confession of the apostle. In fact, Christ *has* been raised from the dead, the first fruits of those who have fallen asleep (1 Cor. 15,20). Paul can breathe again when he looks into the future. Is it an illusion? God's spirit bears testimony that it will become reality.

"Now we have received not the spirit of the world, but the Spirit which is from God, that we might understand the gifts bestowed on us by God" (1 Cor. 2,12). This Spirit guarantees that the hope for the future is no vague and indefinite expectation, no utopian idea, but that it is real. On the other hand this situation leads us to the truth that Christianity is a matter of hope, not of full possession. Our salvation is based on hope. But it is precisely this which divides men (Rom. 8,24; 15,4; 2 Cor. 3,12; Eph. 2,12). Only one who is open to the absolute standards of God and is ready to sacrifice his own can share such hope, and this requires no slight effort. Though the death on Golgotha is the epitome of scandal—the disgrace so public, the divinity wholly concealed—the difficulty really begins earlier, with the whole historical character of Jesus the Savior.

Since Jesus is a man in every aspect of humanity, he is the

child of his people, speaks their language, lives as they live and prays their prayers. If we want to understand him, we must take pains to learn his language. His thoughts move in a form which is different from the western way of thinking, since the latter is determined by the classical Greek forms of thought. The country in which he lived was not one of the great empires. It was not the region of one of the great ancient cultures. For the Roman historians, Palestine belonged to the least known territories of the time of Augustus. It was not a particularly conspicuous event, when a teacher in that country gathered disciples around him: the rabbis did the same. And they were also expected to perform miracles. Nor did his death on the cross point him out as having a special destiny. The Romans executed men frequently in this cruel and shameful manner (J. Zimmermann). Thus indeed, as Paul says, the way in which God appears to men is a vexation and foolishness (1 Cor. 1,23). When Paul himself assures us that he is not ashamed of the cross, we distinctly sense that he is resisting a natural reaction. Only one who, surrendering to faith, stands at God's side and considers the Christ-event from there can understand that what looks like folly is in reality divine wisdom.

The hidden character of divine revelation expresses itself also when, according to St. John's gospel, Jesus refused to answer the Jews when they demanded that he frankly acknowledge whether or not he was the Messiah (Jn. 10,24-39). They thought he should be able to prove his Messianic dignity to them in an unveiled way, which could be attested objectively. When Jesus declined the public testimony of himself which they demanded, he did so not for reasons of opportunism or from ill will, but because it was objectively impossible to fulfill their request. If Jesus had publicly testified to himself, he would have submitted to public standards. That, however, means he would have submitted to a standard inadequate to God's revelation. The content of divine revelation *cannot* be predetermined from a standpoint within the world. Jesus referred to the testimonial of the works which he performed in the name of his father. But the very fact that these works were done in the name of the Father, that God appears in them, can only be affirmed in faith.

The veiled character of divine revelation would be exaggerated if we were to agree with the early Karl Barth that a *contradiction* exists between our natural religious ideas and concepts on the one hand and divine self-communication on the other. This view would lead to the denial of any divine revelation. The paradox accepted by Barth, taken as a principle, would lead to our getting farther and farther removed from God, the more carefully we applied our concepts to him. It would be another form of exaggeration to see in divine revelation only a cipher, engaging the mind but having no further meaning for us.

Let us turn now to a new set of problems: By what means has God carried out the revelation of himself in man's history? He has used a double method, actually one method with two aspects. That is, God has revealed himself to us in historical actions and historical words. He approaches man in his salvific action and his salvific word. Hence we shall speak, in what follows, both of the salvific action and the salvific speech of God, and of the inseparable union of his words and actions.

GOD'S REVELATION OF HIMSELF IN JESUS CHRIST

In Jesus Christ, God's revelation of himself in action and in word is bound together in an indissoluble unity. Consequently it is most fitting and fruitful if we begin by sketching the function of Jesus Christ for the whole of divine self-revelation. In the divine plan of revelation Christ was to be the summit of all that is to be communicated to man by God. Therefore everything else that is connected with revelation revolves around him. Christ was no late arrival in God's plan of creation; he was rather its life-center from the beginning. The importance of this thesis requires that it be demonstrated in detail from Sacred Scripture.

According to the scriptural texts, the man Jesus is the first creative thought of the Father. Everything else was conceived of and planned on his behalf. The world, both cosmos and history, exists because of Christ; Christ was not planned because of the world. He was foreordained in one single divine world-plan as the center of creation and as the revealer of God. This latter function is proper to him because he is the foundation on which the existence of creation rests. Thus the Logos that had become man was intended by God in one single act to be both the center and the savior of the world. He can be the savior because he is ordained by God as the center of the world, from which saving forces radiate out over the entire creation. The question as to the ontological dimension in which Jesus' relationship to created reality lies, particularly whether Jesus should be considered as a part of the evolutionary course of creation, will be discussed later. In the scriptural texts which testify to Christ's relationship to creation, its ontology is not analyzed. They show, however, that the redemptive function of Jesus is founded on his ordination to the world. The texts emphasize that both aspects belong together. But they lay greater stress on the aspect of salvation history and revelation than on the ontological-causal aspect. In this respect St. Paul's letters are as distinctive in expression as the writings of St. John. In the First Epistle to the Corinthians Paul writes: "For indeed, if there be so-called gods, whether in heaven or on earth—as indeed there are many 'gods' and many 'lords'—yet for us there is one God, the Father, from whom all being comes, towards whom we move; and there is one Lord, Jesus Christ, through whom all things came to be, and we through him" (8,5f., *NEB*).

The most enlightening passages are in the epistles to the Colossians, the Ephesians, and the Hebrews. Colossians states:

He is the image of the invisible God; his is the primacy over all created things. In him everything in heaven and on earth was created, not only things visible but also the invisible orders of thrones, sovereignties, authorities, and powers: the whole universe has been created through him and for him. And he exists before everything, and all things are held together in him. He is, moreover, the head of his body, the church. He is its origin, the first to return from the dead, to be in all things alone supreme. For in him the complete being of God, by God's own choice, came to dwell. Through him God chose to reconcile the whole universe to himself, making peace through the shedding of his blood upon the cross—to reconcile all things whether on earth or in heaven, through him alone. (1,15–20, *NEB*)

These words testify first of all to the salvific function of the revelation which God makes through Jesus Christ. But at the same time they tell who this Jesus is. Let us refer again to the marvelous beginning of the letter to the Hebrews with its universal vision (1,1–3, 2,5–10). The following passage is directed to the Christians at Ephesus (Eph. 2,10): "For we are his workmanship, created in Christ Jesus for good works, which God prepared beforehand, that we should walk in them." In Jesus God shows himself in regard to his plan for the world. Heinrich Schlier gives the following interpretation of the connection between Jesus Christ's relationship to creation and his salvific function:

The Church is in its nature oriented towards the whole of mankind and the entire world. In her the mystery of God's will prevails that embraces and cares for "Heaven and Earth." God's will overlooks neither the outermost nor the innermost, neither the nearest nor the farthest things. From the outset the Church is oriented towards and concerned about all times and all places, all men and all powers. In its existence and its activity it asserts the truth of the salvific will of God. Salvation, however, means in this epistle: to raise a humanity alienated from God and divided in itself to the one, unifying vision of God. Salvation means the re-establishing of man and his world in the peace of obedience in Christ. Thus when the apostle speaks of the Church as the mystery of Christ, he has in mind above all that the Church is the mystery of the will of God which in Christ precedes all things, is concerned about all things and elevates everything into peace. This mystery in a certain sense is also that of the creator. As such, it is hidden before the aeons in the God who created the universe (cf. Eph. 3,9). The aeons are the epochs of history that constantly invade the present time from the future. Thus the mystery of Christ which manifests itself in the Church is hidden from history as such. Up to now the mystery has not appeared in history, just as nothing was known of it before the Church came into existence (cf. 3,5). Aeons after aeons rose up and disappeared. The aeon of this mystery remained in concealment, history itself veiled it, ruling powers and men in general did not allow it to appear. History always permitted only its own mystery to be made manifest, the aeon of this world. But the mystery of Christ existed all the same. It is always there wherever there is creation. It is also the mystery of the creator, and finds its being not only in God's eternal salvific will but also in his creative will. For Christ is, according to the apostle, also the one in whom the universe is created and the one in whom it has stability (cf. Col. 1,16f.), so that all that is created proclaims this mystery in its own way. To the extent that creation still goes on in a world that keeps truth imprisoned in wickedness (Rom. 1,18), and which confuses and mistakes the creature for the creator (Rom. 1,23ff.), to that extent is the mystery of Christ visible and effective as the mystery of the creator. With whatever terrors world history may run its course, yet by the very fact that it happens it is ultimately grounded in creation and in God's creative will. And so the mystery, which to a great extent is concealed and falsified by man, rises up resplendent again over creation. The savior, as the apostle stresses in this passage against the gnostics, is no one but the creator. Christ's mystery, therefore, when it comes to light in the Church, also illuminates once again the mystery of creation.

The mystery of God's eternal will that remained concealed from the aeons of history in God the Creator has now, according to the apostle, been revealed in Jesus Christ. The eternal will of God, secretly working in creation to re-establish man in Christ, has now been fulfilled in Jesus in the midst of history. In Christ's death and resurrection, God has realized his own primary mystery in the midst of the world. Thus the apostle in his Epistle to the Colossians also expressly calls Jesus Christ the mystery of God, and the events of his cross and resurrection are termed the mystery of Christ (2,2; 4,3).[5]

The gospel of St. John conveys the same conviction as the Pauline writings. In the initial hymn it says: "Through him all things came to be; no single thing was created without him" (Jn. 1,3, *NEB*). "He was in the world; but the world, though it owed its being to him, did not recognize him" (Jn. 1,10, *NEB*). The world, the cosmos, is understood by John as the sphere of human existence (Jn. 1,10; 9,5; 12,25; 13,1; 16,21; 17,11); John speaks of it only for the sake of God's revelation in Christ. The world is seen as the necessary presupposition for God's activity in Christ in the history of revelation, as the sphere for the historical activity of man. One and the same Logos is the foundation of the creation of the world and of God's revelation in it. He accomplishes his task of revelation in a sphere which is not foreign to him. A vital continuity exists between his two functions despite their difference in quality.[6]

If Christ is the center, the meaning, and the climax of the cos-mos and of history, then everything is either the way to him or a sequel to him. Whatever takes place before his time is his pre-history. He himself signifies the absolute climax of the evolution of the created universe as it has moved onward for billions of years. Apart from Christ, God will not bring about new ways of communicating himself within history to the whole of mankind: God's revelation of himself in Christ has universal significance. What takes place after Christ must be understood, as far as divine revelation is concerned, as a participation in his life. Jesus is not only a phase in the history of religion but the unsurpassable con-summating of God's revelation, valid for all of creation. At the same time, of course, he is a new beginning, marking the decisive introduction of the absolute future. To emphasize the fulfillment-character of Jesus' coming is not to overlook the character of promise which is proper to him. In Christ, or more accurately in the risen Lord, creation has reached its goal—deification; that is, the unconditional self-communication of God to creation and crea-tion's acceptance of this divine gift of himself even within the course of the world. With an inexhaustible dynamism this event will transform the entire creation.

When we reflect on the totality of God's self-revelation, we must look back from Christ's place in history to the secular era preceding him. If we wish to contemplate the effect of God's self-revelation we must look forward, towards the absolute future. Looking back into the past we distinguish between the self-revela-tion of God in divine actions and his self-revelation in divine utterances. In Christ himself salvific action and salvific speech are most intimately connected.

In the totality of his existence Jesus is the revealer and the revelation of God. What he does and what he says are the expres-sions of what he is in himself.

Readings

Bulst, Werner. *Revelation*. Translated by Bruce Vawter. New York, Sheed and Ward, 1965.

Latourelle, René. *Theology of Revelation.* New York, Alba, 1966.
Moran, Gabriel. *Theology of Revelation.* New York, Herder and
  Herder, 1966.

Notes

1 Cf. Josef Blank, *Krisis. Untersuchungen zur johanneischen Christologie
und Eschatologie* (Freiburg, 1964), 69.

2 *RSV: Revised Standard Version.* Except where otherwise indicated, the
Scripture quotations in this publication are from the *Revised Standard Version and the Apocrypha,* copyrighted 1957 by the Division of Christian Education, National Council of the Churches of Christ in the U.S.A., and used
by permission.

3 *The Documents of Vatican II,* ed. Walter M. Abbott, S.J. (New York:
America Press, 1966), 112. Excerpts from the Constitutions and Decrees
of the Ecumenical Council are taken from *The Documents of Vatican II,*
published by Guild Press, America Press, Association Press, and Herder and
Herder, and copyrighted 1966 by the America Press. Used by permission.

4 *NEB:* From the *New English Bible, New Testament.* © The Delegates of
the Oxford University Press and the Syndics of Cambridge University Press
1961. Reprinted by permission.

5 "Die Kirche als Geheimnis Christi," in *Die Zeit der Kirche* (Freiburg:
Herder, 1956), 300f.

6 Blank, *op. cit.,* p. 191.

‹ 4

God's Self-Revelation in Work: His Creative Activity

THE PRE-CHRISTIAN REVELATION OF GOD IN SALVIFIC ACTIONS

If we distinguish God's revelation in action from his revelation in word and consider the revelatory actions in the prehistory of Jesus, we must make one basic observation at the outset. We frequently encounter in theology the distinction between "revelation-through-work" and "revelation-through-word." The creation of the world is designated as revelation-through-work; the revelation which began with Abraham and culminated in Christ is termed revelation-through-word. In scholastic terminology one would have to call the work-revelation "natural," the word-revelation "supernatural" revelation. The distinction, however, is impracticable. By it we overlook the fact that the divine revelation which began in Abraham and culminated in Christ was carried out in actions, although its comprehensive form is the word. The distinction in question, therefore, does not adequately express what is meant. We shall see that the difference between "natural" and "supernatural" must be explained in a different way. Nor would the problem be solved if we tried to distinguish terminologically between the revelation of creation and the revelation of Christ, however many objective reasons may argue for this distinction.

53

According to the doctrine of the Christ-centeredness of all creation, everything is, in a certain sense, a revelation of Christ.

Perhaps the difference might be made clear by resorting to such expressions as "preparation for the revelation of Christ" and the "accomplishment of the Christ-revelation." The preparation for the Christ-revelation includes two main steps: the billions of years before the call of Abraham—to whom, according to the apostle Paul, the gospel was first revealed—and the relatively short period of time since Abraham's call. Such a division into two completely unequal parts should not, of course, cause us to overlook the differences which exist within the pre-Abraham era—for example, between the period in which man made his appearance and the prehuman period, We shall first discuss the work-revelation, or revelation of action, which took place in the era preparing for Christ; and this will be done in such a manner that we shall gradually trace our way back to the beginnings.

The most important event of divine self-revelation before Jesus consists in the liberation of the sons of Israel from the Egyptian captivity by Moses, and the events following their wanderings through the desert, their conclusion of the covenant on Sinai, the proclamation of the law, the occupation of the Holy Land. These events have fundamental significance for the existence of the Jewish people. Consequently, they were festively celebrated in cult. However complicated the origin and early development of the people of Israel may be historically, they still sense a divine power in their becoming a people. In the experience of God which occurred in these events, more specifically in the experience of Jahweh's salvific activity, the religious and national unity of the people of Israel was created. They now exist as a people through and from the awareness that the ineffable God came down to them in freedom, and works in their midst. They know themselves to be chosen by him before all other peoples. With them and with them alone God made a covenant. This people is supposed to show the grandeur of God to other peoples as well; therefore, it also has a representative task. But the other peoples should not be excluded. The People of God was the representative of all mankind and must proclaim the kingdom of God to the others.

The Sacred Scripture which testifies to the history of these events is not meant to teach history in the modern sense. It is no historic chronicle of the events. Its texts are rather objectivizations of the real experience of God and of the faith of the people of Israel. The call of Moses (Ex. 3,1–5) marked the beginning of God's self-revelation in these events. Moses received in Midian, "in the western part of the desert," the command to free his people from Egyptian domination and to lead them into the promised land, Canaan. To the question Moses puts to the mysterious Being, Who is the God who has given him such a difficult and far-reaching task? he receives an answer which is as strange as it is upsetting:

God said to Moses, "I AM WHO I AM." And he said, "Say this to the people of Israel, 'I AM has sent me to you.'" God also said to Moses, "Say this to the people of Israel, 'The LORD, the God of your fathers, the God of Abraham, the God of Isaac, and the God of Jacob, has sent me to you': This is my name for ever." (Ex. 3,14–15)

In another part of this work the name of Jahweh will be discussed in greater detail. At this point we should call attention to the fact that the name "Jahweh" designates God, not directly as absolute Being, but as the inviolable reality (*Wirklichkeit*) in the sense of a principle of operation (*Wirksamkeit*). He who calls Moses proclaims and gives testimony to himself as the one who is and always will be powerful in his chosen people. As he exercised his power among their ancestors, so he will create the future of his people. Thus God's answer to Moses contains the notion of the continuity of God's effective activity as a pledge of his reliability. He who speaks with Moses is said to be the God of the Fathers, of Abraham, Isaac, and Jacob. Thus at the very beginning of its existence Israel becomes conscious of its prehistory by looking back to its origins, the patriarchs.

However the history of the patriarchs may be portrayed in Sacred Scripture, the main issue is its testimonial to faith in saving divine guidance. When God called Abraham away from his homeland, he concluded a covenant with him which contained the promise of a great number of descendants. This covenant was in

preliminary form and was the introduction to the covenant on
Sinai. Abraham's descendants were conscious of being guided
and led by God in a special way. God's protection and planning are represented in Sacred Scripture in conceptual forms
and images which were congenial to the time. The high figures
used in quoting the age of the patriarchs should probably be
understood as symbols of the continuity of the saving providence of God and of the good future awaiting God's people.
The experiences which Israel had with God at the time of the
conclusion of the covenant with him, and the preceding history
of the patriarchs, are recalled again and again in the following
centuries. In innumerable texts in the psalms and the prophets,
the power and generosity of God as the Lord and the Savior
are praised (Pss. 9,18; 48,9ff.; 71,2; 77,15; 106,8; 145,12;
Is.45,7; 51,3; 54,1; 65,17ff.; Jer.16,21; Ez.34,27–30). The
knowledge of God's guidance gives his people hope to withstand the blows of fate, and at the same time it gives them
reason for reflection. The prophets always interpret the misfor-
tunes of the people as God's judgment, but they add the promise
that God will turn to the aid of his people again when they
return to the right path. It was the prophet Ezechiel above all
who, in the rigors of the Babylonian exile, sustained the people
by giving them the hope of being led home in accordance with
God's promise (Ez.37,12; 39,28). The meaning of any affliction
sent by God is: "They shall know that I am the Lord" (Ez.7,27).

    Not only the Israelites but also other peoples are to recognize
God's powerful hand in the course of history (Ex.7,5.17; 11,7;
14,4.18; Ez.25,7.11.17; 12,16; 36,23). All events in history serve
the one purpose of making God known (Ex.14,31; 1Kg.18,39;
Is.45,7; 48,12f.; 63,10). So too in the Christ-revelation the splendor of God is proclaimed; so too, according to the Old Testament,
his glory is revealed by God's communication of himself to his people (Is. 6,3; 42,8; Ps. 29,9; 57,8ff.; 57,11; 97,9; 102,15). The
splendor of the Lord fills the earth. All peoples can see it (Num.
14,21).

    In the course of their history, the Israelites were obliged again and
again to undergo experiences which seemed to be, or which really

were, contradictions of the covenant in which they lived. They knew that they were called to a partnership of grave consequence and of high promise. They knew by experience that among all the divine and numinous beings worshipped at that time, Jahweh, who had appeared to Abraham, who had directed Isaac and Jacob, who had given Moses the command of liberation and had revealed his name to him, was the one and only living God. Such an experience of God was completely unheard-of at that time, and represented a demythologization of the most thoroughgoing sort. In the midst of a completely polytheistic world the Israelites alone were monotheistic because of the experience of God that had been granted exclusively to them. All that was considered divine, anything that was the object of worship, was concentrated in and directed towards Jahweh alone. This God was neither a function of the national temper nor subject to any kind of magical coercion. He was the inexpressible mystery, which in complete freedom devoted itself to men in order to liberate them from their misery.

THE REFLECTIONS OF THE OLD TESTAMENT ON THE BEGINNING OF THINGS

But experience of God as expressed in the covenant conflicted with that of every day. It seems a depressing paradox indeed that while such great promises for future happiness had been given to men who lived in the covenant with God, none of these promises seemed ever to be fulfilled. Even taking possession of Canaan did not appear as a fulfillment. Eventually men began to question whether the hopes placed in God's promises could not perhaps have arisen from a great error, could not have been a mirage of the desert. Such doubts seemed all the more justified, and were all the stronger, because unlike the other peoples of the surrounding countries the Israelites had built their whole life upon the promises of the one God and on their confidence in these promises. As a people they were constituted again and again by their longing anticipation of a future time of salvation. Even when they turned back to their past, as they often did, and remembered how "it was of old" they did so in order to find in the past a pledge for the future. Yet Israel had to look on as one generation of her children after another went to their graves without ever seeing the rising dawn of fulfillment; and their day-by-day experience of oppression, threats, danger, decline, and defeat bore no resemblance to the promised glory.

From the depths of such misery questions were bound to arise concerning the God to whom they had dedicated themselves. Was he not lacking either in power or in mercy? Would not the gods of neighboring tribes with their sensual, seductive fertility cults offer better and more reliable rewards? Desertion from the living God was the extreme expression of such scepticism. Those who grieved most intensely over this problematic situation were inevitably the most faithful members of the group; and they did so in a spirit of faith and hope. The fruits of their meditations are preserved in those writings which recount the history of the people from the very beginning; particularly in the first eleven chapters of the book of "Genesis." We may assume that the basis, even if only a very small oral or written section, of this part of the Scriptures traces its origin to the time of Moses—that is, to the thirteenth or fourteenth century before Christ. The picture which the Old Testament paints of Moses and his historic activities justifies the assumption that again and again this man, with his unique strength and wisdom, stemmed the rising tide of doubt and unbelief in Israel through his preaching and writing. In the face of religious decadence, unbelief, and cynicism, any man who wanted to turn the tide had to bear witness credibly to the power and kindness of God, Israel's partner in the covenant, if he was to awaken courage and confidence, and finally to sound the call for conversion. From the time of Moses on, accretions of texts with similar aims grew from generation to generation, developing along three basic lines. They are usually called the Jahwistic document, the Elohistic, and the Priestly Code. The corpus of Jahwistic literature probably attained its definitive form in the eighth or ninth century, possibly at the court of Solomon; the priests' writings did not take final shape until the years of the Babylonian exile (538–450 B.C.) or shortly thereafter. After the return from the exile an editor, presumably a priest at the temple at Jerusalem, assembled the texts into the unified structure they have today. The Elohistic texts (so called from the name "Elohim" given to God before the event described in Exodus 3,15) represent a different line of tradition stemming chiefly from northern Israel (c. 750–700 B.C.). They are irrelevant for our present question.

However we may pose the question of literary criticism, it is clear that the texts all have one common concern: they attempt to overcome scepticism and unbelief in Israel, and they do this by telling a story. They aim to teach what the situation requires about God and man in order to awaken man and at the same time offer him solace. But they do so not by proposing a doctrine but by telling a story. More specifically, they go back to the earliest beginnings. Thus the story which attests to God's care for the people of Israel becomes a report on the creation of the world. The purpose of the narrative is not to tell how the world originated, but to show that God intended from the very beginning to single out the people of Israel and to establish his covenant of salvation with them (etiological method). Perhaps the significance of this method of presenting doctrine in story form becomes clearer if we compare it with the methods which would be used by a Greek thinker.

Around the same time that the priests' text originated, or perhaps a little earlier, the Greeks were reflecting on the question of the origin and nature of the world of man. They tried to solve the problem by analyzing the essences of things. Thales, who probably lived between 640 and 546 B.C.—i.e., at the time of, or somewhat before, the priests of Jerusalem who authored the priests' text—is the first witness for the Greek method. Like the author of Genesis he saw himself in a situation in which society was dominated by myths, confronted with the question of the meaning of life. Now he too in his turn started out by referring to the origins of the world. According to him the world came from water—an interesting parallel to St. Peter's second epistle (2 Pet. 3,5).

It is illuminating that in the priests' text too the entire organized world rose out of a watery chaos—in a different way, of course, from that envisioned by Thales—namely, through a creative act of God. Imperceptibly, however, Thales' story undergoes a change and becomes ontology. He asserts that not only does everything originate in water, but that everything *is* water. He probably derived this opinion from his practical knowledge of the ocean. But we need not go into that further. Although the ontology of Thales is but a primitive one, it is here that the ontological question concerning essence and meaning was raised for the first time in the history of the West. Since then men have never ceased asking this question. It is not the same as the questioning in the Bible regarding destiny, function, and history, but is rather an inquiry into the intrinsic nature of things, and is accompanied by a more and more refined process of abstraction. The Old Testament manner of thinking differs from this. The Old Testament writers looked back to the beginning in order to understand and explain the present and hope for the future. The future is the most important. Yet they do not shift, as do the Greek thinkers, from history to metaphysics. They see that the true understanding of man and his salvation comes not from metaphysics but from history. In their return to the beginning they are trying to reach back to a point of departure from which a whole network of subsequent events had arisen; from this point they then move forward again up to the present time, and thus they seek to bring into view those crucial events from which the present has resulted, and in the light of which alone it can be understood and mastered. If one looks for a symbol of this kind of thinking, it is the straight line; whereas for Greek thought, with its concentration on the essence resting in itself, the symbol would be the circle. As we move along the historical horizontal plane characteristic of Jewish thinking in the Old Testament, we do find from time to time an ontological awareness, and even some statements concerned with essence. But they derive their meaning only from the fact that they are elements in the historical movement.

From these considerations we see that the narrative of the first eleven chapters of Genesis must be interpreted in the light of the particular situation which was created by the loss of confidence in the covenant which occurred in Moses' time, and even the struggle to preserve belief in God during the period between Abraham (ca. 1800 B.C.) and Moses, and in the ill-fated centuries that followed.

The authors of the texts mentioned were men who in the light of their faith in Jahweh pondered over the problem of how a people who had entered into a covenant with God could find themselves in such a catastrophic situation as that in which they lived and suffered. Their observations are an expression of great religious and theological maturity.

Inspired by a realistic view of everyday experience and yet at the same time by the strength of their faith in God, these men developed a history of faith designed to solve the conflict between faith and reality. In so doing they had to come to grips with the religious views of the world surrounding them, as well as with the religious outlook of their own people. The religious world of their neighbors was dominated by myth. They saw their own people doubting God, and so in danger of succumbing to the mythical religions of their surroundings, with their numerous gods and goddesses. To cope concretely with the demands of their time, therefore, the authors felt obliged to offer assurance and warning to their people in the form of a direct confrontation with the mythical. Naturally the myths they encountered deal with the origin and the development of the world and of man.

When the biblical authors speak of the origin of the world, they are not primarily concerned with satisfying curiosity about cosmic origins; nor do they intend primarily to replace a mythical explanation of the world by one that is anti-mythical. They rather attempt, first and foremost, to tell a story, a story which, by the way it presents the origin of the world and the subsequent course of events, would make both God's guidance and the darkness of their present experience at the same time comprehensible. For they are convinced that despite all appearances to the contrary, God is still present working in the world, that he is still uttering a salvific call demanding a response, that evils have arisen because man despised or refused to hear God's call, and that the covenant has been ineffectual because of the recalcitrance of the human partner in the agreement. The authors intend not so much to inform and instruct as to appeal to men from their own deep feeling of concern and strong sense of responsibility. In doing this they also teach, of course. But their teaching has but one purpose: to issue a summons

—a summons to hope and to unshakable faith. Thus what is termed a report assumes the character of a kerygma—a proclamation of God's glorious achievements in the past, and so of a future filled with promise.

It may help us to understand the text better if we compare it with the Babylonian myth of creation with which the authors of Genesis were probably familiar. Their knowledge of this myth is all the more probable since their account makes a conscious effort to differ from it. The beginning of the Babylonian creation myth reads as follows:

At the time when the sky above was not named and the firm expanse below did not have a name; when Apsu, the original beginning, their creator, and Mumu and Tiamat, the mother of all of them, mingled their waters into one; when the shrubs were not yet interwoven with each other and no thicket of reed was to be seen; when the gods did not exist, not one, when they were not called by names and when their fates were not determined—then the gods were created in their midst.[1]

Then follows the account of the terrifying struggles of the primeval gods, struggles from which the child of the sun god, Marduck, emerged victorious and became the creator of gods and men. This text is a magnificent monument to a great historical epoch. It was written around 2000 B.C. and was still sung every year at the New Year's celebration in spring at the time of Alexander the Great (died 333). Thus the text undoubtedly had an extraordinary historical force. The crucial sentence is, "Then the gods were created in their midst." A mighty, destructive struggle between primeval forces in nature preceded this creative activity—those primal forces of nature of whom the original gods were merely symbolic representations. The gods of light who came forth from this struggle are the children born of the destructive conflict of primeval forces. They were the enemies and at the same time the heirs of their fathers. But where the primeval deities came from, the hymn does not say.

The biblical text is a polemic directed against this and other myths. Naturally, to make a protest of this sort, the biblical account must to a large extent employ mythical terminology, precisely in order to reject the myth itself. If the gods of light and their retinue, the men they brought forth, represent the survivors of a primordial struggle, then one finds intelligible the antitheses in the world between fortune and misfortune, light and darkness, good and bad, virtue and guilt. Then one can accept, in other words, the fact that a metaphysical dualism prevails in the world. Here we encounter a fundamental experience and a basic pattern of oriental thinking. Nevertheless, the biblical text resolutely rejects such a dualistic explanation of the world. It designates Jahweh as the only true God, who effortlessly created the entire world in its diversity. The biblical author says this, not to impart any theoretical knowledge, but to issue an ethical and religious call to his fellow-men. The call might be translated into terms such as the following: "Do not let yourselves be seduced by such gods, but give yourselves to Jahweh. In spite of everything, he is the only true and living God."

We should not overlook the fact that the author declares Jahweh to be the creator of all things, one who has no need to struggle with an antagonistic power, one whom no one can resist, on whom no one can impose limits, whom no one can endanger or threaten. He is characterized as the universal God, whose uncontested and incontestable area of dominion is not one nation but the whole world. He creates the whole world as a stage for the drama of universal history, not just for the drama of any national history. He puts the world in order as he would a house; he lays out paradise as he would a garden; he creates men as a potter shapes his wares on the potter's wheel, without struggle, without trouble, and according to his own decision. The whole mythological heaven of the gods collapses in this tale. In such a demythologized reality no room remains for an original principle of evil, for a metaphysical dualism. The living God cannot be made responsible for evil in the way the gods and goddesses of the myths are saddled with responsibility for the world's disastrous state. Rather, evil invaded human history through man's free decision and contrary to God's original plan of salvation. It was an expression of God's special love for his creatures that despite their rebelliousness he did not abandon them to their fate but cared for them, and repeatedly renewed his offer of salvation to them. The Israelites were to be conscious of the fact that God's plan of salvation had originally included the entire universe, but that gradually, without turning away from the whole of creation, he concentrated with growing intensity on one group of men who were the predecessors of the people of Israel.

Our text, and particularly the priests' text with its six days of work, is by and large a hymn of gratitude to God, who from the beginning until this very hour has arranged everything for our salvation, who did not withdraw from the covenant, despite the obstinacy of his human partners, but who constantly increased his efforts to offer salvation to his people, without ever forcing them to accept it.

The character of the text as a thanksgiving-hymn to God becomes particularly clear when it repeats the statement over and over like a refrain: "And God saw that it was good." This sentence is meant in no way to testify to a metaphysical state of goodness, but rather to witness to the saving power of God's works.

The hymn of praise to God includes the rejection of those concepts of the gods which were prevalent in the thought of the nations which Israel had encountered in the course of its variegated history—the Egyptians, Babylonians, Assyrians and others. Indeed, it was simply unthinkable that within the framework of ancient oriental polytheism, one nation, and one of the smallest ones at that, should believe in and teach monotheism. Polytheism was an ever-present temptation for them, and had constantly to be resisted. When, for example, God is praised in the creation-hymn of Genesis for having created the sun, the moon, and the stars on the fourth day of creation, the hymn becomes for the Jewish believer an explicit repudiation of the pagan gods of the stars venerated in the astral religions of Babylonia. This text, in spite of its peaceful rhythmical flow, responds in a "tremendous anti-mythical pathos" (von Rad) to the question of the reality of the astral gods Marduck and Sin of the Babylonians, and the animal gods of the Egyptians. The authors—that is to say, the priests' text—give the categorical answer that neither animal gods nor astral gods exist. There is in fact only one God, the God of the Fathers. He is eternal, and has created with ease the whole of visible and invisible reality, and has done it in a way which is beneficent for man and designed to serve his joy and his fulfillment in life (A. Läpple).

Thus it is understandable if in the Old Testament the conviction prevails that only a fool could declare that there is no God (Ps. 14,1; 53,2; Job 2,9; Jer. 5,12). The folly is all the greater because even in nature God's splendor shines forth to such a degree that one must be blind not to see it (Pss. 13, 18, 32). A fool like this does not so much deny God's reality as deny the effectiveness of his activity in our life. He does not recall, like the wise men of the Psalms, that God looks down on mankind from heaven in order to discover a sensible man who is seeking God (Ps. 13,2). Such foolishness involves great guilt. The fool asks for a life not bound by any ties of responsibility. "The evil man boasts of his soul's desires, the grasping man blasphemes, the wicked spurns Yahweh. 'His anger is up there, he will not make me pay! There is no God!' " (Ps. 10 (9b), 3f., *J*).[2] The Old Testament condemns even more vigorously the godlessness of the surrounding nations, who do not acknowledge the one true God. The condemnation of these peoples expresses itself at times in pointed formulas: they sit in darkness and in the shadow of death; they have no real existence because they lack God, the true principle of existence. The worship of a multitude of gods is branded as atheism, and in the Old Testament this collective atheism of a people is always considered as sin.

THE CHURCH'S TEACHING ABOUT
GOD'S REVELATION OF HIMSELF
THROUGH HIS CREATIVE ACTIVITY

So seriously did the Church take its responsibility to defend the doctrine that God can be known from nature, that it declared at the First Vatican Council that the one true God, our creator and Lord, can be known with certainty from created things by means of the natural light of human reason.[3] This article of faith had a long prehistory and was the answer to two one-sided positions. On the one hand, several philosophical systems had denied either God's existence or the possibility of knowing him; on the other hand, and again in a deep spirit of scepticism regarding human reason, but with all the greater emphasis on the role of faith, the thesis was advanced that God can be known only through instruction and education, and that tradition alone, therefore, is able to shape and form the religious consciousness. The council left the question open as to how the possibility of knowing God, which it taught, could be actualized, whether by way of proof, by intuition, or by a postulate of practical reason. The oath against so-called Modernism, however, contained the statement that God, the origin and ultimate goal of all things, could be known by the natural light of reason from the visible works of creation in the same way that a cause can be known from its effect, and that therefore his existence could be proved.[4]

The council was realistic enough, however, to separate the question of theoretical possibility from the question of actual realization of the fact. It declared:

At the same time it pleased God's wisdom and goodness to reveal himself and His eternal decisions to the human race in another, supernatural way. . . . It is because of this divine revelation that whatever in divine matters is not intrinsically inaccessible to human reason can be known easily, with certitude and without admixture of error by all, even in the present situation of the human race. But revelation cannot be said to be absolutely necessary. It is needed only because God in His unbounded kindness intended man for a supernatural goal, namely, participation in His own divine goodness, something that completely transcends human understanding.[5]

Man's capacity to know God through the natural powers of his human reason (as stated by Vatican I) has never been realized in fact—indeed it has never needed to be, since from the very beginning God has communicated himself to man in grace and has promised to give himself to man ultimately in direct encounter. Nevertheless, the Vatican doctrine is of incalculable importance. For through it we see more clearly that man is by his very nature open to God, that he has within himself a divine existential as a constitutive element of his being, and that he has therefore the capacity to hear God. It is noteworthy that the council, in the text mentioned, uses the expression "revelation" in a way that suggests that it applies only to what the council calls "supernatural revelation." Yet the entire second chapter of the third session of the First Vatican Council in 1870, which is under discussion here, bears the heading "Revelation." The same is true of the "Canones." Thus it is in keeping with the spirit of the council if we understand creation, too, to be divine revelation. We will see that Scripture also regards creation as divine revelation—not only as the forerunner of God's saving action but as a salvific event in itself. We can of course overlook this aspect of it. Even though creation can be seen as God's representation of himself, man, as a consequence of his present situation of sinfulness, needs a special impulse to recognize the presence of divine mystery in the world. There are many reasons which may prevent him from seeing this most profound mystery at the heart of the world: they can be in man himself, but they can also be ascribed to God's presence being veiled in his creation, and to the wretched condition of the world itself. Even in revealing himself further in a way that transcends creation God has repeatedly impressed upon man the necessity of his interpreting and understanding himself as a creature. It is an underestimation of God's self-revelation as it transcends creation, when Rudolf Bultmann restricts it to man's regaining the understanding of himself as a creature. It is true that it does accomplish this, but it also leads man beyond that point by giving him the power to understand and fashion a mode of existence for himself in the light of Christ. Thus it leads him to union with God—divinization—and opens to him the absolute future.

The Second Vatican Council accepted the basic teachings of the First. But it relates God's revelation of himself in creation more closely to the revelation given in Christ. The former is viewed as an introduction to the latter, the latter as the goal of the former. The first took place for the sake of the second:

3. God, who through the Word creates all things (cf. Jn. 1:3) and keeps them in existence, gives men an enduring witness to Himself in created realities (cf. Rom. 1:19–20). Planning to make known the way of heavenly salvation, He went further and from the start manifested Himself to our first parents. Then after their fall His promise of re-

demption aroused in them the hope of being saved (cf. Gen. 3:15), and from that time on He ceaselessly kept the human race in His care, in order to give eternal life to those who perseveringly do good in search of salvation (cf. Rom. 2:6–7). Then, at the time He had appointed, He called Abraham in order to make of him a great nation (cf. Gen. 12:2). Through the patriarchs, and after them through Moses and the prophets, He taught this nation to acknowledge Himself as the one living and true God, provident Father and just Judge, and to wait for the Savior promised by Him. In this manner He prepared the way for the gospel down through the centuries.

4. Then, after speaking in many places and varied ways through the prophets, God "last of all in these days has spoken to us by his son" (Heb. 1:1–2). For He sent His Son, the eternal Word, who enlightens all men, so that He might dwell among men and tell them the innermost realities about God (cf. Jn. 1:1–18). Jesus Christ, therefore, the Word made flesh, sent as "a man to men," "speaks the words of God" (Jn. 3:34), and completes the work of salvation which His Father gave Him to do (cf. Jn. 5:36,17:4). To see Jesus is to see His father (Jn. 14:9). For this reason Jesus perfected revelation by fulfilling it through His whole work of making Himself present and manifesting Himself: through His words and deeds, His signs and wonders, but especially through His death and glorious resurrection from the dead and final sending of the Spirit of truth. Moreover, He confirmed with divine testimony what revelation proclaimed: that God is with us to free us from the darkness of sin and death, and to raise us up to life eternal.

The Christian dispensation, therefore, as the new and definitive covenant, will never pass away, and we now await no further new public revelation before the glorious manifestation of our Lord Jesus Christ (cf. 1 Tim. 6:14 and Tit. 2:13).

5. "The obedience of faith" (Rom. 16:26; cf. 1:5; 2 Cor. 10:5–6) must be given to God who reveals, an obedience by which man entrusts his whole self freely to God, offering "the full submission of intellect and will to God who reveals," and freely assenting to the truth revealed by Him. If this faith is to be shown, the grace of God and the interior help of the Holy Spirit must precede and assist, moving the heart and turning it to God, opening the eyes of the mind, and giving "joy and ease to everyone in assenting to the truth and believing it." To bring about an ever deeper understanding of revelation, the same Holy Spirit constantly brings faith to completion by His gifts.

6. Through divine revelation, God chose to show forth and communicate Himself and the eternal decisions of His will regarding the salvation of men. That is to say, He chose "to share those divine treasures which totally transcend the understanding of the human mind."

This sacred Synod affirms, "God, the beginning and end of all things, can be known with certainty from created reality by the light of human reason" (cf. Rom. 1:20); but the Synod teaches that it is through His revelation "that those religious truths which are by their nature accessible to human reason can be known by all men with ease, with solid certitude, and with no trace of error, even in the present state of the human race." (The Dogmatic Constitution on Divine Revelation, #3–6)

Reading

von Rad, Gerhard. *Old Testament Theology*, 2 vols. New York, Harper, 1962, 1966.

Notes

[1] Jordan, *In den Tagen des Tammuz. Altbabylonische Mythen* (Munich, 1950).

[2] *J: The Jerusalem Bible.* Excerpts from *The Jerusalem Bible*, copyright © 1966 by Darton, Longman & Todd, Ltd. and Doubleday & Company, Inc. Used by permission of the publishers.

[3] Denzinger-Schönmetzer, *Enchiridion Symbolorum, Definitionum et Declarationum de Rebus Fidei et Morum* (Freiburg: Herder, 1965[33]), 3004, 3026. Hereafter cited as Denz.

[4] Denz., 3004, 3538.

[5] Denz., 3005, Denz. 3538. See also Pius XI, *Studiorum ducem,* June 29, 1923; Pius XII, *Humani generis,* August 12, 1950; and the Dogmatic Constitution on Divine Revelation of the Second Vatican Council.

› 5

Atheism and Scepticism

ATHEISM IN THE OLD TESTAMENT

The more existential statements which the First Vatican Council added to its theoretical theses concerning the knowledge of God which man has by his very nature are supported by an abundance of texts from Sacred Scripture. Here too the concern is not with the theory that man can and must recognize God in his creation— that is, that the world has to be understood as his creation; they are primarily interested in inspiring man to surrender himself to the divine mystery present within creation. It is in this sense that we should understand the passage from this Old Testament text which originated in the Hellenistic period (Wisdom 13,1–9,*J*):

Yes, naturally stupid are all men who have not known God and who, from the good things that are seen, have not been able to discover Him-Who-is, or by studying the works, have failed to recognize the Artificer. Fire, however, or wind, or the swift air, the sphere of the stars, impetuous water, heaven's lamps are what they have held to be the gods who govern the world. If, charmed by their beauty, they have taken things for gods, let them know how much the Lord of these excels them, since the very Author of beauty has created them. And if they have been impressed by their power and energy, let them deduce from these how much mightier is he that has formed them, since **through the** grandeur and beauty of the creatures we may, by analogy,

70

contemplate their Author. Small blame, however, attaches to these men, for perhaps they only go astray in their search for God and their eagerness to find him; living among his works, they strive to comprehend them and fall victim to appearances, seeing so much beauty. Even so, they are not to be excused: if they are capable of acquiring enough knowledge to be able to investigate the world, how have they been so slow to find its Master?

To understand this text we must bear in mind that the knowledge of the one true God, the God of Israel, was a matter of the utmost importance to the author. He is not concerned with natural theology in the Aristotelian or in the post-Tridentine sense. On the contrary, he resists and opposes the surrounding polytheism and develops an apologetic for Jahweh, for Israelite monotheism. The ability man has by his very nature to know God, as the First Vatican Council taught, is thus implied, but not presented explicitly. The text describes the philosopher, who unlike the "fool" does not surrender to passion, thereby denying his belief in God's judgment, but who seeks after truth: the man who strives to find the truth but does not yet attain to it. Although the guilt of these godless scholars of Hellenistic culture does not deserve as severe a censure as that of the godless sinners of the psalms, they are nonetheless not completely innocent. For with all their scholarship they have not attained to the knowledge of the most important truth, that God and the universe are not identical. For the Old Testament, philosophical atheism arises from a culpable decision, not from a pardonable intellectual error.

ATHEISM IN THE NEW TESTAMENT

We find the same existential summons in the Pauline texts of the New Testament, namely, in the Epistle to the Romans (1,18–28), in the speeches attributed to Paul at Lystra (Acts 14,14–18) and on the Areopagus in Athens (Acts 17,22–30). All these are far from being merely instructional statements. They are rather warnings, summonses, appeals to recognize God acting in the world and in worldly events, in the human spirit and in the ongoing process of history, in his works of mercy and his just judgment. Paul stands in the tradition of Israel when he declares to the Romans that the service of idols and the ignorance of God are inexcusable, because what can be known of God is perfectly plain to them. God himself has made it plain to them (Rom. 1,19). But they wanted a God according to their own desires, and so exchanged the true God for idols (Rom. 1,25). These statements are made with the existential purpose of recalling man, by the allusion to creation, to himself—that is, to a genuine and true self-awareness, to an authentic understanding of himself, which then includes awareness and understanding of God. In the Middle Ages the conviction was common that nature was God's book in which only he could read who was able to read God's handwriting —that is, whose eyes were opened by faith (Bonaventure).

ATHEISM IN MODERN TIMES

The forms of atheism evidenced in the Old Testament represent the most important aspects of the atheistic mentality as such. It has, of course, appeared in many variants in the course of human history, but till now it has always had essentially the same motives and causes. This is true even of that form of atheism which is beginning to develop at the present time, although its articulation is certainly different from any hitherto existing form, particularly from those attested to in Scripture, so that the "new" atheists consider old-fashioned the atheism prior to their time.

Among philosophers and in the life of secularized society in general today there occurs, more commonly than this pure atheism, what might be called an "aporetic" agnosticism; insofar as this is not simply a lack of interest on the part of people comfortable in the affluent society and not faced with any crisis, it can result from a strong emphasis on the limitations of rational human knowledge. The typical agnostic of our day is aware that the principal metaphysical questions—the existence of God, human freedom, the immortality of the soul—cannot be answered by the methods of natural science. But he is prepared to leave these matters to the free decision of the individual or to faith. In this he is following the thought of Kant, though there is this difference, that while Kant considers these things to be postulates of "practical" reason, the agnostic leaves the question of their validity and significance open.[1]

At this point it must suffice to give a short survey of atheism within Christian history. In this connection it should be noted that we cannot speak about atheism in the proper sense where, although there is no explicit affirmation of the personhood of God, there is an affirmation of the divine. In connection with the difficulty of the concept of a personal God, we must take into account the fact that in those religious and religio-philosophical systems in which the personhood of God is rejected, especially in the systems of the Far East, it is only the limitation of God connected with our empirical concept of the personal which it is intended to reject. For the rest, one has to say that a living God is appealed to wherever there is not only reflection about, but also the practice of, religion. For the exercise of religion occurs always only in dialogue with God, in the hope that God will grant help and be gracious. One can also differentiate for the sake of clarity between a negative and a positive atheism. The negative consists in a man's never yet having gained a notion or concept of God. The positive is the belief that one possesses proofs that God does not exist.

Already Thomas Aquinas [2] had to contend with two objections against the reality of God which to the present time have found no satisfactory solution, and in fact have not only maintained their virulence but have, if anything, grown stronger. The first objection is that there cannot be a God because the countless evils in the world—sin and pain, misery and need, cruelty and agony, in the lives of men as well as animals—are incompatible with the activity and actuality of a benevolent God. The second objection claims that to explain reality as we experience it the assumption of God is not necessary. It would lead us too far afield here to discuss and to evaluate the answers of Thomas Aquinas. One must concede that the unspeakable suffering in the world indeed represents a depressing perplexity which does not harmonize with the idea of a benevolent God, although there are many explanations or attempts at explanations of suffering (e.g., human guilt, freedom, the biological and purifying meaning of pain, eschatological consummation; with reference to the undeniable and often immense suffering of animals, the solidarity of destiny between man and the rest of the world). One can argue indirectly against this that the rejection of God makes the situation of man still more helpless and hopeless.

With reference to the second objection, we have to say that it was precisely Thomas Aquinas who contributed decisively towards its survival into our time, when, in the interpretation of the Christian concept of creation, he pointed out—quite rightly—not only the dependence of the world upon God but also the world's own reality and value, its independence of God, an independence bestowed on it by God himself. When subsequently, under the influence of naturalistic conceptualizations, only one of these poles was stressed, the atheistic explanation of the world was a natural result.

When Pierre Simon de Laplace (died 1827) stated that he did not need the "hypothesis of God" in his scheme of the world, this phrase had its roots in the Thomistic theology of creation of the thirteenth century. Incidentally, it is worthy of note that Laplace himself had no intention of supporting atheism with his apparently cynical utterance, as he himself later explained.

In modern times there has developed an increasingly widespread atheism on the basis of these two perennial objections to God. Many forces have been at work in this which can be enumerated singly, but in practice cannot be isolated from one another. They can be summed up in general in terms of the movement towards autonomy by which men have attempted to free themselves from the dominance of the Church (cf. the lay movement beginning in the fourteenth century). These attempts towards a secularized "coming of age" were buoyed up and given energy by a confidence in reason which did not believe itself to be in need of faith, and by a highly intensified demand for freedom. These powers became concrete on the one hand in science—not only specifically in natural science but also in philosophy and history (the autonomy of reason)—on the other hand in political and economic, social and civic life (the French Revolution). At first the attacks were directed against the Church, but then they proceeded beyond the rejection of the Church's authority and the significance of Christ for salvation to the denial of God. In the scientific realm atheistic thinking took the form partly of scepticism and agnosticism, partly of a radical rejection of God, as in the materialistic systems. The latter attempted a unified, monistic explanation of the world, as opposed to any form of dualism (God and world, body and soul). Materialistic monism developed from crude beginnings in metaphysical materialism to a refined form in economic materialism (Marxism). In both forms it gained influence in the widest circles and led in the nineteenth and twentieth centuries to the multitudinous loss of belief in the living God, lamented particularly by Pius IX, Leo XIII, and Pius XI.

While Hegel attempted to harmonize the modern spirit of the nineteenth century with biblical faith by a pantheistic conception of God, Ludwig Feuerbach and Karl Marx developed the philosophy of materialistic monism. Nietzsche became its prophet. Because of the extraordinary significance of this trend of thought, it is fitting to sketch it briefly. It is of special importance that with these thinkers an element became determinative which had not previously been specifically formulated, although it was always present and sometimes prominent—namely, the notion that God is not only superfluous but even dangerous. In its most succinct formulation this thesis reads: If man is to live, God must die. If God lives, man must die.

In the thought of Ludwig Feuerbach (died 1872), the particular alone is real, the general is an illusion. The most important science for him is physiology: man is a purely organic creature. Human thinking is a function of the physiological organs. The principle of ethics is the desire for happiness. God is the creation of human psychological needs. Man projects his wishes and ideals, his longings and hopes—unattainable at present—into a higher world, calls these God and prayerfully worships him. As soon as man's happiness has been achieved, this faith in God will disappear. We must, therefore, with all our powers strive to improve the material situation of men, so that they will no longer need faith in God. A religious impulse is not completely lacking in this philosophy, inasmuch as Feuerbach declares that for man, man is God, and it is towards him that he must turn all his efforts.

Marx, in contrast to the individualistic philosophy of Feuerbach, turns to the problems of society. According to him, the world has to be transformed in such a manner that men can live in it without being tormented by suffering. Faith in God stands solidly in the way of such a transformation of the world. Marx proceeds from the assumption that God is imaginary, an empty word, a function—the creation of men who, as an opiate for their misery, project the picture of a benevolent God on the screen of their fantasy and place their hope in this picture. God as created by man is the "sigh of oppressed creation." This picture must be destroyed so that all man's efforts may be directed to the world, and not squandered in the adoration of God. By "world" he understands all that is material, together with the system of reciprocal human relationships. The world is, therefore, the world of industry and technology.

Man forms a unity with the world, which he inherits in order to transform it. Even nature is the nonorganic life of man. Man imposes his own image on nature; and in fashioning nature, he fashions himself. It is only in doing this that he achieves a truly human existence. In his world-fashioning efforts man becomes the lord of nature. Only thus does he gain and exercise his true freedom. Only thus will he become free from every illusion. Such a world condition is not given him with the world itself, but is a task for which every sacrifice must be made, even if it will lead to success only in the distant future. This future rises upon the horizon of human hopes as the perfect society in which no evil will exist. The God of the Bible permits evil and sin. He is truly a long-suffering God. In the Marxist world of the future man will no longer need, as he did in the time of faith in God, to cling to his dreams about a happy hereafter. As a result, he will no longer be estranged from his true and intrinsic nature. If man is to dedicate himself to the task of the future in full mobilization of his strength, it is necessary that every form of faith in God, even the most private in the innermost recesses of the heart, be overcome. Hence religion cannot even be tolerated as a private affair. The most private faith in God always has public implications, insofar as it impairs man's energy in the fashioning of the world. The struggle against religious faith is, therefore, a central concern, and this struggle has itself a messianic character, as is shown by the severity of the anti-theistic statements in which it finds expression.

John Courtney Murray rightly says:

The biblical history of salvation, which began when Yahweh became the living God who came down to rescue his people from the misery of their enslavement in Egypt, looked to a consummation that was at once a reality and a symbol—the entrance into the Land flowing with milk and honey. The new history of salvation, which began when the living God died, in the historical discovery that he is not man's creator and much less his savior, also looks to a consummation that is, however, to be a reality and not only a symbol. The new master of history, the Party, renews the ancient promise, to lead the people to the Land. Only now the Land is within the confines of this earth, and entrance into it will take place in time. The symbols of milk and honey are still valid; there will be abundance for all. But over the whole Land and all its people a new banner will fly, reminiscent of the one that Moses set up after Joshuah's victory over Amalek, except that it will read: God is not here; God is dead.[3]

It needs to be said, in criticism of the theory of Marx and Engels, that their chief error lies in the one-sidedness of their anthropology, an anthropology developed with thorough consistency within the limits of this one-sidedness: man is understood primarily as a biological and social being, thought and feeling are understood as ideological additions, and the individual is undervalued. Man becomes man through labor. Labor is possible only in society. On the other hand, production and exchange are the basis of social organization, so that the divisions of society are decided by the methods of production and the nature of the products. In the capitalist world the worker does not possess what he produces. It is something foreign to him, and so his labor itself becomes something foreign and unintelligible. In fact, he becomes foreign to himself. In his own mind he becomes an object, a piece of goods, to himself; in the face of this abandonment to social forces which he does not understand and cannot master, he comforts himself with faith in a world other than the real one, with a Beyond which he creates for himself out of his own need. In this view, religion and faith in God are only an ideological superstructure resting on the economic situation, and this must be changed. Then religion will die a natural death, says Marx, because in a world of freedom and happiness men will no longer need to create a world of illusions. However, we know from history and experience that faith in God can live or die in any social situation, and therefore that it is not conditioned or created by the economic organization of society, even though this can influence it for vitality or for weakness.

Present-day atheism stands in fact under the banner of Nietzsche's proclamation: God is dead. Nietzsche apparently means by this expression that God at one time, in a sense difficult to ascertain, was not dead. He asserts—We have killed him—that he once was alive. Nietzsche is convinced that with the death of God a new age for mankind begins. He ridicules the *petite bourgeoisie* for not being aware of this. In Nietzsche it becomes particularly evident that atheism is not the result of intellectual considerations but of a decision. From Nietzsche comes the expression: "How would I endure it not to be God, if there were one?" And "The God who sees everything, he had to die."

We can ask whether or not such a decision of the will is present even in those atheistic systems which formally attempt to establish atheism with intellectual arguments. We will in fact even have to say of them that they rest on a decision against God, even if it is admittedly impossible to look into the heart of a man. This atheism has its roots in modern man's consciousness of life and value. God is experienced as confinement; therefore he cannot be allowed to exist. Such atheism has the character of a postulate. The nonexistence of God is demanded by man for the sake of man (cf. N. Hartmann). For its elucidation let us point to a particular example.

In the thought of Ernst Bloch [4] we encounter very strong eschatological accents derived from the Old Testament concept of God. The God who was with Moses and whom he proclaimed is of a different character from the heathen gods of the neighboring tribes. He is not static but is possessed of an immense dynamism acting for the creation of the future. According to Bloch the God of Moses gives at the very beginning a definition of himself which is breathtaking and makes any static view of the world meaningless: "I will be who I will be" (Ex. 3,14). In Christianity too, taken in its central core, the static world-view has been overcome. A human eschatological messianism is the center of its message. But in Bloch's view the only form which a radical hope for the future can take, in the process by which the world becomes itself, is atheism. Because man has considered God all too long as a fixed and static being independent of him, the power really signified by the concept "God" has not been able to enter effectively into world history or into human action in the summoning and strengthening manner in which it should. According to Bloch only an atheism which is fully conscious and explicit, having once for all abandoned the hypothesis of God, is capable of penetrating to the Unconditional and to the total hope-content which the word God has been used to designate. As in the case of Marx, atheism is commended to us here for the sake of the future of humanity—not, however, for the sake of a classless society to be attained through atheism, but for the sake of the Unknown Unconditional.

Sartre considers atheism to be the basic decision for a truly human life. Atheism stands at the beginning of life, it is not the result of thought. While for Marx atheism develops out of the necessity for transforming the world, for Sartre and all those who share this intellectual view the authentic life is a sharing of suffering with the disgraced, the betrayed, the shipwrecked, the enslaved, and the sick. There is nothing we can change about this. Life is essentially a life of agony and anxiety. But even such a life is the real expression of freedom. The deliberate acceptance of the absurdity of the world and of one's own existence, without desire for solace—it is in this that man expresses his true freedom.

In addition to the atheistic outlook on life proclaimed by Nietzsche, there is today another view of the world which for many includes the idea of the nonexistence of God. The world is experienced in its worldliness—its secularity—in a manner never known in the past. The world is, so to speak, released into its worldliness. This is theologically quite a legitimate process, and indeed grows out of the Christian, especially the Old Testament, faith itself. The world as the creation of God must be understood as something that possesses its own laws. It is a theological thesis that the world must be seen and acknowledged in its secularity. Such a view of the world has no necessary connection with atheism; on the contrary, it leaves the path to God completely free. But in point of fact it is combined, for not a few, with the notion that the world is self-sufficient and that nothing exists outside it.

In this connection we must mention that form of contemporary atheism alluded to in the beginning of this section. It differs from other forms primarily in that it calls itself "theological" atheism. Rooted in German Protestant theology, it has come to full-fledged development in the United States, where its representatives call themselves post-existential and post-European atheists. They include William Hamilton, Thomas J. J. Altizer, and in a certain sense also Paul van Buren. This atheism bases itself upon Nietzsche's declaration, God is dead. Its representatives believe that they can find support for their position in the thought of Paul Tillich, Dietrich Bonhoeffer, Rudolf Bultmann, John A. T. Robinson, and even Kierkegaard and the early Barth. The salient feature of this atheism is an extremely radical dialectic which cannot be adequately dealt with by means of logic and which is often apparently mystical.

We can describe it perhaps in the following manner. At one time there was a God to whom homage and adoration were rendered. Today he is no more. For "we are not talking about the absence of the experience of God, but about the experience of the absence of God." These atheists do not want simply to abandon Christianity—above all, not the reference to Jesus. Indeed it is on Jesus that their whole religious interest is focused. They say that Christ himself has killed God. We must believe and hope on Christ: he is an example of freedom and love. Committing themselves to a *coincidentia oppositorum,* they consider that the present task of theology is a dialectical synthesis of a radically secular subjectivity and genuine biblical faith. With this their attention is drawn to the religious world of the East, which is acquainted with a form of holiness that has always been foreign to Christianity. Conversely, we could be prepared for a new form of the incarnation by opening ourselves to the radical secularity of present existence, an incarnation which is to unite the radically holy and the radically worldly. What this new "becoming flesh" of the holy, which is to be a universal kind of faith, will finally look like is still unclear. Hence we must wait upon the absent God, who may return. The category of "waiting" differentiates the radically atheistic theologians from the exponent of ordinary atheism. During this time of waiting, the place for living is the world; not the altar, but the city, with its poverty-stricken fellow-men, and its enemies. This also is the way to Jesus, who calls us into the world that we may serve it. This waiting is not to be confused with a mere social humanism or individualistic existentialism. The world is the world of the city, as Harvey Cox says (*The Secular City*). This means for him power, culture, sex, money, the Jew, the Negro, beauty, ugliness, and poverty.

The thesis of a God who died and remains dead can be logically tenable only if God is understood from the outset not as a being independent of man and the world, but as a force or function, whether in the world, or in relationships between people, or in human thought and feeling. It has its roots in a manner of thinking which is pragmatic and hostile to metaphysics, or one-sidedly actualistic and personalistic. Nevertheless, we can say that this atheistic theology represents basic concerns of Christianity which ordinarily were not stressed clearly and strongly enough— namely, that the world possesses its own existence, law, and value, and the hiddenness of God until the day of his final self-disclosure (cf. the *theologia negativa*). The question, however, is whether the resistance of modern man to outmoded ways of thought necessitates an atheistic view of the world; whether the displacement of God from human life is consequently required for the realization of these basic concerns, or whether their actualization does not have a better prospect of success if it is granted that God lives, that he moves history by working in human hearts, that he acts out of the depths and in the heart of man and at the same time transcends him. Radical demythologization, denumenizing of the world, the complete secularization which allows the world to be itself—this need not imply apostasy from God. It can in fact be a process of neutral value, one which forces itself upon us under different forms and with a varying tempo, especially as science and technology tend increasingly to take possession of the world. It remains, then, an open question whether man will acknowledge the world, which has become his world and is becoming steadily more so, as a creation or not.

The urgent concerns of the atheistic theology briefly sketched here are especially illuminated by their attempt to support themselves on the above-mentioned German Protestant theologians. For the latter take the world quite seriously theologically as a world which possesses its own value and reality. Further, God is spoken of here as a reality representing an ineffable mystery, hence in the way of the *theologia negativa* specifically characteristic of mystics without, on the other hand, the inclusion of the *theologia positiva*. Nevertheless we must firmly reject this atheistic theology, because it interprets its Protestant authorities too subtly and, frankly, mistakenly. For example, Bonhoeffer would be amazed to hear the views being attributed to him. Despite many related formulations and insights there is a chasm between the atheistic theology and the theology of the Protestant theologians whom the former cite. We shall comment only briefly on this point.

Bonhoeffer states explicitly, "God is the 'beyond' in the midst of our life." [5] It is Bonhoeffer's concern and that of the other theologians cited by the atheistic theology to stress man's coming of age and the immanence of God in the world, without denying his transcendence, and to teach the latter without abandoning his immanence. Bonhoeffer develops positively the movement begun in the Renaissance in the direction of human autonomy (in science, politics, society, art, and even in ethics and religion). The worldly man is for him the man come of age, but not by that token a godless man. In a dialectic of faith he writes from prison before his martyr's death: "So our coming of age forces us to a true recognition of our situation *vis-à-vis* God. God is teaching us that we must live as men who can get along very well without him. The God who is with us is the God who forsakes us (Mk. 15:34). The God who makes us live in this world without using him as a working hypothesis is the God before whom we are ever standing." [6]

The Protestant theologians cited were of the opinion, and generally continue to be so, that earlier theology did not do justice to the dialectic of immanence and transcendence, that it had conceived of God as one reality among several, as a being among beings; indeed, that it had actually localized him above and outside the world. Actually, such representations of God occurred only in certain misguided figures of the earlier theology. Even in their times Augustine and Thomas, to mention only two names, designated God as at once the height and the depth and the "within" of man. It is instructive when Tillich observes that when it is said that God is in heaven this does not mean that he lives in some special place but that his life is qualitatively different from the life of creation.

It is true that Tillich criticizes the traditional conceptions and designations of God severely, though without always doing justice to what they really meant. However, it is not his intention simply to do away with the traditional concept of God. Rather he attempts to translate it into terms intelligible to people of today, using the means provided by the philosophy of existence. He considers God as Absolute Being. Although he is skeptical about using the concept of person, and even the concept "God," he insists that we should pray. His concern is to relieve man of anxiety in the face of a God who simply makes demands on him from outside, as it were—that is, to free man from any heteronomy; and so he emphasizes the immanence of God much more strongly than his transcendence, although he does not by any means simply deny the latter.

Tillich writes elsewhere, in words which opened Bishop Robinson's eyes,[7] "And if that word has not much meaning for you, translate it, and speak of the depth of your life, of the source of your being, of your ultimate concern, of what you take seriously without reservation." [8] The term "God," according to him, describes the final transcendent depth of our being, the creative ground and the meaning of our whole existence. Of course, we must free the picture of depth from any spatial significance—that is, it must again be demythologized. It seems, however, more compatible with modern man's experience of life, more expressive of God's otherness, his transcendence and at the same time his immanence, than the spatial image of height. (We talk, for example, about the depth of truth and the depth of suffering, but not about the height of suffering and the height of truth.) The following quotes from Robinson are especially characteristic: "The question of God is the question whether this depth of being is a reality or an illusion, not whether *a* Being exists beyond the bright blue sky, or anywhere else." [9] "God as the ground source and goal of our being cannot but be represented at one and the same time as removed from the shallow, sinful surface of our lives by infinite distance and depth, and yet as nearer to us than our own selves." [10] In another instructive passage Robinson states, "I pray to God the Father. The prayer of the Christian is the opening of one's self to that totally gracious personal reality which Jesus could only address with the word Abba-Father. I am not in the least interested in a God who is described in some vague, non-personal, pantheistic concepts. The only God whom I need as a Christian is the God of Abraham, Isaac, and Jacob, the God and Father of our Lord Jesus Christ and not the God of the philosophers." [11]

It can scarcely be denied that Robinson, in his concern to save the Christian faith for mankind today, pushes the transcendence and the personality of God so much into the background that they are in danger of disappearing; as a result the worship of God seems to exhaust its meaning in relationships between persons, in each existing for the other. Consequently his position is not ultimately clear.

For the evaluation and overcoming of theological atheism the question must be asked in any given instance whether it is simply a rebellion against an incomplete conception of God—that is, whether God is not in fact affirmed, but in uncommon terms. Thus, for example, the statement that God is that reality which concerns us ultimately and which we take seriously without reservation can be understood entirely in a theistic sense, even though in the process the term "God" is omitted or even rejected. Further, it must be asked whether the expression "Waiting for the return of God" is possible for the human spirit apart from the presence of faith in God in the depth of consciousness. Hence in argument with theological atheism it is the factual question which must first be clarified.

For the rest, the Christian knows of God through revelation. Through Jesus Christ he becomes certain of the fact that one God in Three Persons exists. Hence he speaks his "Yes" to God out of the conviction of faith. That does not mean that for him the "natural" knowledge of God is eliminated. It is rather, like everything natural, put into its place in the revelation of Christ. The natural ability to know God is not only not denied by faith, it receives from it an impulse and a direction by being encompassed by it. We should, therefore, not minimize the natural ability to know God. Nor does it contradict the "Yes" of faith to God.

In the effort to know God from nature there is no question of men attempting to take possession of God or to control him, as some Protestant theologians fear. God actualizes in man the ability which he himself has implanted in the human spirit to reach out after God, to ask about him, and to turn to him. This asking and seeking is already to be understood as the beginning of man's answer to that divine call and summons which the world, as the creation of God, represents for the man living in it. Because, apart from revelation, God shows himself to man in the world in an indirect way; thus making himself the object of knowledge, he makes man the subject of this knowledge. It leads, however, if true to its nature, not to an objectification of God, but to an obedient and loving encounter with him.

On the other hand, it is doubtful if a man has ever come to the conviction of the existence of God by way of natural proofs. This doubt is not a contradiction of the above-mentioned decree of the First Vatican Council. For the latter declares the existence of objectively valid thought processes which are rightly concluded with the sentence: God exists. We must differentiate between the objective validity of a truth and its subjective appropriation in personal conviction. The objectively valid reasons for the existence of God would maintain their value even if no one had ever become convinced of the existence of God by this method. They would still show that faith was capable of vindication. We should not, however, in our evaluation of the psychological effectiveness of the proofs for God's existence, overlook the fact that they involve extraordinarily difficult and complicated thought processes and require good will as well for their evaluation and affirmation, since they are not, of course, compelling mathematical proofs. Indeed the question must also be raised whether a purely theoretical knowledge of God ever does exist or can exist. *Vis-à-vis* God man cannot remain neutral.

The idea must be firmly rejected that religious faith so far as it originates in man himself must be destroyed before faith in Christ can arise. Against this view, held by the early Barth, Bonhoeffer, and others, is the fact that faith as it occurs in non-Christian religions is a form of expression of man's devotion to God. Further, we do not know to what extent this faith is wrought by the grace of God. Even if it can be a position out of which man feels justified in rejecting the message of Jesus Christ, it can, nevertheless, and at the same time, be a point of contact for faith in Christ, since it is an actualization and realization of man's openness to God.

If we are to come to grips with God's communication of himself to man in Jesus Christ, and the prehistory which led up to that, we must remember that in the course of history, God shows himself at any time only in ciphers and signs, not in the immediate fullness of his being—that is, in a form which is not his own but is foreign to him—but that a future is promised in which he will show himself without intermediary. Therefore all knowledge of God exists in a condition of unrest and movement towards the future. Every present form of faith in God is exposed to temptation and to doubt. But it is open towards the future. When God reveals himself in the fullness of his being, the knowledge of God will no longer be a problem (1 Cor. 13,12). Faith in God must therefore move in a twofold direction, towards the transcendent and towards the immanent. If it leaves either out, it is subject to doubt and despair, and is liable to be overwhelmed. It can live only as a movement towards a God who is future and therefore, by that fact, present.

We must stress lastly that atheism as a social phenomenon will not be overcome in the end by mere theoretical deliberation, but only by Christian action—perhaps by the war against poverty and against slums, by the solution of the race question, and by the other methods urged by the so-called theological atheists.

With regard to the relationship between theistic theology and so-called theological atheism, the attitude of the former in relation to God is also one of waiting; not a waiting upon the return of God, simply, but a waiting for the coming of God in the future. The Christian theologian looks towards the future and expects from it the final and unmediated self-disclosure of God. Although he knows himself bound to God by God's gracious call, he nevertheless experiences him as a hidden God. This hiddenness of God can in no way be removed in the course of human history. Ardent longing and fervent effort cannot penetrate the veil which conceals God from the human spirit. The open and unmediated exchange of God with the world and each individual man in it represents just this absolute future to which we have alluded so often. So waiting for God acquires the characteristic of a hope for the future, not a passive but a creative hope. The contents of this hope may be essentially different for theistic theologians and for the so-called atheistic theologians; its structures, nevertheless, are similar.

German Protestant theology is threatened with the danger of a one-sided immanentism in this area of discussion, so far as it is represented by the hermeneutical school based on the views of Bultmann (for example, Ebeling, Fuchs, Juengel, Braun, etc.). It is motivated by a pastoral concern: the message of Jesus

Christ must reach modern man, and hence must be brought home so effectively that it really touches him. The message of the gospel and the contemporary situation of man must not be permitted to fall asunder but must find each other. This direction, then, adopts to a large extent the thought structure of Heidegger. In a special way it considers programmatic for theology Heidegger's statement that it is above all in language that Being both comes to light and is concealed.

Let us cite some of the most important examples. According to Gerhard Ebeling, God is only present for us in that he speaks to us—that is, in the Word-Event. The word, as Ebeling rightly stresses, is not just information, but an opening up of reality and of the future. By the word of God, as he puts it, God is not only illuminated so as to become visible for man. Rather, the word radiates from God and illuminates our existence in this world. By its light the world becomes changed. Thus the world is seen to be God's summons to us. Since the world concerns us, our speech in the world is always already an answer to God's call; indeed, human language is a manifold echo of God's word. While Ebeling is concerned with the world and what belongs to it, Ernst Fuchs understands language as the coming to light of being (*Lichtung von Sein*) within the framework of Christology. God brings man to speech in Jesus Christ. With the success of the language-event man becomes a being for whom the question of God is silenced, and whose existence becomes one of gratitude. Should the language-event fail, however, then the question of God arises. Our self-understanding is placed under the criticism of a self-understanding derived from the biblical text on the basis of God's word to us. Jesus becomes a helper here, not by transmitting objective or useful information, but by his word of summons (*Anrede*), which reaches us ever anew in the preaching of the gospel.

The most radical among the hermeneutical theologians is H. Braun. In his view it is necessary to bring the message of the Bible down from the heights of the so-called world of God to the profane ground of authentic humanity. God is to be found in our fellow-man; he does not exist for himself. He is, rather, to be understood as the Whence of human agitation. This agitation is characterized by the words "I may" and "I will"; thus at the same time by security and by obligation. But both security and obligation originate with one's fellow-men. This means that man as man, man in his fellow-manhood, man as true community, implies God. God should be understood, then, as a particular kind of community. This is a far-reaching alteration of the biblical message, or at the very least a one-sided interpretation of it.

H. Gollwitzer stresses especially that knowledge of God should not remain attached to mere ontological or objectifying statements, but must move on to the element of the personal; that is, finally must find its fulfillment in dialogue with God. Discourse about God, says Gollwitzer, to be appropriate to God, must take note of five conditions. (1) God, as eternal "Thou," is a person, never in any manner an "It" structure. He addresses man as his counterpart. The truth of God occurs in personal encounter. (2) God is comprehensible only in relationship, never outside it. He is comprehensible in the covenant history of Israel and in the history of Jesus of Nazareth. (3) Man cannot bring God within the sphere of his own powers, since that would make an object out of God; he can only encounter him in event and in history. (4) God confronts man in the act of speaking to him, in the word. Even his action has the character of a word. God is never truth in the sense of an object or a general idea. (5) God's word does not control man, but creates space for a genuine freedom of response on the part of man.

In all these views the thesis that God is only a reality existing outside man, that God is only *extra nos*, is opposed. On the other hand, the thesis that God is God for us is emphatically defended; indeed, that he is God in us. The concern which this expresses is warranted. Yet the question must be asked whether this concern is not advocated in such a one-sided manner that the transcendence of God is lost sight of. If this is the case, then an encounter between God and man cannot occur; man remains closed in on himself, able to carry on only a monologue, and that within his own narrow dimensions.[12] The devil is being driven out by Beelzebub. If God is understood as immanent either completely or one-sidedly, he becomes simply a structural element of human existence. Ontology is sacrificed to functionalism or structuralism.

Whoever attempts to establish the existence of God on the level of theoretical considerations can avail himself of the lines of argument worked out in the course of the history of Christianity, particularly by Thomas Aquinas. He must, however, include the developed considerations of modern philosophy and science. Perhaps we can, for example, advance from the ontological difference between being as such (*Sein*) and being in the sense of that which is (*Seienden*), to Absolute Being through the medium of being which is in itself indeterminate (*das an sich unbestimmte Sein*), since it is only in the light of Absolute Being that that being which is given in all the particular beings (*Seienden*) of our experience can be explained.

In particular, the anthropological perspectives of the present day can become a point of departure for the way to God. Both in a positive and negative way man today has become a puzzle to himself. In the movement of the spirit in which he seeks himself—often, for lack of reflection, unaware that he is seeking himself—he always finds that he is swept beyond himself towards the Thou, towards the community, towards the world; at the same time he experiences his inability to escape from the care and anxiety that hound him and to find the absolute security and absolute justice he longs for. Consciously or unconsciously the longing for encounter with his fellow-men, if it is deep enough, becomes a way to God. Thus, if man is to understand himself rightly, he must continually go beyond himself, and indeed to that unlimited horizon where alone he finds an answer to the questions which trouble the depths of his being.[13]

An honest confrontation with atheism will show that its justifiable concerns—freedom, brotherhood, engagement in the world—not only are not threatened by faith in God, but find their deepest foundation, obligation, and legitimation precisely in it. For God embraces both nature and history with creative power and leads their movements, without inhibiting interventions, towards the fullness of the future. We are not faced with the alternatives God or freedom, God or our fellow-men, God or the world; there is only the unity of God and nature, God and history—unity with God through our fellow-men and through the world.[14]

According to Scripture, God's revelation of himself in creation and his revelation in Jesus Christ, with its preliminary stages from the time of Abraham, are not two separate divine actions running parallel to one another but a single divine action which develops in various phases. The divine self-revelation made first of all through the whole of creation is both diminished and augmented in a constantly ongoing process during the course of history. It is diminished in that it narrows down its focus of concentration further and further to individual groups and to particular individuals, until it is concentrated in one individual, Jesus Christ. At the same time it is augmented by being intensified in its concentration, so as to attain its highest and unsurpassable fullness in that one individual. The divine self-revelation which begins with Abraham, ascends, in Moses, to its climax in the Old Testament, and points out Christ as the promised One in whom it will be fulfilled is the continuation on a new plane of the divine revelation which had begun with creation. God's self-revelation, which originated in the act of creation, is not superseded by the phase of revelation which begins with Abraham. Rather, the one phase is taken up into and preserved in the other and at the same time carried beyond itself. Between God's self-disclosure in his creation of the world and his self-concealment in Abraham, Moses, the prophets, and Christ there is no contradiction, but a continuity in discontinuity.

WAS THERE A "PRIMITIVE REVELATION"?

The question has often been discussed as to whether there was a "primitive revelation" of God associated with the origins and the primeval fate of the first human beings—a revelation transcending that accomplished in the fact of creation. While this question was generally answered affirmatively in the theology of the past, such a thesis meets with serious opposition today. The objections are that it is impossible to prove, and that it is difficult even to imagine how such an original revelation could have been preserved throughout the millennia of human history. While the first objection is self-evidently valid, the evaluation of the second depends upon imponderables which everyone will evaluate according to his own temperament. Therefore we can only answer our question with the statement that there probably was no such primitive revelation—at least, there are insufficient grounds for assuming one. Moreover, even if not impossible, its assumption is superfluous. The real "primitive revelation" was addresssed to Abraham and Moses.

Readings

de Lubac, Henri. *The Drama of Atheist Humanism.* New York, Sheed and Ward, 1950.

Lepp, Ignace. *Atheism in Our Time.* New York, Macmillan, 1963.

Notes

[1] Cf. H. R. Schlette, "Der Agnostizismus und die Christen," in *Wahrheit und Verkündigung* (Paderborn, 1967), I, 123–147.

[2] Cf. F. van Steenberghen, *Ein verborgener Gott* (Paderborn, 1966).

[3] *The Problem of God* (New Haven: Yale University Press, 1964,) 112.

[4] *Geist der Utopie,* 1918; *Das Prinzip der Hoffnung,* 1954.

[5] *Prisoner for God* (New York: Macmillan, 1954), 124.

[6] Bonhoeffer, *op. cit.,* pp. 163–164.

[7] John A. T. Robinson, *Honest to God* (Philadelphia: Westminster Press, 1963), 21–22.

[8] Paul Tillich, *The Shaking of the Foundations* (New York: Scribner's, 1948), 57.

[9] Robinson, *op. cit.,* p. 55.

[10] *Ibid.,* p. 59.

[11] *Loc. cit.*

[12] See K. Luethi, "Evangelische Theologie," in *Wort und Warheit,* 11 (1966), 677–681.

[13] F. Seiler, *Das Dasein Gottes als Denkaufgabe* (Lucerne, 1965).

[14] H. Beck, *Der Gott der Weisen und Denker,* die philosophische Gottesfrage (Aschaffenburg, 1968³).

The Fulfillment
of the Old Testament
Work-Revelation
in the Works of Jesus

God's self-revelation reaches its ultimate expression in the works of Jesus Christ. According to the testimony of the synoptic gospels, the actions of Jesus had for their purpose the establishment of the kingdom of God. This concept sums up what Jesus wanted to achieve. It will be discussed in greater detail in the treatise on the Church. God's kingdom means, at the same time, salvation for man. For it is precisely when man submits himself to God that he attains his own true life. This becomes clearer when we recall that God is creative love. God's reign in man means that that love which lives in the depths of man's being but also transcends him becomes the principle of his activity. This question will be explored in greater detail in another context.

God's manifestation of himself in the works of Jesus can be illustrated by a few examples. John the Baptist, from prison, had his followers ask Jesus whether or not he was the Messiah: "Are you he who is to come, or shall we look for another?" Jesus answered them, "Go and tell John what you hear and see: the blind receive their sight and the lame walk, lepers are cleansed and the deaf hear, the dead are raised up, and the poor have good news preached to them." (Mat. 11,3–5). This text implies that God becomes visible in the actions of Christ—the feeding of the hungry, the healing of the sick, and the resurrection of the dead. Since these salvific works were brought about by words, they will be discussed later in the context of revelation by means of the word. At the center of all the revelatory acts of Jesus, however, stand his death and resurrection. Paul's letters center on these two events. He had not met Jesus during the latter's historical life, so for him it is not Jesus' public activity but the completion of his life on Golgotha and the events of Easter morning which are of significance. These phenomena make Paul ask repeatedly what the God must be like who acts in this fashion. If Paul sees a revelation of God in Jesus' death and resurrection, it is because he was driven to it by that complete change of mind called forth in him by God's initiative. It is God's action, first of all, in the events of Golgotha and of Easter morning, which deeply impressed the apostle. But then these events led Paul again and again to the question of who this Jesus is who interfered so decisively in his life, and who the God is who acts through him. Is it the same God he knew from his pre-Christian faith? Is it the God who spoke to Abraham and Moses?

According to the gospel of St. John also God revealed himself in Jesus Christ's works of power. We will discuss that when we analyze the revelation in word, to which John bears witness. Frequently the New Testament emphasizes that God revealed his glory through Jesus Christ: Lk. 2,9; 2,14; 9,32; 24,26; Jn. 1,14; 2,11; Acts 22,11; Rom. 6,4; 2 Cor. 3,18; 4,4;1 Tim. 1,11; Titus 2,13; Heb. 1,3; 2,4; 2,11; 3,3; 1 Jn. 1,2; 3,5; 3,8; 4,9; 1 Pet. 4,13 Jas. 2,1 Apoc. 21,23.

REVELATION IN WORD

Divine revelation through action is necessarily connected with divine revelation through word. The "word of God" is a dominant theme throughout Sacred Scripture. It forms the beginning and the end of God's salvific action. It was by his word that God created the world, according to the Priestly Code, and it will be by his word that the world will end. Only when the call "Come" resounds (Apoc. 22, 20) will history, which was established, continued, preserved, and developed by the word of God, come to an end, brought to completion in the immediate self-communication of God to men.

The Emphasis on the Word in the Second Vatican Council

In Catholic theology it is only recently that the significance of the word of God has received the attention which is its due. More stress was put on the salvific sign than on the salvific word. This is not to say that the salvific function of the word was ever entirely forgotten. We need only remember that the proclamation of the gospel in the celebration of the Eucharist always ended with the prayer: "Through these saving words may our sins be forgiven." Furthermore, it indicated a habitual faith in the word of God that the Catholic Church always preserved Sacred Scripture, which not only contains God's word but in a certain sense even is God's word. Nevertheless, the word has not been given the emphasis and the place it deserves. It would be inexact, however, to say, as is sometimes done, that the Protestant Church was the Church of the word, the Orthodox Church that of the sign, and the Roman Catholic Church that of the sign and the word, implying that listening in faith was the mark of the first, perceiving in faith that of the second, and both listening and perceiving in faith that of the third. In point of fact none of the three Churches mentioned has ever completely lacked either of these functions. The difference lay in the weight ascribed to the one or the other factor.

How much the atmosphere has changed can be seen from the fact that in the Preface to the Dogmatic Constitution on Divine Revelation the Second Vatican Council takes the word of God as its point of departure. Since this is a basic matter, let us quote literally:

Hearing the word of God with reverence and proclaiming it confidently, this most sacred Synod takes its direction from these words of St. John: "We announce to you the eternal life which was with the

Father, and has appeared to us. What we have seen and have heard we announce to you, in order that you also may have fellowship with us, and that our fellowship may be with the Father, and with his son Jesus Christ" (1 Jn. 1:2–3). Therefore, following in the footsteps of the Councils of Trent and of First Vatican, this present Council wishes to set forth authentic teaching about divine revelation and about how it is handed on, so that by hearing the message of salvation the whole world may believe; by believing, it may hope; and by hoping, it may love.

Also the conclusion:

In this way, therefore, through the reading and study of the sacred books, let "the word of the Lord run and be glorified" (2 Th. 3:1) and let the treasure of revelation entrusted to the Church increasingly fill the hearts of men. Just as the life of the Church grows through persistent participation in the Eucharistic mystery, so we may hope for a new surge of spiritual vitality from intensified veneration for God's word, which "lasts forever" (Is. 40:8; cf. 1 Pet. 1:23–25).

The Structure and the Forms of the Word in General (the Word as Function of Man)

Before the function of the divine word for God's self-revelation is analyzed, two presuppositions must be clarified. One concerns the word as a function of man and of God; the other concerns the relationship of seeing and hearing.

Let us first recall the fundamental fact that it is the capacity for using words which constitutes man and reveals him as man. At first it is only a capacity, which must be developed and exercised. If a man does not exercise his ability to communicate through words, he will fall short of full humanity. This ability is primarily an exercise of the mind and heart, and only secondarily an exercise in expression. The capacity for using words is coordinated with the ability to hear. The latter, too, is in the beginning only a capacity which must be developed. The true word is first formed in the mind of man. The spoken word is an embodying, an incarnation, of the inner word in which man soliloquizes. Only if man undergoes the labor of inner speaking—that is, the effort of thinking—will the spoken word have mental and spiritual content.

To the structural elements of the word belong not only its origin within the speaker but also its arrival in the listener, not simply in his ear but in his mind. Its arrival within the listener is as constitutive of the word as its origin from the speaker. Speaking and hearing together build a unit of meaning. The one who speaks the word and the one who receives it are a unit, even though the listener may reject what the word expresses.

In our everyday life we can distinguish several forms of the word. The most important are the simple statement, praise (doxology), call, command, proclamation, exclamation, and finally self-revelation. It is not possible to separate these forms clearly, but they must be distinguished.

The word of statement has an instructive, informative function. It is the kind which the teacher offers in school, the catechist in religious instruction, the communications media in their reports. It must be precise. It aims at the assent, at the conviction, of the listener. It creates a community of consciousness. It serves the formation of educated society, whose members thereby learn what is going on in today's world and hence know how to act in it. But it is certain that modern man often finds the naked truth hard and bitter, and he is frequently tempted to reject or overlook it when it does not coincide with his own experiences and wishes. Thus the word which states the truth may produce scepticism. This danger can be avoided when the sense is conveyed that the statement is not only the product of cold reasoning, but emerges from a background of experience in which the heart has a role.

In consequence of man's being imperfect and imperfectible, all his statements are imperfect, and essentially imperfectible. Therefore, the way a report or description is received always and necessarily depends to a certain extent on the good will of the listener. This is particularly true of statements concerning human affairs; the danger is less for statements concerned with the processes of nature. The form of the word as call or command is directed to the will; the response to it is willingness, obedience. The word that asks for obedience must not, however, be presented purely in terms of the will, for this would not be worthy of man. In the interest of man's dignity such words must be invested with a perceptible meaning, even though this meaning may not be so self-evident as to be accessible to everybody.

Above all, love must be effective and perceptible in such a call. For every call and every command ought to serve that movement in which man is becoming himself, individually and collectively. A call without love, a command for command's sake, is a dictatorship unworthy of man. True authority aims at being an author—that is, an originator and deepener—of life, but it can add impetus and motivation to this life only if it does not destroy the freedom of the person addressed. On the other hand, it may not refrain from urging, warning, challenging, and commanding if it is to inspire the person called to make the right use of his freedom—that is, to bring about, in a responsible fashion, what is right, true, and good, and thus to fulfill that human dignity which is rooted in God. A brutal, completely unloving command is just as inhuman, just as damaging to humanity, as is blind obedience. If love is effective in the word of call, strength is given to the receiver to do what the word asks. For love is creative, always and everywhere. It creates what it loves where this does not yet exist. It strengthens what it loves where it does exist. It lifts the person who is called above himself to a new existence.

We usually define the word of praise as the honoring of God in our words and deeds. But we must not exclude from the honoring of God the honoring of his image in creation, man. Respect and acceptance are the life breath of every man. Every man, because he is a creature, and even more because he is a sinful creature, experiences himself as endangered and failing and hence lives in insecurity of mind and heart. Consciously or unconsciously, he longs for recognition by the community, even though this recognition should take the form of constructive criticism.

The word of proclamation is one which delivers a message of salvation to man, whether in the earthly-political or the eschatological-religious sphere. The exclamatory word in which man expresses his joy and his suffering, his delight and his despair, seems far removed from the real purpose of the word, which is to establish community. In reality, however, it too is related to community, because there is no complete solitude within history—radical solitude is a characteristic of damnation. The cry of a tormented or of a jubilant heart is a cry out into the congregation of brothers and sisters. It bears testimony to the overflowing fullness and power of certain human experiences which can scarcely be expressed in words.

The most significant and most intense form of the word is the word of self-communication. In this word the "I" reveals itself to the "thou" in an act which enables the "thou" to receive into his own life the "I" which discloses itself to him, and, conversely, enables the "thou" to enter into the "I." The "I" is also revealed to a certain extent in every other form of word inasmuch as every word is an expression of the person of the speaker. Even in objective and objectivistic reports the reporter shows himself for what he is: as honest and reliable, as hypocritical, shameless, or cynical. Acknowledging the intense personal character of the word of self-communication, we often say: Only this person or that could have spoken or written in this or that way. But in reporting or summoning or commanding we can detach ourselves from our own word. We can even listen to it. We can confront it like a stranger. Even a scoundrel can announce a message of salvation repugnant to himself. So also with the human face: the most pious can mask depravity, the most worldly a saint.

In the word of self-disclosure, however, the person of the speaker is existentially involved. Through it he entrusts himself to the "thou." This word is caught up in the movement of love. It is a word of caring, of concern, not for the instruction of the hearer, as in the case of the word of statement, but for the other's very life. This form of word creates in a special way the sense of community. Such a word of self-disclosure involves a great risk. Its whole success and significance is staked on the expectation of one answer: I reciprocate your love. If the answer is otherwise, the word can only return, in shame and fear, to the one who spoke it. A second great danger lurks in such a word: not only the risk of rejection and denial, or mockery and contempt, but that of the loss of the self involved in abandoning one's true "I" and advancing upon the listening "thou." This grave peril can be avoided only when reverence lies at the heart of the words "I love you." Man cannot escape the danger of self-loss by refusing to speak the word of love out of caution and the desire to avoid involvement, for then he is closed in on himself, made a prisoner of his own littleness. In fact, it is not possible for a man to find the narrow path between the abyss of self-loss, on the one hand, and the abyss of self-imprisonment, on the other, on which he can walk without falling. Rather, he must strive to achieve self-surrender in self-possession and self-possession in self-surrender, without ever completely succeeding. Only that way of life which we call heaven—that it, God's communication of himself in immediate self-disclosure and man's response to this—will enable him to be completely present to himself and at the same time completely present to the other.

A special form of word is that which we call faith, in the sense of man's response to God. This is not just an acceptance of certain information which God gives him about mysterious truths. Rather, it is a response to the divine word of self-disclosure by an act of surrender to God, in a decision coming from the depths of his person. Faith, therefore, in its fullest meaning has the character of an encounter. The element of knowledge is included in it. It is, however, a "knowing" in the sense used in Sacred Scripture—that is, in the sense of a union of person with person. Therefore faith is not a lesser form of knowledge, but a higher form of encounter, which includes knowledge.

Forms of the word discussed thus far can occur either as spoken or as written. Herein lies an extraordinarily far-reaching problem. The normal thing, in the sense of normative—i.e., closest to the norm (though not necessarily in the sense of the commonest)—is the spoken word. The dispersion of men across space and time makes it necessary to communicate the word of information or call or proclamation or exclamation and even self-communication through the written or printed word where the spoken word cannot reach. Writing and printing are ways of replacing the spoken word. That is not to say that they are insignificant for human society; it is simply to see them in the right perspective. They are means of extending the limits of human language. They are necessary and even indispensable substitutes, but they are only substitutes. The immediacy of encounter is lacking. As substitutes for the spoken word, they are governed in general by the same rules and laws as the latter. The most important difference lies in the fact that the listener becomes a reader, resembling a spectator who can return at any time to the picture he contemplated. The reader, however, reads correctly only if he assumes the attitude of a listener. This is particularly true when the words in question concern human affairs —it is less important when the subject matter is mathematical, physical, and chemical formulas. When, for example, the reader reads the sentence: I love you, the only way to receive the text meaningfully is not to be silent but to answer to himself: I reciprocate your love. To be sure, the printed word lacks to a certain extent the power to impel which is inherent in the spoken word. On the other hand, it has one advantage over the spoken word: duration. Written and printed words can be taken up and reflected upon by the reader at any time, while the spoken word is transitory.

All these considerations will help us to understand God's word more concretely.

The Word within God

Ultimately, the human word can be understood only if it is seen as the expression and manifestation of that word which God himself speaks in his divine life. God is love, as we are told in the First Epistle of John (4,8). He is this, not in a sort of exalted solitude, but in the form of a dialogue. The love which, according to John, is God's definition must be understood as a productive or fertile act of the absolute, divine spirit. He knows himself in the breadth and depth of his own being and without undergoing any process of development, and thereby expresses himself fully in a word that contains in itself Absolute Being. In fact, the Being of God consists precisely in the act by which he utters this Word. We are accustomed in theology to speak here of the first divine "person," although the word "person" in this context may not be entirely satisfactory. Since the word spoken by God in the act by which he exists is itself personal, and is brought forth as a person—a Son—by God in an act of self-communication, we can also call God "Father." The word formed by God in this act of self-communication has the quality, beyond our comprehension, that it turns back to the Father in love and knowledge—that it has therefore the character of a word-in-reply (*Ant-wort*). It is simultaneously spoken word and reply. If we use the expressions "Father" and "Son," we may say that they carry on an eternally fulfilling dialogue which never ceases or diminishes. We may even put the matter briefly by saying that they are nothing other than a subsisting dialogue. This dialogue springs from love, and at the same time finds its climax in an eternal love which unites the two partners. Love as Father-God is the source, the wellspring, of the dialogue. Love, at the same time, is its blissful expression. Insofar as this heavenly love is the fruit of the divine dialogue, we call it the Holy Spirit. Thus this short reflection enables us to see God, the ultimate and absolute reality living in the depths of man's being and at the same time transcending him, as an eternal dialogue of love.

When, earlier on, we characterized man in terms of his capacity for using words, we meant that he possesses this capacity by virtue of the fact that he participates in the mystery of the eternal dialogue of love which we call God. The human word is an echo of this dialogue, and from this it derives its great dignity.

Hearing and Seeing

We come now to another presupposition for the understanding of the word and its significance for the human spirit. Important as the word is, its significance must not be stressed one-sidedly. The ultimate promise given to man refers to the vision of God—that is to say, the sight of Absolute Being, which is Absolute Love itself. We must not think of this as a gazing in wonder at the never-changing splendor of God. It is, rather, a living exchange with God, who discloses and gives himself directly to man. Thus it becomes that fulfillment of life which we call dialogue. For Augustine and for Bonaventure it was part of the decisive significance of the incarnation of the Word of God that the Word was no longer only audible but became visible as well. If the word is directed more to hearing than to seeing, nevertheless the Word of the Father become man differs from all other words through the fact that it is both audible and visible. The basic element of the Christian message of salvation is that the incarnate God became visible in human history and began to converse with men as a visible person. This visibility has by no means been rendered superfluous by the audibility of God's word, for man is made to see and hear, and by no means only to hear. It would be too high a price to pay, if one could hear God only by losing the vision of him.

It is doubtful whether we can maintain that the act of hearing the word is more spiritual than that of seeing it. Such a question can be decided only by asking what is meant by hearing and seeing. If we mean only the sensory process, it seems reasonable to say that both modes of perception are of the same rank, acknowledging that man approaches the world differently with each of his several senses. If hearing and seeing are understood as intellectual activities mediated by the senses, they seem even more to be of equal rank. In any case it is striking that it is not the hearing but the seeing of God that is promised to man as his ultimate future: God's immediate gift of himself to his creation is represented in terms of vision. A more precise analysis leads us to say that this vision will take place in the form of an exchange, which takes place in a fulfilling and ever-growing dialogue between God and creation. According to the testimony of Scripture, even those who are especially close to God have longed to see him. Also, in the past, God's revelation of himself in word has frequently been connected with vision, as in the case of the prophets. God spoke with Moses face to face out of the midst of the fire (Dt. 5,4). Here it becomes evident that within history we cannot see God directly, but only indirectly. This may be why, in the calling of the prophets, the vision of God became less frequent, and its place was taken more and more by the word alone. It is more in keeping with the relationship of man to God within history that men should listen to God, for he is a hidden God of whom no image can be made. Nevertheless, the seeing of God is the absolute future which has been promised to man. We may observe, with reference to this point, that it is a matter of human experience that man is more in possession of himself in the act of seeing than in the act of hearing. In the act of seeing he can in a certain sense seize the initiative—if an object is objectionable to him, he can close his eyes or look past it. But he can hear only when someone talks to him; and he cannot close his ears to an annoying word, as he can close his eyes. When God turns to man in speech, the relationship of the creator to the creature is expressed in a particularly powerful way.

We must not forget that ultimately God offers himself to man directly and unveiled. Hence theologians speak of the "beatific vision of God" as the ultimate future of man. But this vision of God is of an inexpressible dynamism and, as we have said, in its turn takes place in dialogue.

God's Word as Real Address

When we begin to analyze the "Word of God," which pervades the entire Scripture and is the beginning and the end of God's revelation of himself to man, we must remember again that we are concerned with a type of thinking which is different from that of classical Greek philosophical thought. Here too the concept of "word"—"logos"—occupies an important place. However, it denotes "meaning" or "significance" which can be discovered by thoughtful reflection. In Sacred Scripture, however, "God's word" is always a matter of the direct influence of God on man. When God speaks, his word enters into the very life of the one addressed.

God's word to man appears in all those forms which we have ascribed to the human word. It can instruct, praise, call, command, proclaim, exclaim, and be self-disclosure. Above all, however, and in all its forms, it is a word of promise. In this expression the apostle Paul summarizes all that we owe to God's people of the Old Testament (Rom. 9,4): They lived in the era of the promise. God's word was spoken at several stages in the history of salvation in an especially concentrated form; for example, in the call of Moses, in the conclusion of the covenant on Sinai and the events connected with it, and in the call of the prophets of the Old Testament. On Sinai it went forth as the word which established the covenant and instructed the people in the covenant; to the prophets it came as a word of guidance and as a word of promise (H. Schlier). It appeared as a person in Jesus Christ. Among the writers of the New Testament it was Paul and John above all who reflected on and proclaimed the word of God. One might even call the Acts of the Apostles the history of God's word in the early Church.

If the question is raised, What exactly is to be understood by the phrase "Word of God"? it cannot be denied that this is an anthropomorphic expression. It serves to express the personhood of God and the personhood of man touched and caught up by his grace. It indicates that an encounter takes place, an encounter of the free God with free man: an event which includes both distance and community, remoteness and nearness, and in which the ineffable mystery present in man emerges into the field of his experience, yet without overpowering him. In this connection it is of decisive significance that the word spoken by the man under divine inspiration is itself termed the word of God.

With a view to the further understanding of what takes place here we may touch on a problem of our natural knowledge. From long philosophical wrestling with the question we know that the world as it is known to us, the world in which we live, consists of two components: the object itself, on the one hand, and our own mind on the other. We cannot know the world as it is in itself. What presents itself to us is always the world as we know it, and therefore the world as it is molded by our knowledge. Contemporary microphysics presents us with an instructive example. It has been demonstrated that we know only those subatomic particles on which we have exerted our influence—i.e., that it is impossible for us to know them apart from the mode of being which we have given to them. What they are like of themselves, and apart from us, we do not know.

If it can be said that Kant exaggerated the power of integration exercised by the subject in the process of knowledge, we must also add that Thomas Aquinas, according to the usual interpretation of his doctrine, underrated the integrating power of our mind, although he did not by any means overlook it. He does say, after all, that we know things *modo nostro*. Both thinkers agree that only the world we know is our world. These reflections indicate that the world cannot be understood simply objectively as something which exists statically, but must be understood as something which is continuously happening as a result of our own endeavors. The world is the result of what we find and of what we form.

Perhaps an illustration from every day experience can make this even clearer to us. Friendship and love bestow upon man a vision which enables him to see the world differently from the way he would ordinarily see it. The difference is that he experiences it in relation to the other person. This changes his entire world. By analogy, God's word can be understood as the result of divine and human action. God acts as God and man acts as creature, each in his own way and according to his own dynamics. Inspired by a divine call and God's grace, the person called translates into the spoken human word, in a direct spiritual process without natural contemplation and reflection, what God wants to tell mankind through him. This word, of course, is temporal and participates in the social and cultural situation as well as in the personal temperament of the man moved by God. Yet we may say that it is God who places the word in the mouth of the man. It is in this way that the word of Jahweh becomes the word of the prophet (Is. 6,8; Jer. 1,4f.; 23,21f.32; 26, 12–15). Even the intensity of Jahweh's feeling is transferred to the prophet (Jer. 6,11). Thus, the prophet really speaks Jahweh's word (Num.24,13; 1 Sam.15,16; Jer.23, 32). Therefore he proclaims only what Jahweh says, and all that Jahweh says.

Let us cite the call of Jeremiah as a particularly revealing example. In the first chapter of the book occurs the following passage:

The words of Jeremiah, the son of Hilkiah, of the priests who were in Anathoth in the land of Benjamin, to whom the word of the LORD came in the days of Josiah the son of Amon, king of Judah, in the thirteenth year of his reign. It came also in the days of Jehoiakim the son of Josiah, king of Judah, and until the end of the eleventh year of Zedekiah, the son of Josiah, king of Judah, until the captivity of Jerusalem in the fifth month. Now the word of the LORD came to me saying, "Before I formed you in the womb I knew you, and before you were born I consecrated you; I appointed you a prophet to the nations." Then I said, "Ah, Lord GOD! Behold, I do not know how to speak, for

I am only a youth." But the LORD said to me, "Do not say, 'I am only a youth'; for to all to whom I send you you shall go, and whatever I command you you shall speak. Be not afraid of them, for I am with you to deliver you, says the LORD." Then the LORD put forth his hand and touched my mouth; and the LORD said to me, "Behold, I have put my words in your mouth. See, I have set you this day over nations and over kingdoms, to pluck up and to break down, to destroy and to overthrow, to build and to plant." (1, 1–10)

We can also point out many other passages where, as it is said, "God puts his words into the prophet's mouth" (e.g., Num.22,38; 23,5.12.16; Dt.18,18). It is God himself who makes the prophet hear and see. He opens the prophet's ears, so that he can hear and take to heart Jahweh's word (Ez.3,10.17; Is.50, 4f.). He himself opens the mouth of the prophet (Ez.3,17;33,32). The prophet takes God's word into his very body and thus falls under the power of the word and into Jahweh's hand. So we find in Ezekiel:

"You must deliver my words to them whether they listen or not, for they are a set of rebels. You, son of man, listen to the words I say; do not be a rebel like that rebellious set. Open your mouth and eat what I am about to give you." I looked. A hand was there, stretching out to me and holding a scroll. He unrolled it in front of me; it was written on back and front; on it was written lamentations, wailings, moanings. He said, "Son of man, eat what is given to you, eat this scroll, then go and speak to the House of Israel." I opened my mouth; he gave me the scroll to eat and said, "Son of man, feed and be satisfied by the scroll I am giving you." I ate it, and it tasted sweet as honey. Then he said, "Son of man, go to the House of Israel and tell them what I have said." (Ez. 2,7–3,4,J)

An instructive example for the dynamics of God's word could be quoted from the prophet Amos (3,8): "The lion has roared, who will not fear? Jahweh has spoken, who can refuse to proclaim his message?" (Compare Num. 22–24; 1 Kg. 18,46; Is. 8,11; Jer. 15,17; 20,7; Ez. 33,22.) As God places the word in the prophet's hearing, the prophet actually speaks God's word. He is God's mouth (Jer. 15,19; 42,21). We cannot overlook, on the other hand, the fact that God's word is uttered only in the words of men.

God's Word and Man's Word

Here we encounter two very important questions. One is: What is it that makes a word God's word, when, physically speaking, it is a man's word? The second is: How can a human word be recognized as God's word? We might attempt the following answer to the first question. In speech man makes himself present; he expresses himself, creates a representation of himself. It comes, or can come, from the center of his person. Insofar as man is a creature himself —i.e., insofar as he is continually being created by God both in his existence and in his activity—he is an expression and a manifestation of God. Scripture even calls him the image of God. From this aspect the word, the self-expression of man, is indirectly an expression of God and therefore in this sense God's word. If one argues in this way, then in this sense, any human word is simultaneously God's word. This is particularly true of that human speech by which man expresses the transcendental horizon of his existence—namely, the inexpressible mystery which we call God.

In our context, however, the expression "God's word" means not natural knowledge of God, but that self-revelation of God which is accessible only to faith and which has reached its preliminary climax in Christ; that is, that speech of God in which he promises himself to us in order to communicate his life to us. This word of God can only be received by man—to follow a line of thought of Karl Rahner's—when God creates the very receptivity for it; that is to say, when he bestows on man an interior illumination by grace. In such a case God not only allows man to speak about him authoritatively but, participating as a partner in the activity by grace, he constitutes the word which the man speaks. By his action in constituting the human word, God gives it the character of a word of God.

This leads to a new problem, however: that of co-operation between God and man. We can trace this problem through the whole of theology, yet it cannot be said that a satisfactory solution has ever been found. The answer would be one-sided if we ascribed the action to God alone or to man alone. It would be equally incorrect to ascribe part of the activity to God and another part to man. We must say, rather, that the whole is done by both God and man, in each case in a different way, appropriate to the one who is acting.

The man who speaks the word which God, as uncreated grace, has constituted within him experiences himself as one addressed by God through the very grace he has received. Thus he speaks out of an experience of God; that is, of the unlimited transcendental horizon which has appeared concretely in space and time in human words. On the basis of this experience of God, he sees the connection between God and the communication he has received. According to this analysis God's word, though human, is created by God in a threefold way: he is its ultimate origin, he is its content, and he is the subject who in partnership with man constitutes it.

The word which the individual human being receives as God's word is usually not intended for him alone, but for a community. We can therefore call it a public and official word. If other people are to understand and accept the word of an individual as God's word, an interior illumination from God is also necessary in their case.

The attitude of both the recipient of God's word and those addressed by him, and who accept it, is not an insight into the correctness of its contents, but is an openness to God: it is faith. Faith in this sense means a human response to God in which man commits himself to God, who in turn graciously promises himself to man; thus man enters into a community of life and, consequently, a community of thought with God.

With this statement we are already engaged with the second question: how the listener can recognize that a human word is God's word and therefore should be accepted. How is he to know that he need not fear that a prophet who claims to offer the word of God may be proclaiming it incorrectly, diminishing it or falsifying it, or simply expressing his own fantasies? The interior illumination given by God does not dispense us from the need to ask such questions. Towards a solution of the problem the following thoughts are offered. First of all we must acknowledge that no human being is capable of communicating God's word adequately, because the inexpressible mystery which is God is also present in every activity of God's, and therefore cannot be imprisoned in human concepts or words.

Looking at it positively, the fact that the prophet has been called by Jahweh guarantees objectively enough that he is no false prophet. In being called, the prophet is (very often against his original life-plans and expectations) singled out by God and reserved for God's service throughout his existence. He is also equipped and prepared by God for his difficult office (Is.6,6; Jer.1,9; Ez.3,8f.) Jahweh remains with him and grants him life and support (Is.8,10; Jer.1,8.18; Ez.3,8f.). Jahweh lives as God "for him." For the listener, however, the problem is by no means solved simply by maintaining that this is the objective situation. For him it is a life-or-death matter whether or not he personally can distinguish for himself the false prophet from the genuine (Jer.23, 16.25). Frequently, those called by God can prove themselves by special signs which we shall discuss later. But then, signs must be understood. Thus the question of how the true proclamation of God's word can be distinguished from the false accompanies the entire history of prophecy in the Old Testament. When Hananiah stood up against the prophet Jeremiah, whose preaching before the tribunal he rejected, and spoke instead what the people wanted to hear, Jeremiah could at first only reply: "Amen! May the Lord do so; may the Lord make the words which you have prophesied come true!" (Jer.28,6).

This irony was justified by future events. The false prophet states what he had fabricated in his own dreams. "The prophets who lived long before you and me prophesied war, famine, and pestilence, but the prophet who prophesies salvation can show himself a true seer, sent indeed by the Lord, only when his prophecy is fulfilled against many countries and great kingdoms" (Jer. 28,8f.). The mendacious prophet can be recognized from the fact that he attempts to entice the community away from Jahweh to other gods. In the last analysis, only the future will tell whether a prophecy is true or false. "When a prophet speaks in the name of the Lord, if the word does not come to pass or come true, that is a word which the Lord has not spoken; the prophet has spoken it presumptuously, you need not be afraid of him" (Dt.18,22).

The same difficulty obtains in the New Testament. Here, too, the false prophets resemble the true messenger, Jesus, to such an extent that they may be mistaken for each other. Even Satan can assume the disguise of an angel of light. He who is truthful, however, and acts truthfully, who listens to the word with a purified heart, is able to distinguish the one from the other. As John says, the sheep will recognize the call of the good shepherd with infallible certainty, will stay close to him and will not follow the stranger (e.g., Jn.10,3–5, 27–29; 18,37; 2 Cor.11,14; Gal.1,6–9). It is the faith of the New Testament that God's word was indeed sent to the children of Israel (Acts 10,36), the Word of God which is Jesus himself, a word proclaimed by God and at the same time by Jesus, and then by his apostles, through whom it is made available to the whole of mankind, both Jews and heathen (Acts 13,26; 15,35; 18,11).

Occasionally the attempt has been made by means of philological and historical investigations to distill the word of God itself from the unity of God's word and man's word. Painstaking research, however, has demonstrated that, as regards the Old Testament, it is impossible to distinguish between Jahweh's words and the prophets'. The words of the prophets are at the same time entirely divine and entirely human. God's word is present in the word of man: it pervades this as a spiritual power. The prophet speaks with Jahweh's words (Num.24,13; 1 Sam.15,16; Jer. 23,22; Ez.3,4). He announces only what Jahweh says and what Jahweh commands (e.g., Num.24,13; 1 Kg.22,14; Dt.18,18). The prophets of the Old Testament again and again introduce Jahweh's word with the formula: "Thus spoke Jahweh"; as a rule they also finish with the expression "saying of Jahweh."

Similarly it is true of the New Testament that the divine and human word are inseparable. The word which is Jesus himself is proclaimed to all men by means of human words which are the creation of the men who preach and bear witness to Jesus. This is the gospel of Jesus, of his salvific death, and of his resurrection. But through it the Holy Spirit speaks, sent by Jesus. In him, on the other hand, speaks the risen Lord, present in the Spirit. Thus the witness of the apostles is Christ's witness to himself. This will be treated in detail later.

For the proclamation of the message of salvation concerning the crucified and resurrected Christ, the first Christians used language and expressions which had been formed in the Jewish synagogue and the Hellenistic world, in order to tell their listeners that God had spoken to the world through Christ once for all. The fact that in such human language, spoken by men and heard by men, the word of God is spoken can only be known when its power is experienced, its power to transform and to convert. To those who shut themselves off from this, the gospel remains hidden, since the significance of the word cannot be estimated according to the standards of everyday human life. Those, however, who accept in faith the word proclaimed discover at the same time the honesty and the reliability of the prophet who proclaims it (2 Cor.4,2f.). If the prophet has no defense against the accusation that he is giving out his own invention as the word of God, and hence is perverting the truth, this is because he shares in "the form of a servant" of Jesus Christ, the Word himself in person. In this case Christ's statement applies, "He who hears you, hears me, and he who despises you despises me" (Lk.10,16). The only grounds Paul can give in support of his preaching is his claim that he has been sent by Christ, and if this apostle occasionally speaks of "his" gospel, he does not mean ideas he has invented, but the message of salvation which was entrusted to him (Rom.10,17). He understands his own preaching as a proclamation of Jesus Christ, and his work of salvation—that is, his preaching—is itself an eschatological event.

According to St. John's gospel, Jesus' testimony and that of his witnesses form an indissoluble unity. As a messenger of God who comes from above, Jesus testifies to what he has seen and heard with his Father. Through his witness he communicates to those who believe a share in his own seeing and hearing. Thus they can become witnesses, in union with Jesus the revealer and through him, but in such a way that it is the revealer himself who speaks in their witness. This becomes even more evident if we add St. John's thesis that the Spirit sent by Jesus makes the Christ-witness and the Christ-event present in the word of Christ's witnesses.[1]

The Interpretative Function of God's Word

When we begin to investigate the function of God's word in human words we find two facts: God's word functions as interpretation and as action. Certainly these two functions cannot be mechanically separated. They are, rather, an indissoluble whole. But in this whole we can distinguish the two functions mentioned.

As we saw earlier, God reveals himself by acting in history. It would, however, be entirely erroneous to try to recognize that a particular historical event was revelatory from the simple fact that it happened. Even though we understand God's revelation as history, as indeed a whole course of historical events, beginning with Abraham and completed in Christ, we cannot directly experience this, much less experience it as divine revelation. We cannot simply say that faith is basically and essentially confidence in history, or devotion to past deeds of God, or a universal, historical, and concrete hope for the future action of God. Though faith in God has its foundation in history, and not in metaphysics, it can develop out of history only insofar as this is interpreted; that is, understood in a particular way and so expressed in words. Whether a fact of history should be understood as God's revelation (in the supernatural sense) or simply as a part of God's creative action, continually advancing the world's progress, will depend on the word which interprets it. (God's action in creating and advancing the world also involves a certain divine self-communication, but this is not the same as the way in which he took hold of Abraham, or in which he appeared definitively in Christ.) It is the interpreting word which *creates* the difference between the revelatory deed of God in the strictest sense of the word and his other creative actions. But in our context let us first emphasize that it *uncovers* the difference. In his word God himself provides the interpretation. For example, political catastrophies are interpreted as judgments of God. The prophets, from the sixth century before Christ, proclaim again and again that political and economic catastrophies are not simply the consequence of specific historical settings, but are salvific visitations of God. Such an understanding of history is arrived at only through

Jahweh's proclaimed word. Without it, how could we know that Israel's history was any different from that of other nations? The Philistines and the Syrians, for example, were also liberated; the former from Kaphtor, the latter from Kir (Amos 9,7). Nor are Jesus Christ's death and resurrection comprehensible without the word of proclamation. As we have mentioned several times before, there were at the time of Jesus numerous executions by crucifixion. The apparitions of Jesus after his death might themselves be misconstrued as visions or illusions if the word of proclamation did not reveal them as matters of fact. As Sacred Scripture shows, Jesus' cross can be rejected as no more than the just end of a false prophet. The Easter message can be called into question by spreading the rumor that the disciples had secretly stolen the body from the grave. Only through the interpreting word, both through Jesus' own word and through theological reflection on his person, can the salvific events be understood in the right light. We can see from his letters with what incessant care Paul tried to understand, to interpret, and to proclaim the event of the cross as the form of the divine plan of salvation, and the resurrection as the original datum of the Christian faith. According to Paul, faith is derived from hearing, not seeing (Rom.10,17; see Jn.20,29). This function of the word is not contradicted by the fact that Christ declares in John's gospel: If you do not believe me, then believe my works (Jn.10, 38). Both according to Jn.10,25 and also according to Jn.5,36–47 his works are clear confirmation of his words. But they in their turn only become understandable through his word. Only through the word can they be known as works which he performs as messenger of his Father. Only the word tells us that his works testify for him, and that through them the Father himself gives witness for him.

The Action Function of God's Word

We come to the second function of the word. It is not only, not even primarily, significant as interpretation and teaching, but as action. God's word has effect. It is effective action even where it is intended as teaching. Teaching and action form a unity in the word of God. God's word works with power. This power, however, is no brute force, but a power filled with spirit and with light, for in the word God himself acts. This will be better understood if we recall that God cooperates with man in constituting the word. The active character of the word can be illustrated by the Hebrew expression "dabar," which signifies both "word" and "deed" (see, e.g., Gen.15,1). In Acts (10,36) it is said that God sent his "word" to the Israelites (see also Lk.2,15; 3,2). By this expression is understood Christ's whole work of salvation. Isaiah, among others, also bears witness to the active power of the word when he has God say: "By my own self I swear it; what comes from my mouth is truth, a word irrevocable: before me every knee shall bend, by me every tongue shall swear . . . ." (45,23,*J*). Let us also recall the passage previously quoted from Jeremiah 1,1–10. When, on the other hand, a prophet announces something in the name of the Lord which is not fulfilled, this is a certain sign that it was not the Lord speaking but the prophet speaking presumptuously (Dt.18, 22). God literally casts his word amongst the people, that it may be a force in history. Even where the word meets resistance, it reaches its goal: "For the word of God is alive and active. It cuts more keenly than any two-edged sword, piercing as far as the place where life and spirit, joints and marrow, divide. It sifts the purposes and thoughts of the heart." (Heb.4,12,*NEB*) The word bestows grace and judgment upon Israel (Jer.23,29; Is.50,2).

The character of the word as action and power is expressed by the fact that it creates history. It not only appears at a certain moment in history, it produces history out of its own dynamism. It is always conditioned by a historical situation, and it advances history. God certainly does not depend upon the situation in which he speaks his word, but neither does he overpower men with divine arbitrariness. He speaks to men in a fashion which corresponds to the level of their development. Only when the time is ripe, that is, when men are capable of being spoken to by him, and insofar as they are capable, does God speak to them. Then, however, he leads them to a new level of existence and a new understanding of God and of themselves. God's word produces history insofar as it moves men to definite actions. It can be said that since the days of Samuel the decisive power in Israel's history has been the word of God (1 Sam.3,10ff.; 9,27; 15,26; 2 Sam.7,4ff.).

The interlacing of the historical effect of the word with the his-

tory of the word itself is shown in the fact that the word of God was
spoken in a number of stages, as we see from the opening of the
letter to the Hebrews (Heb. 1, 1–9). There were many and long
periods of history in which God addressed no word to men. Each
time God communicated only a certain measure of himself to
man until the fullness of his self-revelation was reached in Jesus
Christ. There are two aspects to this. On the one hand, divine revelation constitutes a great unity, from its first moment to its culmination in Jesus Christ. This is true, although there are long periods of
divine silence between individual pronouncements of the word.
Each individual level of the word is open to the next level, however
distant that may be. It is received by and preserved in the next level
until the time arrives for a new and higher level. Out of the fullness
of God's love, each stage is enabled to transcend the one preceding
it, the new is not a necessary development from the previous one.
Each step is rather an expression of a free divine decision, but each
has its place in God's general plan for man's future. Each stage is
both a fulfillment of what went before and a promise of what is to
come. Thus even in the Old Testament there is not only promise
but also fulfillment; and yet, viewed as a whole, the Old Testament
does have the character of promise rather than of fulfillment:
Christ is the fulfillment, yet he too points to God's last and definitive self-revelation. Thus even the event of Christ, despite its
character of fulfillment, is also a beginning and a promise, the
promise of an absolute future.

The second aspect is that God's mystery was disclosed to man
not in a single act, but step by step. It is not surprising, therefore,
that many revelations which are perfectly clear in the New Testament are shrouded in darkness in the Old Testament; that many
pressing questions, such as the fate of man after death, remained
unanswered for a long time and only gradually became relatively
clear. Only one who does not see the historical character of God's
plan can be scandalized by such things.

When we emphasize that God's word is history and creates history, we must make one fundamental distinction. God's word both
established and advanced the history of the Jewish people. With
the incarnation of the Son of God this particular type of historical

effectuality of the Word of God came to an end. The Word of God which appeared in Christ as a person has certainly been promised to man until the end of history, and in it God demonstrates his saving power. But it no longer establishes the history of a nation. Thus we must distinguish between the character of God's word as power and its character as history. The former can exist without the latter but not the latter without the former. With regard to the character of God's word as power let us quote a passage from Leo Scheffczyk:

The first impression given by the reports of the preaching of the apostles is that of the extraordinary power of this word. At the first speech of Peter mentioned in Acts, given under the influence of the pentecostal Spirit, his hearers were "cut to the heart" (Acts 2,37), and as a result about "three thousand souls" were baptized (Acts 2,41). This apostolic preaching, introduced by the formula "my words" (2,14), is experienced as a power which offers salvation. At another time the same power heals the man born lame (3, 4–26) when Peter invokes the name of Jesus (3,6). Here, already, Peter indicates that this effect was not accomplished by his own power or piety (3,12). Rather, the name of Jesus invoked over the sick man and the faith which rose up in him "brought him strength" (3,16). Thus, the word of the apostles confers strength from God upon the willing listener.

The apostolic preaching has the same success with the nonbeliever, as can be seen in the proclamation of the "good news of Jesus" to the Ethiopian chamberlain by Philip (8,35), and the sermon of "those who had been scattered after the persecution that arose over Stephen," before the Greeks in Antioch. "The power of the Lord was with them." Peter's speech in Jerusalem justifying his action in the case of Cornelius (Acts 11, 5–17) expressly quotes from the message of the angel to the pagan captain the allusion to Peter's words: "He will declare to you a message by which you will be saved, you and all your household" (11–14).

The creative effect of the word with its power to save is even more clearly expressed in the portion of the Acts of the Apostles devoted to the activity of Paul, as well as in his own writings. In the latter a kind of theological reflection on the word of God is already apparent. The nonbelievers "were glad and glorified the word of God" (Acts 13, 48), which came from the mouth of Paul, the word of God's grace (Acts

14, 3; 20, 32), which goes forth accompanied by signs and wonders, leads to the conversion of the heathen and bestows salvation upon men. It is "the message of salvation" (Acts 13, 26), which edifies the congregation (13, 15) and leads to the conversion of the unbelievers (19, 17–20).[2]

The dynamics of the divine word must not be understood one-sidedly. God's word comes to man not only as power, but also as content. We wish to emphasize this again; it can be seen in both the Old and the New Testaments. We have remarked several times how the apostle Paul struggled for a correct understanding of Christ's death and resurrection. The result of his theological reflection is a many-sided doctrine. A one-sided dynamism and actualism would contradict the meaning and the importance of God's word.

Summary of the History of God's Word as Interpretation and as Event in the Old Testament

The revelation of Sinai (Ex. 19ff.) occupies a central position among all the revelations of the Old Testament. In this event Moses was God's appointed mediator, whose task it was to deliver the message of God's promise of himself to the people of Israel. On the basis of the experience they had had with God in their history, the people of Israel understood God's action as a word-event. Thus it was natural enough for them to ascribe even the origin of the world and its preservation of God's word. Admittedly the problem of the origin of nature is secondary in Old Testament thought to the interpretation of history as a divine self-revelation. Furthermore, the texts which deal with the origin of the world are never concerned with cosmological problems, but always with the question of man's salvation. In the Priestly Code (Gen. 1, 1–31) as we saw before—the origin of the world is described as the beginning of God's salvific action. The authors do not trouble to distinguish between a natural and a supernatural dimension within creation. This distinction which was elaborated by later theology, and which has its importance for understanding revelation, did not concern them. We serve the spirit of the Old Testament best when we emphasize that although it did not know the concept of the supernatural, the reality designated by this world in medieval theology was present right from the beginning, and present not by reason of the world's own dynamism, but by reason of the dynamism of Christ taking effect in anticipation. The fact that, according to the Priestly Code, God created the world through the word seems to indicate that it was God's intention right from the beginning to enter into an intimate conversation with his creatures. This is shown also from the fact that although, according to Genesis, man broke off the conversation with God, nevertheless God persevered in the dialogue, reopening it again and again.

The authors of Genesis know only one word of God, which unfolded itself in many stages. They do not distinguish between the divine word that created the world and the word that called Moses to liberate his people. God called the things and they came. Through God's call they are also kept in existence. How closely the word through which God created and preserved heaven and earth is connected with the word to Israel can be seen from Psalm 19. In Psalm 147 too, Jahweh's creative and his salvific action form an integral unity. For Deutero-Isaiah the creative word of God from which things take their origin is not only the first historical miracle of God but a salvific event in itself. It is the foundation of all further divine deeds of salvation (Gen. 1,1–31; Ps. 33,6–9; Is.40, 26; 48,13; Ps. 147,4; 148,5; Sir. 39,17f.; 42,15; Judith 16,15f.). In the New Testament also God's creative word is seen as closely connected to his salvific word: Rom. 4,17; 2 Cor. 4,6; Heb. 11,3; 2 Pet. 3,5ff. It is the prologue of John's gospel above all, however, which identifies the personified Word of salvation promised to mankind with the foundation of creation (Jn.1,10).

According to both the Jahwistic and Elohistic texts, Abraham was called by God out of his homeland and out of his father's house. A great number of descendants and a blessed country were promised to him (Gen.12; Gen. 15). Furthermore he is told that in him all the peoples of the earth will be blessed. God's covenant with Abraham was the precursor of his covenant with Moses. In the so-called historical credo this connection is solemnly confessed

(Dt.6,20–34; 26,5b–9; Jos.24,2b–13). The history of Abraham, guided by God, is the beginning of the history of Israel, God's people.

By his word God definitively established the covenant with the people chosen by him (Ex.24, 1–8). Moses was the mediator. After him no prophet appeared like him (Dt.5,4; 34,10ff.). The basic law of the covenant is the decalogue (Ex.20, 3–17, Dt.4,13; 10,4). This relationship is solemnly proclaimed in the so-called short historical creed (Dt. 6,20–24; 26, 5b–9; Jos. 24,2b–28). This history of Abraham, directed by God, is the introduction to the history of Israel, the people of God.[3] The one central thing of all that God demands of his people is that they love him (Dt. 4,37; 7,6ff.; 10,12ff.; 11,1.13.22; 30,16.20). The decalogue is entitled the "Ten Words" (Ex. 34,28). They are considered to constitute in essence the whole of the salvific proclamation of Jahweh's will to Israel. We possess traditions of these events in several forms. In Exodus we read:

Yahweh came down on the mountain of Sinai, on the mountain top, and Yahweh called Moses to the top of the mountain; and Moses went up. Yahweh said to Moses, "Go down and warn the people not to pass beyond their bounds to come and look on Yahweh, or many of them will lose their lives. The priests, the men who do approach Yahweh, even these must purify themselves, or Yahweh will break out against them." Moses answered Yahweh, "The people cannot come up the mountain of Sinai because you warned us yourself when you said, 'Mark out the limits of the mountain and declare it sacred.'" "Go down," said Yahweh to him, "and come up again bringing Aaron with you. But do not allow the priests or the people to pass beyond their bounds to come up to Yahweh, or he will break out against them." (Ex. 19,20ff.,*J*)

In the Priestly Code we read:

And Moses went up the mountain. The cloud covered the mountain, and the glory of Yahweh settled on the mountain of Sinai; for six days the cloud covered it, and on the seventh day Yahweh called to Moses from inside the cloud. To the eyes of the sons of Israel the glory of

Yahweh seemed like a devouring fire on the mountain top. Moses went right into the cloud. He went up the mountain, and stayed there for forty days and forty nights. (Ex. 24,15ff.,*J*)

The editor interprets the event, in which the people perceived claps of thunder, flashes of lightning, the sound of the trumpet and the smoking mountain, stood far off in fear and trembling and asked Moses to talk with God:

All the people shook with fear at the peals of thunder and the lightning flashes, the sound of the trumpet, and the smoking mountain; and they kept their distance. "Speak to us yourself" they said to Moses "and we will listen; but do not let God speak to us, or we shall die." Moses answered the people, "Do not be afraid; God has come to test you, so that your fear of him, being always in your mind, may keep you from sinning." So the people kept their distance while Moses approached the dark cloud where God was. Yahweh said to Moses, "Tell the sons of Israel this, 'You have seen for yourselves that I have spoken to you from heaven.' " (Ex. 20,18–22,*J*)

The ten words are interpreted, explicated and applied to different situations (Ex. 21–23; 25,1ff.; 35,1ff.). Of especial importance is the centralization of worship.

Jahweh had Moses present the covenant to the people for acceptance (Ex. 24,3). The covenant was to be agreed upon freely by both partners. The people answered: "All that the Lord has spoken we will do" (Ex. 24,7). The covenant was written down so that it would be a constant reminder to Israel of their election by God in grace and the basis of all his future dealings with them (Dt. 4,2.5ff.; 31,24ff.).

In the time of the prophets the people were reminded of the covenant again and again by prophetic utterance. When they abandon the covenant God sits in judgment on them, not in order to reject them, but in order to call them back to faithfulness to it. The prophetic word therefore has the function of keeping alive in the people awareness of the covenant, or reawakening it in them, and to show the future.

The "I am" formula represents a special form of divine self-revelation in word. It appears above all in Deutero-Isaiah in the form of a lawsuit between Jahweh and the gods, that is, in confrontation with the polytheistic environment of the Jewish people. In this lawsuit the question at stake is the existence of one true God. According to Isaiah 43,10, that which must be recognized, believed and understood is this truth: "I am he. Before me no God was formed, nor shall there be any after me." God himself calls the members of his people as witnesses that he is the one and only God; that he is the first and the last; that there is no other God besides him (Is.43,12; 44,8f.; 44,6ff). Jahweh alone can send prophets. The gods cannot show for themselves one prophetic word that has been fulfilled or that acts as a salvific deed deciding the course of history (Is.44,9). By his word then, creating history, Jahweh gives testimony to himself in Israel, and Israel thus is the witness that Jahweh is God, and he alone.

Readings

Urs von Balthasar, Hans. *A Theological Anthropology.* New York, Sheed and Ward, 1967.

————— *Word and Redemption.* Translated by A. V. Littledale with Alexander Dru. New York, Herder and Herder, 1965.

————— *Word and Revelation.* Translated by A. V. Littledale with Alexander Dru. New York, Herder and Herder, 1964.

Notes

[1] L. Scheffczyk, *Von der Heilsmacht des Wortes* (Munich, 1966); H. Krings, H. Schlier, and H. Volk, Art. "Wort," in H. Fries, *Handbuch Theologischer Grundbegriffe*, II (Munich, 1963), 835–876; E. Lohse, "Deus dixit," in *Evangelische Theologie* 25 (1965), 567–585.

[2] *Von der Heilsmacht des Wortes* (Munich, 1966), 185ff.

[3] See W. Richter, "Beobachtungen zur theologischen Systembildung in der alttestamentlichen Literatur anhand des kleinen geschichtlichen Credo," in *Wahrheit und Verkündigung* (Paderborn, 1967), 175–212.

◄7

Jesus as the Completion of Revelation through the Word; Miracles and Signs

GOD'S WORD A PERSONAL REALITY IN HISTORY

The entire Old Testament is directed towards the time when God's pre-existent Word will become present in human history. The day of Jahweh is announced (Is. 2,12; 49,8; Joel 2,1; Mal. 3,2), a day on which God himself will appear as an acting subject in human history. In Jesus Christ, God's word is proclaimed no longer simply as a power guiding history, but as a personal reality in history. When the New Testament calls Christ the Word, it is not concerned primarily with God the Father's expression of his inner self within the divinity, but with God's communication of himself to the world. The New Testament presupposes the understanding of God's word unfolded in the writings of the Old Testament, which it takes up and carries further. The sayings of the prophets are quoted as God's word (Mt. 1,22; 2,15; Acts 28,25; Lk. 1,70; Acts 3,21; Heb. 1,1ff; 10, 15ff.; 2 Pet. 1,21). In particular the

123

laws given by Moses are considered God's word (Mk.7, 8–13; see Heb. 12,19.25f.). Also in the New Covenant God's creative word appears in very intimate connection with the salvific word (Rom. 8,21f.; 2 Cor. 4,6; Heb. 11,3; 2 Pet. 3,5ff.; Jn. 1,10).

The oldest texts of the New Testament do not call Christ God's Word. This designation is only the result of a long theological reflection. It is presented to us in the writings of John. The synoptics declare that by his words Jesus interprets the Father in heaven and brings men salvation. According to these texts of the New Testament the word of God which Jesus speaks seems, in the first place, to have no other significance than the word of the Old Testament which God spoke through the prophets and through Moses, the prototype of all that is prophetic. Yet the situation is completely altered, for Jesus announces his proclamation with an incomparable authority (Mk.1,15; Mt.7,28f.; Lk.4,32). Unlike the prophets of the Old Testament, he does not refer to a divine mandate. On the contrary, he speaks on his own authority (Mt. 7,28). Furthermore, acceptance or rejection of his word makes the difference between salvation and disaster (Mt. 10,13–15). "For whoever is ashamed of me and of my words in this adulterous and sinful generation, of him will the Son of man also be ashamed, when he comes in the glory of his Father with the holy angels" (Mk.8,38; see Mt.10,32f., Lk.12,8f.). He is the sower who sows the seed of the word (Mk.4,13ff.). In the word of Jesus we find again that he claims to speak for God. This is why his word demands an ultimate decision. He who rejects Jesus' word rejects God himself. What no prophet and no teacher would have dared to do, Jesus does, in saying to those who are lost and despised: "Your sins are forgiven" (Mk.2,5) and in interpreting definitively the meaning of the Scriptures. What the Old Testament ultimately meant remained open until Christ came; it was only through him that it received authentic explanation.

We can understand that Jesus' words were considered foreign and irritating. It is of special importance that his words are creative especially in the remission of sins—that is, they bring about a right relationship between God and man. The words of Jesus themselves prove to be salvific acts. Where Jesus' word is pronounced, events occur which have a salvific power. When he proclaimed the beginning of God's dominion, the signs of its coming began to appear and the future announced by him started to have an effect on the present (Mk. 1,5; Mt. 3,1–3). From the eleventh chapter of John's gospel it is evident that Jesus' word seeks to transform the entire human being, not only his thought and his will but his entire physical existence. After reporting Jesus' statement that he is the resurrection and the life, and that whoever believes in him has passed over from death to life, the evangelist relates the resurrection of Lazarus, thus demonstrating how God's word works creatively and has power over the entire man (E. Lohse).

Thus the evangelist Luke can place on the lips of the risen Christ: "These are my words which I spoke to you, while I was still with you, that everything written about me in the law of Moses and the prophets and the psalms must be fulfilled" (Lk. 24,44). After these words he enlightened the minds of the apostles, according to the further words of Luke, so that they could understand the Scriptures. He explained the meaning of his death and resurrection. From this it becomes clear that "the words" are nothing but the events of Golgotha and Easter morning. In those events God promised himself to mankind in a definitive way. Even though the synoptics do not formally call Jesus God's Word, the theological interpretation which they give of Jesus shows that for all practical purposes they consider him as the definitive word of salvation directed by the Father to men, which can no longer be surpassed and is intended for all men. What Jesus says emanates from the center of what he is. Because his words are salvific, a sacramental significance can be ascribed to them. And as they are nothing but a manifestation of himself, he himself may be called sacramental.

In a special fashion Paul, too, knows that he is called to serve the word. The word is entrusted to him (Gal. 2,7). Through the bestowal of the office of apostle the task of proclaiming the word has been laid upon him (1 Cor. 9,16ff.). Service of the word requires personal dedication from the apostle. He must not set obstacles to the word by selfishness in his aims, or by offering human wisdom or his own spiritual experiences. In a spirit of faith in the word he must lead a Christlike life, and must be prepared to suffer for the word, in order to testify through his existence to Christ's suffering which he proclaims (2 Cor. 1,3ff.; 4,16; 11,23ff.). The word which Paul proclaims is God's own word (1 Thess. 2,13). God is not only its object or content but also its subject, the one who utters it. It is the word of the Lord (2 Cor. 13,3). But the word which Christ speaks is at the same time the word which the apostle proclaims (2 Cor. 5,20; 1 Thess. 1,8; 2 Thess. 2,14). Beyond this word no further word of God will be given to men. He is God's "Yes" and "Amen" to his previous promises (Rom. 10,16f.; 2 Cor. 1,19f.). In the word which Paul preaches the salvation which he preaches is already present (1 Cor. 11,26; Rom. 1,17; 2 Cor. 4,4; 2 Tim. 1,10f.) That is, Christ himself is present in the word which preaches him. Indeed ultimately he himself is the one who does the preaching (Rom.8,2; 1 Cor.2,13; Eph.6,17f.). Admittedly it is only those who believe who experience the salvific power of God's word (Rom. 1,16; 1 Cor. 1,18;15,1; Eph.1,13; Col.1,5 *et al.*). Yet even those who deny it experience its power, only in this case for disaster and destruction (Rom.11,28ff.; 1 Cor.1,18ff.; 2 Cor.4,3ff.; 2 Thess.1,8). In any case it is a decisive power. Its purpose is to bring reconciliation, truth, life, hope and freedom, with Christ and in Christ.

In Jesus God's word has become definitive. Through this definitiveness it remains perpetually relevant. It is, as the epistle to the Hebrews shows, a great event: God's speaking to the fathers through the prophets, God's speaking through the Son on the last day, the Lord's initial speaking, the confirmative speaking of the listeners, the *parakalein* in the assembled congregation and finally the *logos parakleseos* of the epistle to the Hebrews itself (see Heb. 1,1f.; 2,2–4; 3,15; 10,25; 13,22). Yet from the moment that God speaks to us through the Son, all speaking circles around this Son, and thus fills the last days, bringing a constant reminder of the significance of the present, and the offer of the sabbath, and the rest once again, for a little while (Heb. 3,17ff.; 4,3f; 10,37).[1]

The concept of the word seems to be most fully developed in the writings of John. In the apocalypse of John the exalted Lord is called simply the "Amen." He is the last and irrevocable confirmation of all God's promises of himself to man. He is the reliable and true witness, the beginning of God's creation (Acts 3,14). In John's gospel the person of Jesus himself is called God's "Word." Word and person are identified. According to John, Jesus is the very word itself which the Father has directed to men. In him the Father himself has become visible. The theological synthesis of what Jesus was, said, and did in the "Word" or in "God's Word" is the creative achievement of John's theology. Closely connected with the concept of the word is the concept of witness. When Jesus speaks, he gives testimony, testimony to the Father in the world. Particularly interesting is the following text:

He who comes from above is above all others; he who is from the earth belongs to the earth and uses earthly speech. He who comes from heaven bears witness to what he has seen and heard, yet no one accepts his witness. To accept his witness is to attest that God speaks true; for he whom God sent utters the words of God, so measureless is God's gift of the Spirit. The Father loves the Son and has entrusted him with all authority. He who puts his faith in the Son has hold of eternal life, but he who disobeys the Son shall not see that life; God's wrath rests upon him. (Jn. 3,31–36, *NEB*)

This text indicates that John begins with Jesus' being in order to explain his witness to God. Here we encounter a mode of thinking which is the opposite of Paul's. Paul begins with the experience of Christ's work and effectiveness, and reflects back from this on Jesus' being. John by contrast begins with the being of Christ, and this leads him to explain Christ's achievement. By analyzing his achievement, it is true, he again gains a deeper understanding of Christ's being. Jesus is God's self-communication to the world.

In order to understand this statement, it is necessary to say a few words about John's view of the world. John speaks about the cosmos not to shed light on the cosmos, but to shed light on man. The cosmos is the place created by God through his word for man's existence (Jn.1,1–10; 9,5; 13,1; 12,25; 16,21; 17,5.11.13.15. 24; 1 Jn.4,7). The world is seen here as an indispensable presupposition for man's historical activity. According to John it is the same *logos* who is the foundation of the world, and who then raises in the world the summons which is God's revelation. Basically the one revealing does not enter a sphere foreign to him, but one which belongs to him (Jn. 1,11). According to John it is only through man that the world becomes what it really is. It is not sinful in itself. But man's sin conceals the fact that it was created by God. Its character as a creature is no longer obvious. The fact that the world has been long burdened by sinful human action leads to a state of severe tension between Jesus and men—that is, the world. The world can no longer remain neutral to Jesus, its very foundation. He must be accepted as belonging to it or be rejected as a stranger. In contradiction to the structure of its being, it closes itself off from Jesus. Thus John is aware not only of the contrariety between that which is above and that which is below, stressed by gnosticism, but also and more decisively he presents the drama of salvation which is enacted between Jesus the Son of God, who became man and appeared in the world, and the world itself—that is, human history.

John understands Jesus Christ as God's messenger. His function as messenger is accomplished in the historical work which he performs in obedience to his Father's will. This brings salvation to those who believe, disaster to those who persevere in unbelief. Jesus's salvific work as a whole is a word of God to man. In his work, however, Jesus also reveals himself in his own individuality. Thus, his work is self-testimony and at the same time evidence of God's will that man be saved. The self-testimony of Jesus and the testimony he gives to his Father are an integral whole. In testifying to himself as God's messenger Jesus bears witness to the Father also, but only by testifying to himself as one sent from above. Thus God is present for man only in his Son.

The self-testimony of Jesus, which includes giving testimony to the Father, is reliable, because he speaks of what he knows. John says: "Jesus replied, 'My testimony is valid, even though I do bear witness about myself; because I know where I come from, and where I am going. You do not know either where I come from or where I am going.'" (Jn. 8,14,*NEB*)

Jesus knows his eternal origin and his eternal goal. He also knows his path on earth. He can reveal the Father because he knows him. This testimony of his cannot be judged by earthly standards, because nobody knows the Father as he knows him. Through him the Father is revealed. What and who he is is shown in Jesus. Thus Jesus is at the same time the revealer and the revealed, subject and content in one. His two functions as the one who reveals and as the revelation itself cannot be separated. If we acknowledged only the first element, we would succumb to a pure dynamism and actualism. If we acknowledged only the second element, we would incur the danger of an exclusive objectivism. In both cases we would miss John's concept of revelation. On the other hand, in unifying him who reveals with the revelation itself we express again the fact that Jesus cannot testify to himself except by bearing witness to his Father: he can only testify to himself by testifying that he is the Son of his Father. It is decisive for the structure of John's concept of revelation that it unites Jesus' witness to himself and his witness to God. At the same time it is clear that Jesus Christ as God's Son is constitutive of revelation in two respects: for revelation as God's approach to men, on the one hand; and on the other, for revelation as man's path to God—that is, for faith in God and the knowledge of God opened up by faith. Therefore belief in God is necessarily faith in Jesus Christ. To say that Christ is constitutive of faith means not only that faith must actually begin with Christ, but that Jesus Christ remains the constituent center for all human belief. It is he who makes faith possible, provides the foundation for it, enables it to seek and question, and leads it to completion.

These structural connections become evident in a concept which is characteristic of John, namely, the concept of truth (Jn. 14,6; 18,37). Christ testifies to himself as the truth, and this testimony must also be understood as testimony to God. Truth is not something that lies outside Jesus, it is present in him and through him. He is not a witness distinct from it. He is truth itself, in the sense that in him the living God has left his inaccessibility and drawn near to man. Therefore, whoever rejects Jesus closes himself off from the God who shows himself in Jesus, and so is an unbeliever.

The God to whom Jesus refers is no unknown quantity. He is the God, well known to his listeners, to whom Abraham and Moses testified. It is one and the same God who spoke through the Fathers in the Old Testament and who now speaks through the Son. In the light of the present revelation in his Son, we can see whether or not we understand God in his earlier words. For what he intended to reveal, and what his goal was, *is* precisely the one who has now appeared in the world. God's self-revelation, accomplished in Jesus, actualizes and completes all previous revelations testified to in the Scriptures. Since Jesus Christ, the Old Testament can only be understood as God's word if it is comprehended as a foreword to Jesus, the definite word of God.

Thus, Jesus can apply to himself the ultimate expression of self-communication in which God expresses himself in the Old Testament—namely, the formula "I am." This hallowed phrase by which God gave testimony to himself, "It is I," finds its fulfillment in the word "It is I" pronounced by the Logos become man. It is paradoxical that a historical human being should be entitled to claim for himself in all strictness the highest form of God's self-communication. It is as if Jesus said: "I am Jahweh's self-revelation. I am the place of divine presence and of revelation in history." This formula transforms Christ's earthly *kairos* into eternity, and eternity into an earthly *kairos*. In view of this statement there can be only belief which seizes the *kairos,* or unbelief which rejects it. Those who have to do with Christ have to do with the "I am who I am"; with him who reveals and represents Jahweh in history, and thus with Jahweh himself. The confrontation of the Jewish people with Christ becomes a confrontation with their own history, because it is the God of the Old Testament who has become present in Jesus, once for all in a unique manner. The entire claim of God over Israel, repeated again and again as it had been in the course of history, is now centered in Christ, and yet is also strangely remote; it is after all "a man" who makes the claim (J. Blank).

The Acts of the Apostles describes how God's word took root and grew in the first Christian generation (Acts 6,7; 13,49; 12,24). It shows us, above all, how Peter and Paul proclaimed it and what effect it had. First, it describes the effectiveness of the word among the Jews of Jerusalem; then the establishment of the mission to the pagans at Antioch; and finally the proclamation of the message among the heathen, especially Paul's missionary activity. In recent decades there has been much discussion about whether the speeches reported in Acts were actually delivered as they are handed down to us, or whether they are embellished and stylized creations of the author, built on a historical foundation. This problem is not of great significance for our question. The event which God brought about through Jesus of Nazareth, from his ministry in Galilee to his appearances after his resurrection, is the starting-point and the main argument of all the speeches in Acts. Through the apostles the word of salvation reaches Jews and pagans (Acts 10,36f., 40f.; 13,26). It is God himself who speaks and acts in the preaching of the apostles (Acts 17,30; 21,19). But Jesus, too, as the risen Lord, addresses those who believe in him, through the words of his apostles (Acts 13,38f.; 26,23). The Apostles speak God's word; they bear witness to what they have seen and heard (Acts 1,8. 22;2,32). They are the servants of what they have seen and heard. The word of God retains its sovereignty over them therefore, it does not become subject to the power of men. Through the words of the apostles, the Holy Spirit makes possible a true understanding of Jesus Christ (Acts 1,8).

The contents of the apostolic message are always essentially the same. The apostles speak of the salvific death and above all of the resurrection of Jesus Christ (Acts 1,22; 2,32; 4,1f., 8,35; 15,35; 18,11; 19,10; 26,8). They interpret the resurrection of Jesus Christ as the fulfillment of the promise made in the Old Testament. It belongs to the essential structure of the apostolic kerygma that Jesus was raised "according to the Scriptures"— that is, as the Old Testament had foretold (Acts 2,39;13,23. 32f.; 26,6.22). By his resurrection Jesus becomes the Lord and the bearer of salvation. Salvation will be decided through belief or unbelief in him. Also, he is the judgment to come (Acts 10,42).

According to the biblical data, the word of God cannot be separated from the person of Jesus. He is the epiphany of the

eternal Word of God. This is expressed in the statements by which
Jesus proclaims the foundation of the kingdom of God. While
Catholic theology for a long time gave too little emphasis to the
"word of God," Luther gave it so much that it almost became a
hypostasis separable from Jesus. The word by itself, he said, must
be enough for the heart: the earthly Jesus is not the ultimate
ground of faith. True faith holds to the word.[2] This undervaluing
of the person of Jesus in regard to faith, and the isolation of the
"word," made Bultmann's demythologization possible.

MIRACLES AND SIGNS

We return to the question of the recognizability of revelation.
As we emphasized, there is no cogent proof that an event or a
word, or an event happening in a word, is an act of divine
self-revelation. Thus an atheist historian can, without difficulty,
understand the history of God's people in the Old Testament as a
purely political and cultural development. We mentioned above
some elements of the knowledge process which are immanent in
revelation and in men. If we considered that these were the only
means of comprehending revelation, then the charge of pure
immanentism, of "modernism," might be warranted. However,
such is not the case. God has bestowed on revelation itself certain
characteristics which have objective significance. It belongs to the
essence of revelation that these reach man. They are, however,
not merely objectivistic data possessing a significance apart from
man. Whether man acknowledges revelation in freedom, or rejects it, is dependent on whether or not he feels it is related to
him, or foreign. But this is an objective process. Thus while man's
inner experiences with the revealed God have their importance,
they need to be supplemented. We have need of external testimonies, and the ones mentioned by the First Vatican Council are
miracles and prophecies.[3] The council did not define the concepts
of miracle and prophecy. In scholastic theology it has been customary to treat the concept of miracle from the point of view of
natural law, understanding it as a process which surpasses the
natural possibilities of man not only in practice but in principle.

Thus an attempt was made to provide a physico-metaphysical explanation of miracles. In its extreme form this interpretation of miracles maintains that the law of nature is suspended by God's omnipotence. In view of present scientific and technical possibilities it is difficult to establish in fact when there is a miracle in a concrete case. Added to this is Theodor Lessing's objection that it is difficult to prove that accounts of miracles alleged to have taken place in the past are historically trustworthy in the strict sense.

In treating this question we will do best if we follow Scripture and the fathers and concentrate our attention on the sign-character of miracles. For example, in a sermon on John's gospel Augustine says:

The miracles by which God governs the world and guides the whole of creation have been rendered so commonplace for us by being everyday occurrences that hardly anyone considers worthy of notice the miraculous and amazing work of God we find in each grain of corn. Therefore in his mercy he has reserved it for himself to bring about, when the time is ripe, certain things which lie outside the usual course and order of nature, so that men who are insensitive to the miracles of everyday events will be impressed by seeing what is not greater, but is less usual. In point of fact, the ordering of the entire universe is a greater miracle than satisfying five thousand people with five loaves of bread. And yet nobody is amazed to see the former, while the latter astonishes men, not because it is a great miracle, but because it is rarer. Who is it who feeds the entire world even now, if not he who makes whole crops ripen out of a few grains of wheat? Jesus acted, therefore, like God himself. With the same power whereby he gives increase to a few grains to produce a harvest, he multiplied the five loaves in his hands. The five loaves of bread were like seeds, which were not, however, entrusted to the earth, but were multiplied by him who made the earth. This miracle took place before our senses, in order to edify our minds. It was shown to our eyes so that our intellect would reflect on it, and we would perceive with astonishment the invisible God in his visible works. Then, awakened and purified by faith, we would long to see in an invisible way him whom we have learned to know as the Invisible One through visible things.[4]

According to the testimony of both the Old and the New
Testaments, miracles, as a symbol of God's power, cannot be separated from revelation. We may therefore consider miracles a basic
element of the biblical witness to revelation. The men chosen
by God for his revelatory acts show themselves to be such by
historical actions occurring in the world of experience. Their purpose is to awaken faith; not, however, to force it upon people.
Against unbelief they have no guaranteed effectiveness. Faith
remains a free decision, even in the face of miracles. Signs are
intended to draw people's attention and obtain a hearing for those
who preach the gospel. But of course there is also the faith
which has not seen and yet has believed. As divine symbols,
miracles can be understood only by those who are open to God.
If the a priori, transcendental readiness for God is absent, it is not
possible to see a miracle as a miracle. Where this disposition is
lacking, a miracle can even produce hostility (Mt. 11,6; Lk. 6,11,
and Jesus' resurrection itself). Therefore Jesus considers it point-
less to work miracles where men are shut up in their own darkness
and self-satisfaction, and so incapable of understanding them.
Faith does not produce the miracle. Faith is an effect of miracles,
but it is also, in an incipient form, a presupposition for recognizing them for what they are.

The miracles of the Old Testament are concentrated in the
events connected with the exodus from Egypt, the conclusion of
the covenant at Sinai, and the internal and external strengthening
of the people of the covenant. They are intended as divine signs to
lead the people to believe in God as their helper and savior, and
so to abandon polytheism and dedicate themselves to monotheism.
Miracles thus have a theological significance, and have their
place where the progress of the history of salvation encounters
difficulties and resistance which can be overcome only by God's
power.

As regards the form of the miracle in the Old Testament, it is
always unexpected and impressive help from God in a difficult or
hopeless situation. Especially in the miracles decisive for Israel,
God reveals himself convincingly as the great one, the mighty one,
the good one, to whom man can surrender himself in confidence.

Thus Israel experiences itself—its becoming a people and its continuance as a people—as the real miracle. Israel was not saved by the intervention of a miracle; the salvation itself and the preservation of the people was the miracle (Ex.14,31; 19,4f.) Gen.25,21; 29,31; 30,1ff. 22f.). This theological meaning of the miracle would not be diminished even if the miraculous events reported in the Old Testament were representational means used by the authors to praise God's gracious providence. The concept of miracle in the metaphysical sense was unknown to the authors of the Old Testament (J. Haspecker).

As regards the New Testament, the powerful deeds of God are related here also as signs of his presence among men. The biblical signs of the New Testament have their climax in the raising of Jesus Christ from death. Through this event, as Peter states in his sermon on Pentecost, God made Jesus, who had been crucified, the Lord and Messiah (Acts 2,36). Here is the beginning of a new creation—that is, the transcending of the present form of the world into a new world-form which takes its character from the absolute future towards which it is directed. The goal of the whole process of evolution, effected by God and yet immanent in the world itself, towards a radically new form of existence has already been reached at one point within the world. The raising of Jesus is the standard and the norm for all the miracles reported in the New Testament. The resurrection of Jesus is the expression of the innermost dynamism of his existence. In his resurrection a breakthrough took place, and now this exercises an effect which is unforeseeable upon the course of human history and upon the cosmos. The raising of Jesus shows what God intends to do with creation. The world is not a closed system, but is open to that form of existence which has already appeared in Christ. Just as the world before Jesus was directed to him, so now in him and by him it is directed towards resurrection.

In the raising of Jesus and in the other miracles reported in the New Testament the laws of nature are not broken, but preserved and led beyond themselves. Perhaps this will be seen more clearly if we reflect that each of the different spheres of existence is directed towards the higher one, where it is preserved and taken into service. Thus, inorganic matter transcends itself towards organic matter; the organism towards mind; and the human mind transcends itself towards God. The higher being stamps its character on the lower one that it assumes, without robbing it (the latter) of its own law-structure.

On examination it becomes clear that the primary function of the miracles of Jesus (raising from the dead, healing the sick, multiplication of the loaves, etc.) is to reveal the salvation promised by God. They are not a show put on to entertain the crowd, they are intended as signs of the presence of God. For this reason Jesus does not work miracles where the people are not ready for God: in such a situation a miracle would be meaningless. Jesus' deeds of power are performed in the service of mankind. If we look at them from the point of view of evolution, they are stimuli to a surer and more rapid progress towards that ultimate condition in which a changed world will be totally at the service of man resurrected and united to God. Jesus brought this about not by disrupting the laws of nature, but by giving the world, in obedience to the laws of its nature, new energy, in the power of his human and divine spirit. In particular cases, perhaps, he so set in motion the spiritual and mental powers of the man concerned that these had a more forceful effect on his body than is usual in everyday life.[5]

It may be mentioned in passing that the view proposed by contemporary science that natural laws are only probability functions cannot be used to explain miracles. Whether the laws of nature are laws in the strict sense or only probability functions is a matter of indifference for the explanation of miracles. The decisive thing is that the one sphere of existence is always open towards the other, and that all creation is open to God, the inventor and creator of its laws.

Reading

Rahner, Karl. "Christology Within an Evolutionary View of the World" in *Theological Investigations,* V. Baltimore, Helicon, 1966.

Notes

[1] H. Schlier, "Wort" in H. Fries, *Handbuch theologischer Grundbegriffe,* II,864.

[2] P. Althaus, *Die Theologie Martin Luthers* (Gütersloh, 1962), 53; P. Hacker, *Das Ich im Glauben bei Martin Luther* (Graz, 1966).

[3] Denz. 3009.

[4] *Tract. in Joannem* 24, 1.

[5] See B. Huber: "Einheit und Mannigfaltigkeit des Lebens" in *Studien und Berichte der Katholischen Akademie in Bayern,* 4 (1958), 89–105.

‹ 8

The History of Salvation

DEFINITION

Divine revelation is given to serve man's salvation. The words by which God discloses himself to man are words of salvation (e.g. Ex. 3,6ff.; 18,8; 19,4–6; 34,27; Os.12,13; 13,4). In Deutero-Isaiah (45,7) we read: "I form light and create darkness, I make weal and create woe, I am the Lord, who do all these things." According to Jeremiah (29,11), God reassures those exiled in Babylon: "For I know the plans I have for you, says the Lord, plans for welfare and not for evil, to give you a future and a hope." The prophet Ezekiel expects the reinstatement of Israel as Jahweh's last deed, which will make him recognizable as God(37, 12f.). For him the meaning of the exile is not lasting misfortune for the people, but the bringing about of a new knowledge of the Lord in salvation and peace (Ez. 39,28f.).

By the very fact that the hidden god, who is incomparable to any human being, lives among his people their salvation is assured. The absence of God is disaster; his presence is salvation. From the New Testament we may cite the following passages indicating the salvific character of God's word: Acts 5,20; 13,26; 14,3; 20,32.

Since salvation not only occurs within history, as it were in a time container, but takes place in historical acts themselves, we can speak of a history of salvation in reference to the word of God's revelation. The definition of this term "salvation history," which originated in the nineteenth century, is by no means completely clear, and it is therefore controversial. However, it has become indispensable, and has found an accepted place in theology. In our days it has perhaps become the "leitmotif" of modern theology.

The concept of salvation history has two components. It is not immediately evident what the word "salvation" means, because the term has several dimensions. How it is interpreted depends essentially on how we understand the term "man." Man can be seen as an individual or as a social being or as individual and social. We can consider him as performing a function—*homo operator*—or as a person; or as simultaneously being a person and fulfilling a function; as *homo faber*—that is, an economic being; as *animal rationale* or *homo sapiens;* or as *homo orans*—that is, a being transcending himself. In the world of today salvation is seen above all in welfare, in freedom, in education, and in peace. These ideas of salvation move in the human sphere. They take their course, so to speak, on a horizontal line. In the Scriptures they are not neglected, but they have no exclusive dominance there. Peace is mentioned very frequently as a fundamental part of salvation, and what is meant is peaceful relations between men, united in fraternity. But primarily, when Scripture speaks of peace, it has in mind a vertical movement—namely, the movement of God towards man, and man's response in faith; that is, harmony between God and man. The peace which is sought on the horizontal plane has, according to Scripture, an essential condition, namely, peace with God; that is, recognition of the incomprehensible mystery which pervades and transcends the world, the depth dimension of the world understood as personal. To run counter to this provokes disaster, according to Scripture.

The authors of Genesis reflected on the problem, how, in spite of the covenant with God, the world could be abandoned to the powers of disaster, and recorded their thoughts in the story of paradise. Genesis sees an essential connection between sin and disaster and represents it in an image which had at least an immediate appeal to their own time. The heart of the story is formed by the thesis that all disaster begins with sin, and that sin has now become an inexhaustible source of disaster. In such a view, salvation is conceived of primarily in terms of ethics and religion, not of material well-being. Not that this is excluded; on the contrary, it receives considerable emphasis. Man is supposed to cultivate the earth and fashion it with mind and hand into an environment suitable to him. But he can do this rightly only when he transcends himself towards God. In the New Testament we find the same idea expressed in the words of Jesus (Mt. 6,33); "Seek first the kingdom of God and his righteousness, and all these things shall be yours as well." "All these things" are by no means considered superfluous or worthless, they are simply assigned structurally to a secondary position; or rather, understood as the consequence of seeking God. Christ is speaking of a structural order in which nothing is lacking or may be lacking, but everything is in its proper place. The whole of human existence is seen as a unity, which is yet full of tensions. From these considerations we can perhaps understand that Scripture sees salvation primarily as God's promise of himself to man—that is, in the encounter of man with God; but at the same time it omits nothing that belongs to the world.

Scripture testifies to the fact that God wants the salvation of all creatures. He can even be defined as that being transcending the world, yet present in it, who in creative power accomplishes the salvation of all creatures, yet without subjecting human freedom to coercion. The world is ultimately governed by God's will to save, not by the forces of evil and destruction—insofar as evil is not caused by man's free will. God's salvific action consists in an offer of salvation, that is, in a salvific dialogue with men. His will to save can be turned—against his will—into evil, if man refuses his offer. In that case there is no zone of neutrality in which God and man might ignore each other, but only a condition of alienation and catastrophe for man.

God offers salvation by revealing himself, and by establishing his sovereignty in the sphere of historical human existence by means of his active word. This explicit establishment of God's sovereignty, which in the course of human history was experienced for the first time by the people of Israel, is expressed by the term "kingdom of God." Divine self-revelation serves the establishment of God's kingdom, and by that fact at the same time the salvation of men. Only when God in his grace gives himself to man, and when man accepts God's gift of himself—when God thus prevails as creative love in man—only then is that achieved which is meant by the word "salvation." In the course of history God has promised himself to men in various ways; in absolute and radical, historical finality in Jesus Christ. This promise of himself by God to men, in spite of its historical finality in Christ, is itself again only a beginning, signifying a promise of an absolute future—that is, of a definitive self-communication of God to his creatures in transfiguration and deification.

The second component of the term, namely the concept of "history," includes the ideas of freedom, purposefulness, futurity, the significance and the unity of an event—whether that event involves the whole of mankind or some particular group of men—the historicality of man; that is, the fact that he spends his life not only within history but in the accomplishment of historical action.

THE GENERAL AND THE SPECIAL
HISTORY OF SALVATION

If we wish to understand the history of divine revelation as salvation history, it is useful and in fact necessary to distinguish two forms of it, which cannot be separated from one another but are nevertheless distinct; we are accustomed to speak of a general and a special history of salvation. The special history of salvation is that which began with the call of Abraham, had its Old Testament climax in the liberation of Israel from servitude in Egypt, and reached its completion in Christ. The history of salvation which occurred before and contemporaneously with this special history of salvation is termed general salvation history. The concept of a general salvation history is meaningful only if it is admitted that there is salvation outside the "special" salvific action of God. We are justified in making this assumption by the testimony of Scripture that God desires the salvation of all men, and also by reason of the Christocentricity of the world, discussed above. Furthermore, since man has bodily existence and always lives in society, his relationship to God always has a concrete and historical character, and as a result salvific institutions and salvific communities are to be found everywhere. For this reason, even outside the dimension of the special history of salvation, we can speak not only of salvation but also of a history of salvation.

These reflections allow us to see the intrinsic difference between general and special salvation history. In the first place it must be emphasized that the difference is not like that between "natural" and "supernatural." This means that we cannot properly interpret the history of salvation by distinguishing it in a merely exterior manner from world history. The differentiation between salvation history and world history, with which it coexists, needs an inner principle. This can only consist in the fact that God, by his word, declares human history to be salvific history, and by this declaration creates it as such. As regards the general history of salvation, we can point to the words of promise recorded in Genesis, which God spoke to the first men and to Noah in particular. As regards the special history of salvation, we know through God's revelatory word that the history of Israel was at the same time salvation history. Precisely by this word, however, Israel's history was constituted salvation history; it became the history of God's gift of himself to the people of Israel. Salvation history is not distinguished from world history by differences in political, cultural, and social forms, but only by God's word. It is essential, of course, for this that God's word be experienced as God's word by those to whom it is directed. In other words, his people must realize that they are a people established by God. Thus Israel experienced God as their protector and partner in the covenant, in the events which accompanied the liberation from Egypt. There is no history of salvation without dialogue between God and man; the experience of God takes place in faith in him. He who does not open himself to God, in readiness to believe, will see in the special history of salvation nothing but a piece of world history.

It would lead to unnecessary repetition to sketch the course of salvation history, since it is identical with the course of the history of revelation. The Pentateuch (or Hexateuch) presents us with a most impressive conception of salvation history. Of course, if revelation is understood in a restricted sense as applying only to that word of God which was directed to Abraham and his descendants, then the concept of salvation history is wider than the concept of the history of revelation. The restriction of the concept of revelation to God's word to Abraham and his decendants, however, does not quite correspond with the picture Scripture offers us. According to Scripture, God also called forth the world by his word, and in his mercy led and guided men in the ages before he called Abraham. From the creation of the world down to God's revelation of himself at the time of Moses, one continuous course of revelation unfolds itself, in different stages and forms. Therefore, the sphere of revelation must be extended as far as the sphere of salvation history, and *vice versa*.

The determination of the relationship between general and special salvation history is of the greatest significance, as is also the related question whether and to what extent there is or can be salvation outside special salvation history once this has been inaugurated.

No doubt there is a historical connection. The question is whether there is a logical connection, and if so what is its nature. In the discussion of these questions the view is sometimes put forward that general salvation history represents the ordinary way of salvation established by God, while special salvation history is an extraordinary way of salvation. Although this terminology can be understood correctly, it deviates so much from the traditional that it almost inevitably runs the risk of being misunderstood. Therefore, it is preferable to refer to the special way of salvation as the ordinary way willed by God, and to the general way of salvation as an extraordinary way, which he has made possible.

THE HISTORICAL RELATIONSHIP

It is incontestable that the special history of salvation has its roots in the general history of salvation and has grown out of it. If the people of Israel at the time of Moses became aware that it was owing to an act of God that they became a nation, they could look back on previous historic experiences and understand them as a path towards the emergence of their nation. We saw earlier that the hardships experienced even during the time of the covenant caused faithful believers to ask how such things could occur in spite of their partnership with God. At first the tales of the patriarchs, the stories of Abraham, Isaac, Jacob, and Joseph were interpreted in the light of the covenant with God. What we read about them in the Sacred Scriptures of the Old Covenant are testimonies of faith, which are not, however, mere inventions of their authors but have a historical core—particularly the migration of Abraham into Egypt at the beginning of the second millennium. The epoch preceding the time of the patriarchs was also understood, as we saw, as a path leading to the covenant of Sinai. The people of Israel were conscious of the fact that a long development lay behind them, which God led to the goal he had planned for it in the covenant. This evolution had its beginnings in the obscurity of the origin of the world.

What we know from scientific research about the evolution of the world and man, Sacred Scripture presents in terms of faith in the enduring, universal power of God over history. The authors of Scripture are not interested in describing in detail the history of the universe, of the earth, and of men. Scripture is not intended to be a textbook of physics or biology or history. Its numerical statements on the ages of the first men, especially the patriarchs, serve as symbols in the history of salvation, not as historical data. The writers wished to proclaim with believing hearts that from the beginning God planned the salvation of his people, and that he purposefully pursued and realized this plan in spite of all difficulties and setbacks. In reality it was not a matter of a few millennia but of billions of years of evolution of the cosmos from original particles to the breakthrough of mind, in which man came into existence. Our purpose does not require that we state the age of the earth, or of the cosmos, or of man on earth on the basis of modern scientific research. What is to be said concerning the history of salvation is just as true whether men lived for thousands or for millions of years.

The evolution of matter from original energy was a movement forward, towards a new future, and at the same time a movement upward, towards a higher and more complex form of existence. It took its origin both from its own immanent forces and from the abundance of the always creative God. It was a matter of great significance when, in this process of complexification and concentration, a structure was reached in which life arose. It was of even greater and more decisive significance when, in the movement of matter beyond itself, that structural stage appeared in which, through God's creative action, mind was formed, and entered matter as a new principle of development; and *vice versa* brought matter to a new unity of existence. When man stepped forth, the course of evolution, which had taken billions of years, reached its provisional climax. In man the orientation of the entire process and the meaning of creation became apparent. Man stands at the peak of the universe. In its continuous self-transcendence matter required innumerable evolutionary stages, drawn both from its own immanent forces and from the dynamic fullness of God, and an immeasurable period of time, before it reached its climax in man. Because he possesses mind, man can understand himself as a creature, can turn to the Absolute as his origin, and at the same time can sum up the entire world in himself as the climax of the whole, in order to bring it back to God. We hear an echo of this truth in numerous ancient myths which express the conviction that man must sacrifice things in order to possess them as a gift for his own salvation; they bring disaster when he withholds them from the gods.

Sacred Scripture reports, in the Priestly Code which forms part of Genesis, that God himself turned to man so that man could surrender himself to God as his creator, and could thus become his true self. The peak of cosmic evolution is reached each time a human being is born. Every human being is a realization of the goal aspired to by the whole. (This statement is not meant as a foundation for solving the question of monogenism and polygenism, but only attempts to emphasize the significance of every single human being in the process of evolution.)

Although evolution reached its climax in man, the course of

development by no means came to an end with that. The process does not come to rest. If the assumption of scientists is correct that, generally speaking, a zoological species has a life-duration of fifty million years, then men are only in the morning of their life. It is reasonable to expect, however, that the decisive characteristic of man, his ability to reflect on himself, on the world and on God, will not be surpassed in the course of evolution. Nevertheless there can be radical changes in the way in which these things take place. Therefore as man, through a creative call, came forth out of the infinite life of God who has no beginning, namely (as we shall see later) out of the infinite loving dialogue between the Father and his Word, so that he is a finite self-revelation of the Father by his Word, he continues into infinity. His path goes from the infinite to the infinite.

In the moment in which man stepped forth, a new evolutionary factor became effective, mind. Its characteristic was the power to carry on and to intensify the upward movement of matter and of life in freedom of decision. The relationship of object to subject was formed, insofar as man was able mentally to penetrate the world, and to transform it into a true and suitable environment on the basis of his cognition—that is, to create the world of man by means of the matter offered by God, and that in the sense of leading it into the future. No arbitrary boundary was appointed to his knowledge. Only one limit was set to him, that of being human. For all knowledge, according to Scripture, is meant to serve the building up of human existence. This fact is so decisive that we can say that the idea of history could only have developed out of the biblical conception of things. Structurally, the idea of history represents a Christian reality or category grown on Jewish-Christian ground, one which preserves its vitality even when its Christian contents have disappeared. It is of the greatest significance that the entire universe reached in man, in whom it fulfills itself, the capacity to transcend itself consciously and reflectively in the direction of the Absolute. This is not merely transcendence into an always indefinite "beyond," but is an incessant unfolding of itself towards the absolute future, which stands before man, and calls him, and is at the same time his origin. Thus the universe progresses not only horizontally but, at the same time, vertically. Once this goal is reached, the cosmos, also, will rest in itself, for then it will be wholly unfolded and will possess itself in its developed fullness, having returned to its Origin. But even this will not mean the end of the movement. For in full, though not identical, unity with God, man will be penetrated by the dynamic existence of God unendingly. If we find man continuously driven by inner pressure, by desires and ideas, by dreams and hopes, by uneasiness and restlessness, these are sign of the evolutionary forces which propel him towards his absolute future.

We know from the witness of Scripture that the dreams of men about the future are basically not empty illusions but anticipations of reality. For God as the Absolute has opened himself to man and calls him into his own abundance of life. In the light of such considerations we can, if we characterize God as an eternal dialogue of love, describe the world as a process of development towards future participation in this dialogue.

The paradise narrative shows us that man's dialogue with God —that is, his consciousness of God and his devotion to him—is constitutive for man, even if the dialogue were to develop in a negative direction. The latter did in fact happen. At this point let us only say about it that the rupture caused by man in the dialogue with God was a catastrophic setback for the progress of the world. The forward drive of the cosmos was interrupted by the sin of man. At the summit of creation a reversal took place. The author of Genesis assures his contemporaries that the anti-theistic attitude of man had fateful consequences for the lives of individuals and for their relationship to one another and to the world. The cast of man's mind was changed by sin; his vigor and power of concentration were weakened. He could no longer work for the future in the pure joy of creativity, but became a victim of weariness, pride, insecurity, violence, hatred, and cruelty, so that struggle, war, murder, and destruction entered into the process of evolution. These negative effects are described in various ways—in the motif of the serpent, in the story of Cain, of the Deluge, and of the Tower of Babel.

For example, in the mythical thought of that time, the serpent

was considered the symbol of wisdom and life and symbolized the
gods and goddesses who granted wisdom and life. In opposition to
this myth, the author of Genesis declares that the serpent is not a
salvific animal but an accursed one which brings death. The motif
of the serpent represents a general attack upon the whole world
of myth. Disaster strikes men when they leave the one, living and
true God in favor of the gods. But God does not leave man in this
desperate state: he himself seeks after him, to resume the dialogue
with him. God's concern for the world he has created, and which
man has endangered, is so deep and universal that he attempts
again and again to bring the trend of the world's development forward once more. The tales of Cain, Noah, and the Tower of Babel
are testimonies of faith in the development of the history of salvation until the time of Abraham and even of Moses. These testimonies of faith lighten the darkness of human history, not by
scientific or historical but by theological means. Even in a world
placed in jeopardy by man, God remained a saving God, gracious
to man.

We can attempt to clarify, briefly, how these events are evidence
of God's persevering will to save. Cain's turning against Abel
shows that the first men did not acknowledge themselves as creatures of God and did not obey him, but wanted to decide for themselves in inordinate autonomy what was right and what was wrong.
The decisive fact is that God, though he passed judgment on
Cain, did not withdraw his loving care from him. Cain obdurately
repudiated God's choice of him, but God still did not reject him for
ever, and did not deprive him of his mercy. The history of salvation
continues, in spite of having been endangered by Cain.

The same point is expressed even more clearly in the story of
Noah. Men get farther and farther from the meaning of life—
namely, from concord with God. In Noah's time God is shown as
making a new effort to re-establish the right order. He threatens
judgment by way of a catastrophic flood, from which Noah and
his family will be saved. However we understand the story of the
deluge, Noah appears here as another First Parent of mankind. Disaster had struck through Adam: through Noah a new partnership
with God, and thus new salvation, was initiated. This is expressed

in the words: "Behold, I establish my covenant with you, and your descendants after you" (Gen. 9,9). Noah appears here as the representative of mankind. Sacred Scripture again testifies in faith that God does not want disaster but salvation. The whole of creation stands within the horizon of God's will to save. Scripture calls the rainbow the symbol of the covenant between God and men (9, 11–17). According to the sacred text, God says that the covenant with Noah will be the beginning and the foundation of an everlasting salvific relationship between God and men. In particular, note Genesis: "Never again will I curse the earth because of man, because his heart contrives evil from his infancy. Never again will I strike down every living thing as I have done. As long as earth lasts, seed time and harvest, cold and heat, summer and winter, day and night shall cease no more." (Gen.8,21f., *J*) This text bears witness to God's covenant of peace with all mankind, with all of creation. The rainbow is supposed to be the concrete sign of this, to remind both God and man of the covenant. From the rhythm of nature, promised for the entire future, men are intended to recognize that God is the giver and maintainer of life, and that reverence and gratitude are due to him. In this text God himself appears as the founder of religion. It is not theologically adventurous to recognize in this process the biblical authority for the great religions of history. Although each of them contains errors and abuses, yet the core, the reverence for God and the divine, has been maintained. Thus the process of the world's development moves forward again in a positive way.

In the description of the building of the Tower of Babel a new danger is dealt with. The sacred writers see that the various peoples of the earth do not unite in a large and peaceful human family but attack each other in strife and hatred, and they see rebellion against God as the cause. The human hybris which makes men reject the true God and create mythical gods produces confusion, war, and decline among men. The history of the Tower of Babel does not retract what was promised in the scene with Noah, but it makes clear how seriously progress in history is endangered by human sin.

Thus it becomes understandable that God concentrated his attempts to help the world more and more on one individual man, Abraham, and on the latter's family and the nation which took its origin from them; namely, on the patriarchs and the people of Israel. His promises given to Noah, however, continue also to have validity apart from this people which he created and led with special care, even though they constantly suffer new setbacks due to human pride. We have the impression that the more men resist and hinder the course of creation, the stronger God's efforts become. We know that they attained their provisional climax in Moses' time. But the covenant with Moses and the people of Israel was exposed to numerous crises right from the beginning. The prophets had often to interfere—warning, stirring up, and threatening, but also consoling. Most important was their eschatological vision of the future, giving hope for a final and definite time of salvation. Jeremiah, particularly, proclaimed a new, a perfect covenant (Jer.31,31f.). It became more and more evident that the promises did not aim at an objectively new order, but at a person who was expected to bring to pass a new form of existence. This promise was fulfilled in Jesus Christ. He is the real peak of creation. If we said before that every man is a peak at which the universe aims, we must say now that in Christ the tendency of the entire process of evolution towards this goal is concentrated in one individual figure. This thesis needs some comment in order to avoid the impression that Christ is the physically necessary result of world evolution.

In the first place it must be affirmed that the whole course of evolution is directed towards Christ as its goal. The development which preceded him converges in him to its climax. This development began first with a very restricted form of being, original energy or particles; unfolded itself then into a multiplicy of forms and a manifold variety of life, including at last human life; and subsequently, as a result of God's free salvific plan, it began to be restricted, first to the "faithful remnant," and finally to Christ as the one great point of convergence. From here the stream of evolution broadens out again to embrace the human race in its entirety, and the cosmos itself.

The role of Christ in the evolution of the cosmos can be defined not only in terms of the goal of the process, however—i.e., intentionally—but also in terms of the very matter in which it takes place —i.e., physically and organically. For in his human nature, through his mother Mary, he belongs to a particular group, and through this group to a nation and to the human race; its origins are his, and reach back to the billions of years during which there was merely material and organic life. Thus there is a direct evolutionary relationship between him and the entire cosmos. His body is matter from that matter which stood at the beginning of the entire process.

It is also a moving thought that Jesus' spiritual soul, immediately created by God like every spiritual soul, was not fashioned without an organic relationship with his mother, which means with the entire process of evolution; and by this his whole manner of thinking, willing, and feeling was conditioned. The unity of body and mind in Jesus was shaped by billions of years, and by the history of his people and his family, in which lay the roots of his human life. But in him human nature transcended itself towards God in a unique and definitive, in an unconditioned and unsurpassable, way; his human nature was accepted by God in such an absolute fashion that he exists in God and God in him with a singular intensity. In theology this way of existing, one in the other, is described as the "hypostatic union." The "once for all" (*eph' hapax*) of the incarnation of the eternal Word of God must not be understood statically; it must rather be understood dynamically, in the sense that the incarnate Logos led a human life from conception to death, and had to follow a path of the utmost significance for himself and for the whole of creation. The evolutionary process does not come to a halt with the incarnation, but gains a new effectiveness by it (Jn.8,14).

During his earthly life Jesus still had the ultimate form of his existence—the glorification of his body—before him, in the future. In all the statements which John ascribes to him, he is always, so to speak, ahead of himself and of the entire world, because he speaks with reference to his own future. If Jesus, who existed so completely and unconditionally in God, nevertheless died the death of the cross, this was not inherent in the structure of his being but was the task he was given to perform. We shall have more to say about that later. But in his resurrection from the dead the true structure of Jesus' existence broke through and became apparent. The glorification of his human nature is the consequence of Jesus' unconditional union with God. God so fully possessed Jesus that his physical and spiritual nature could without restriction become transparent for the divine.

What happened in Jesus was not only of significance for himself. He lived not only for the sake of all the others but also as their representative. One might apply to him the illuminating phrase which has become common in some recent theology, "corporate personality."

Through Christ, his death and his glorification, a completely new phase was introduced into the history of salvation. According to Paul, Christ became the second Adam of mankind. Salvation history in the strictest sense, that sense in which we encountered it in the time of Moses and in the times of the prophets of the Old Testament, is over. Christ is its fulfillment and therefore its end. Jesus of Nazareth is the promised Messiah, Christ, the Lord. That is the proclamation which we find throughout the New Testament as a basic element of the kerygma of the early Church. After Christ, God's revelation of himself will not take the form of shaping and guiding one particular people. We may therefore wonder whether we should designate the time after Christ by the heavily burdened concept of "salvation history." If we wish to use the expression here, we can use it only analogously and in a sense different from that intended before. If we want to avoid confusion, and also to express the definitiveness and finality of the special salvation history, it is better to speak now of the "time of salvation" rather than of the "history of salvation." This terminology does not lead to an underestimation of the time after Christ, but rather expresses the differentiation between the epochs of divine salvation. Insofar as God now turns himself to the individual, the individual history of salvation has begun.

Since God's revelation of himself in Christ cannot be repeated but is final, it follows that it must also be characterized by universality. Christ himself knows that he is the fulfillment of the

ages. With him the time of the law and of the prophets comes to
an end. The apostles in their preaching call him the one who fulfills and brings to maturity (e.g., Gal.4,4; Heb.1,1f.; Acts 2,17;1
Pet.1,20; 1 Cor.10,11.). Therefore he must be proclaimed in
the entire world. They know themselves to be the responsible
guardians and heralds of the doctrine entrusted to them, and they
admonish their followers to remain faithful to tradition (Gal. 1,9;
Rom. 16,17; 1 Tim. 6,20; 2 Tim. 1,14). Christ is the foundation
laid by God himself. No one can lay any other (1 Cor. 3,10f.).

The finality of Christ's revelation, however, does not mean that
the apostles can not and must not interpret Christ in the Holy
Spirit, and therefore, say more than he said. Just as Christ interprets the Old Testament in regard to himself, so that its meaning
remained open until he came and was unequivocally established
only through him, so likewise the apostles interpret the event of
Christ in the Holy Spirit (Jn. 16,12–15), so that one may say that
only with the end of the apostolic epoch was revelation definitely
finished insofar as it was intended for all men, and since that time
God has not granted any further revelation that would be generally
binding.

We may ask why God in his self-revelation has left us unin-
structed on many things which are significant for our lives. He has
left in darkness many things which forever oppress man. This
situation would be incomprehensible if God's self-revelation were
exclusively a doctrine or teaching, if it were meant to be an intellectual solution to the enigmas of life. More, however, is involved;
above all, God's communication of his own life to man, which
means existence in an immediate and deifying dialogue with God.
This higher form of existence was attained in the glorified Christ.
The time following him serves to let all men and the entire cosmos
come to participate in his glorified existence. Such a thesis could
at first give the impression that the time following Jesus had a purely
pragmatic character, intended only to serve a principle established
once and for all; that it was nothing but a continuous and perhaps
even somewhat monotonous repetition of the same thing, namely
of man's self-surrender to the glorified Christ, in whom the goal
of world development—that is, the absolute future of the cosmos

—had been already reached once for all. But in fact the epoch in the history of mankind after Christ, the duration of which is unknown, is concerned with a highly dramatic event. As we saw, God's revelation of himself in the time before Christ occurred not in a continuing historical process but in individual thrusts. We may, therefore, speak of the *kairos* of divine revelation. Between the individual *kairoi*, then, are long periods which, judged from the standpoint of theology, lie in complete darkness.

The succession of stages which characterized God's revelation of himself in the time before Christ has been replaced, in the time following him, by the call of Christ to all men. Christ, in the event which we call his ascension, did not travel to some vague place beyond this earth, unknown to us; what he did do was to withdraw from our sight the new form of existence—his glorified life—which he gained in his resurrection, and to remove it for the duration of human history. But he nevertheless remains in the world in this mysterious form of existence. It would be naive to want either to localize him or to seek him outside the cosmos. In this form of existence he gives himself to one generation after the other, and each time calls it into his own life. Man answers this call by faith, and it is in this that the specifically Christian form of existence comes into being which Paul describes with the words "being in Christ."

If Christ thus calls us into his own glorified form of existence, which means into immediacy with God, he does not call us back into the past of Golgotha and Easter, but ahead, to himself. It is true that he turns our glance backwards so that in the whence, the whither of our way may become visible. In the past, to be sure, the future is anticipated, but only for Christ himself. For the life of glory and the unmediated vision of God is that radical future which has been promised to us, and was exemplified in Christ. We know from Paul's letters that this future is a profound mystery, which we can interpret only by means of inadequate images. That we shall attain this future, despite the fact that it is radically different from all our earthbound hopes for the future, is guaranteed by our present existence in faith, an existence which is nourished by the past and is "in" and "with" Christ. The glorified Christ, present in the world, places man by his call before a decision which is a matter of life and death. Since the event of Christ, decisions of immeasurable significance occur every day.

Thus the time after Christ is pregnant with a dynamism never before present in the world. It influences the lives of individuals and societies, and even the cosmos itself. Every man is, as we have noted, a vertex of the universe. Whenever an individual reaches the goal in and with Christ, the universe, too, reaches its goal of entering into God. On the other hand, the rejection of Christ's call towards the future means not only a catastrophe for the individual but also peril for the community and for the cosmos. For wherever a human being resists this call, the progress of mankind's movement is retarded.

The question of whether a person follows Christ into the absolute future also has consequences for Christ himself. As men are related to Christ, he is also related to men. Consequently the purpose and meaning of his existence is not realized simply by his physical glorification: it is fully realized only when men in their turn participate in this glorification. Christ, although he calls back from the future which he has already reached to men who are still traveling in pilgrimage through time, urging them forward towards himself, is turned towards the future not in anxious hope but in a sure knowledge. Nevertheless it depends upon the free decision of men, whether or not Christ himself attains his goal in a universal sense. As he represents all mankind, there is something lacking to him as long as not all men have come to him. The fact that this absolute future has not yet been reached in its fullness is certainly not a substantial defect for Christ, but only one from the point of view of the history of salvation—a functional defect. His salvific meaning is realized step by step as, in the time following his temporal existence, one man after another allows himself to be called forward by him, until that situation is reached in which the individual Christ, who represents all, becomes the whole Christ. (The problem presented by the possession of the direct vision of God without physical transfiguration will be discussed later.)

Yet even arrival at the absolute future does not mean the end of the world's movement forward. For the life of direct intimacy with God will be steadily intensified as God unveils new depths of his being, and the dialogue with him will become more profound, more intimate, and more concentrated. This intensification will never come to an end. God will show himself more and more transparently in man and in the cosmos. God will enter into the world with a love showing itself ever more intensely, pervading and embracing everything. The world will, with the possibilities which God grants it ever anew, enter into God in a more and more vital fashion. When Paul says that the state of fulfillment will be called "God all in all" (1 Cor. 15,20–28), we can restate this as "God in the world" and "the world in God." This is a conception of breathtaking dynamism.

If man, as the peak of the process of evolution, is on his way towards such a future, it is to be expected that we should find in him a longing for infinity. The principal thesis put forward by Ernst Bloch in his book *Prinzip der Hoffnung* is included in the Christian expectation of the future. According to him, man is always nourished by the dream of a better, radically different, life to come, and it is this dream which expresses itself in his fairy tales, in his desire for constant change, in his experiences of nature, in his philosophy and music, in his poetry and painting, in his technology, and in his journeys of discovery. This longing of mankind is not only not rejected by the Christian conception of the future, but it is encouraged further to transcend itself into that dimension in which it will be fulfilled and surpassed, without ever ending. What, according to Augustine, is true of historical life—that we look for God in order to find him, and find him in order to seek him again—is true also of the radical future, although in a different way. God will be found in order to be found again. Likewise we shall find all our fellow-men grown together into a true community as our brothers and sisters, and we shall find them such only to find them such ever anew.

THE OBJECTIVE CONNECTION BETWEEN GENERAL AND SPECIAL SALVATION HISTORY

There arises here a question of great significance concerning general salvation history: whether the general salvation history has been abrogated by the special salvation history introduced by God. If we answer no, the special history of salvation seems to lose its character of being absolute. If, however, we answer in the affirmative, the salvation of innumerable men seems to be placed in question: since then, of course, the thesis will be literally valid that there is no salvation outside the Church.

But upon a more detailed analysis of the question, we reach the conclusion that even if the general history of salvation has been abrogated through Christ, there are still possibilities of salvation for those who do not belong to the Church. Because of his universal function in creation and in history, Christ is the universal mediator of salvation. He is the center from which the dynamism of salvation spreads out in every direction. Since Christ lives only as the head of his body the Church, it is a simple conclusion that the Church must mediate salvation for those also who do not belong to the Church, even though it does not reach them either through signs or words. Hence it seems evident that people who live according to their conscience and honestly endeavor to seek God have a desire for God which is only unexpressed (*votum implicitum*), and thus a salvific faith, a *fides qua,* though not a *fides quae;* by it they can attain salvation, even though they belong to non-Christian religions.

We must ask further, however, whether it is not precisely *through* these religions that their members reach salvation; that is to say, whether the general history of salvation continues to run its course, alongside the special history and in spite of it. The former, if it continues to exist after Christ, presents itself in many religions, especially in the great world religions of Asia with their cults, rituals, doctrines, and laws. The fact that the question of truth does not play a special part in them causes a difficult problem here. For it cannot be denied that in divine revelation truth is significant for salvation; that not only the *fides qua* but also the *fides quae* plays a salvific role. At present this problem cannot be solved satisfactorily; but it loses its acuteness if we consider that the non-Christian religions, in a few statements which they make regarding the divine, represent preliminary steps, if only distant ones, of the statements regarding God made in the revelation of Christ. Thus

those religions do not lack all the elements even of a genuine
fides quae. What they do possess finds its fulfillment in the abun-
dance of truth in Christianity. The world religions are now becoming increasingly conscious that they represent an alternative to
Christianity. They even frequently claim to be superior to the
Christian faith both in the ethical and the spiritual dimensions.
They point out, for instance, that in spite of its long duration
Christianity has not succeeded in banishing war from the world.
Although the great world religions are in our days burdened with
certain grievous errors, we must take their claim seriously, as
seriously as have Popes John XXIII and Paul VI and the Second
Vatican Council.

In general—and speaking, as it were, optically—we can distinguish two basic conceptions: the Asiatic-oriental, predominantly
Buddhist-oriented, and the European-occidental, predominantly
Christian-oriented (H. R. Schlette). With this optical or geographi-
cal distinction the basic question is not yet decided or even posed.

In order to approach the problem we must remember that
according to the Christian faith Christ is the highest, the unsurpassable and universal, self-revelation of God. Consequently the
Christian faith is intended for all men, and *vice versa* all non-
Christian religions are valid only in relation to the Christian faith.
Thus they are not definitively but only provisionally legitimate.
When will this legitimacy end? In principle obviously with the
appearance of Christ and the establishment of the Church, the new
people of God. The Church is oriented towards surpassing the
non-Christian religions, and at the same time receiving into itself
their value in a purified form. Thus all members of these religions
are "potential" Christians. The Christian faith itself is enriched by
receiving the other religions into its own sphere of belief. And Non-
Christian religions are not simply abolished in the process, but
purified and brought to fulfillment—they are abolished only in the
sense that their religious values are preserved and fulfilled by being
led beyond themselves (Hegel). This process of integration cannot be accomplished in a mechanical way. That which is new in
the Christian faith depends upon men for its realization: it must
be proclaimed. Yet it is problematic whether or not the proclama-

tion of Jesus Christ to all mankind will ever fully succeed, whether the general history of salvation will ever be fully integrated into the special history of salvation, enriching the latter and fulfilling itself.

In this context it is particularly significant that the world religions cannot be addressed by the Christian proclamation; only the individual believer can be reached. Thus Christianity can receive the world religions into itself only through their individual members.

These relationships show that even after the advent of Christ the non-Christian religions enjoy, if not legitimacy in principle, at least a conditional legitimacy. This is sufficient to permit their coexistence with the special history of salvation. But they always remain in a state of subordination to the special history of salvation, and thus in a condition of provisionality. This relationship was described in the time of the fathers by the expressions "before Christ" and "after Christ," the "before" and "after" being understood in a chronological sense. Certainly this is an acceptable interpretation, although a limited one. The expressions "before" and "after" indicate primarily a situation, not a period in the course of history. In this sense all other religions have a provisional and preparatory function in relation to Christianity. They exercise it whether or not they are aware of it, and this establishes their legitimacy.

For such a conditional legitimacy there are a number of testimonies from the Scriptures; that is to say, from texts which belong to the special history of salvation. Let us recall again the biblical report of the deluge and the covenant with Noah. Of course no historical connection can be demonstrated between this event and the origins of the great world religions, but there is an inner, objective connection, insofar as, according to the biblical texts, God can be found by man in nature. Let us add that according to the sermons of Paul in Lystra and on the Areopagus in Athens, men can find the traces of God in history and in their own conscience (Acts 10,35; 14,15–17; 17,22–28; Rom. 1,9–25; 2,14–16).

The great religions are expressions of these transcendental possibilities of faith. Add to this, that God has never left men without grace, but that he has realized the potentialities in man which call for realization by giving to man the gift of himself—that is, by grace. It is part of the historical and social character of man that religious faith is put into practice in communities and in their doctrines and cults. On the basis of such reflections it would be false to characterize the non-Christian religions as graceless religions. God's grace is always the grace of Christ, of Christ as the Savior of the world. We must distinguish between the basic fact that special salvation history has superseded the general and the possibility which the individual member of a non-Christian religion has of being saved.

We may say that the members of the great religions reach salvation not in spite of, but in a certain sense because of, their membership in them or, more exactly, because of the faith realized in their religions. In the background, it is true, stands always the salvific dynamism of Jesus Christ. Only in the event that a non-Christian were to be confronted with Christ in such a way that a decision could not be avoided, and he decided against Christ, would his salvation be imperiled. Information about Christianity is not the same thing as confrontation with it. Decision is demanded only when Jesus Christ is proclaimed in a credible manner as the only and universal bearer of salvation.

These reflections are valid, too, in relation to a new religion founded after Christ's birth. Even conditional legitimacy would have to be denied to it if it was established in conscious contradiction to Jesus Christ. For this reason in the first epistle of John, that form of gnosticism which maintained that there was a way of salvation in opposition to Jesus Christ is rejected.

In concrete life, of course, no human being can tell whether, if a man makes his decision against Christ, he does so with or without guilt.

These reflections lead us to two further problems. First the question arises whether the absoluteness of Christianity is compatible with such a point of view, or whether it does not promote an anti-Christian indifferentism. The second question is whether, in such a point of view, the missionary activity which the Church has carried out from the beginning does not lose its meaning.

As far as the first question is concerned, we must say that the absoluteness of Christianity consists exactly in the fact that Christ, the unsurpassable and universal self-revelation of God, exists for the sake of all men. Thus Christ is not, as the word "absolute" taken literally seems to suggest, without relationships. On the contrary, in the whole of creation he is the figure who is richest in relationships and possesses the most intense relationships. In him God has not only accepted creation unconditionally, in order to communicate himself to it; he has in fact, in Christ, given himself to his creation unconditionally and without reserve.

As far as the problem of missionary activity is concerned, our reflections do not by any means suggest that it is superfluous. Although the general path of salvation still has a conditional justification, alongside the special one, the latter is meant to broaden out to such a degree that all men can walk it. This, however, is accomplished by missionary activity. It is the task of the Church to give to all men testimony to God as he has revealed himself in Christ. The Church has thus been entrusted with a representative function. The people of God of the Old Testament had to proclaim the honor of the one God to all other men. Likewise the Church must proclaim the definitive revelation of God to the non-Christian religions, and stand up for it in faith and love. In this manner honor is given to God, and the absolute future is proclaimed which God through Christ has revealed to his creation. The Church's preaching is intended to bring the whole of mankind into motion towards that absolute future in faith and hope. The proclamation of the absolute future is of decisive significance also for salvation itself. By the very fact that God is proclaimed, the fullness of salvation is offered to men.

Although the general way of salvation has the power to lead men into this absolute future, there are many divine aids on the way of the special history of salvation which are lacking to the other, so that in comparison with the Christian faith the possibilities of salvation which it can offer are relatively sparse. The proclamation of God is therefore at the same time service of man's salvation. The effect of such a view of missionary activity is not to release it from the task of caring for the salvation of individuals, but to put it into the broader communal context of absolute eschatology. The

service which it performs for the salvation of mankind is seen in
this way to be even greater. Such a view encourages us not to give
in to weariness or defeat. The missions are essential for the Church.
A Church without a missionary activity would be a contradiction.
Those who take the burden of the missionary on their shoulders fulfill a task which belongs to the very essence of the Church. In their
work it is the Church itself which is at work. In the end the general
and the special salvation history will converge, if not within history itself, at the hour of Christ's second coming. From then on
they will not be separated again, since each of them will have forever reached its goal.

Readings

Barr, James. "Revelation through History in the Old Testament and in
    Modern Theology" in *New Theology No. I,* edited by Martin E.
    Marty and Dean G. Peerman. New York, Macmillan, 1964. Pp.
    60–74

Cullmann, Oscar. *Christ and Time.* Translated by Floyd Filson. Phila-
    delphia, Westminster, 1950.

Rahner, Karl. "Theological Principles Concerning the Hermeneutics of
    Eschatological Statements" in *Theological Investigations,* IV. Balti-
    more, Helicon, 1967.

———— "History of the World and Salvation-History" in *Theological
    Investigations,* V. Baltimore, Helicon, 1966.

———— "Christianity and Non-Christian Religions" in *Theological In-
    vestigations,* V. Baltimore, Helicon, 1966.

———— "Christianity and the 'New Man' " in *Theological Investiga-
    tions,* V. Baltimore, Helicon, 1966.

◂ III

Revelation in the Church

‹9

Within the Church

THE CHURCH AS THE UNIVERSAL WORD

When Jesus Christ calls men towards the future, to himself, and to his Father, he does so not in the stillness of interior mystical communication but in tangible, audible and concrete forms—that is, in historical and social structures. He calls man by means of an audible word. This both presupposes and creates history and community. As God's word of revelation has come to men through the word of man, so in its turn Christ's salvific call reaches man in a concrete and historical manner. Since his visible departure from us he lives on, working in sociological structures which exist within history and are subject to history.

The Church originated from the word of Jesus Christ (Rom.1, 1–8; Lk. 8,21; Eph. 5,26). The purpose for which it exists is to hand on in its turn, out of its own living center, the word of Christ. It is intended to be a medium through which Christ becomes present and acts. We may say: "The Church is called by God, and hands on God's call. The Church is the place where God calls and the place to which he calls. Thus it becomes the place where God speaks, where his word is proclaimed, heard and followed." [1] Because the Church is the creation of the Word of God become man, it has itself a word-character. Through his salvific speech and action during his life, and especially through his saving death, resurrection and sending of the Spirit, the Church was fashioned

165

in a hierarchical form, corresponding to his will, and, as soon as
the Spirit was sent, began the task assigned to it of proclaiming
Jesus as the promised Messiah, his death as a salvific death and
his resurrection as meaning new life for men. The Acts of the
Apostles give us ample descriptions of this.

The Church is the heir of the Old Testament people of God.
When these did not acknowledge Jesus of Nazareth as the Messiah
sent by Jahweh, Jesus created from the "remnant" who had become believers a new people, which drew its character from his
own saving activity. The new people of God is fundamentally different from the old, firstly because it sees in Jesus the savior announced in the Old Testament and secondly because Jesus himself
remains personally present in his people. Paul expresses the new
situation by describing the Church as the "body of Christ," with
Christ as the head, the Lord and the source of the Church's life.
Christ becomes present, as he had promised (Mt.18,20; 28,20),
in two ways: through the word of proclamation and by making his
saving death and his resurrection present in the central celebration
of the Church, the Eucharist. Since this celebration is principally
carried out by means of the word, and it is the word which makes
Christ present, it is the presence of Christ in the word which is of
basic significance. If we designate Christ as the original or basic
Word of God, we can call the Church the universal word of God
to men, which derives its character from his original Word.

Christ gives himself to the service of the Church, but this does
not mean that the Church attains any sovereignty over Christ; its
function is that of a servant, Christ remains the Lord. The Apostles,
who formed the kernel of the Church, were very conscious of their
function as servants of the divine word. It was their deep concern
that through their word God's word should be expressed, and not
man's word (2 Thess. 3,1). They were constantly preoccupied with
the thought that Christ, as God's Word become man, should,
through their word, reach men without restriction or distortion
(2 Cor.3,5; 1 Cor.9,27; 9,12). Therefore it was a part of their
work of preaching to live their lives "in holiness and sincerity"
(2 Cor. 1,12). On the other hand, God's word has an indestructible
independence, and it cannot be ultimately deprived of its effect
even by the shortcomings of men (Phil. 1,15–18).

If Jesus uses the Church as God employed the word of the prophets, this means not only that he selects this person or that to speak to men, but that he has created an institution with a definite structure in which and by which he proclaims his saving word to men throughout human history. It would be a one-sided interpretation of his saving action to understand it in a merely actualistic fashion—that is, as an action which simply comes down vertically from above in isolated instances. Christ is served by a permanent institution, which he has created and which endures through time; that is, by an "office." The significance of this office lies in the fact that it is the place and medium in which and by which Jesus Christ's word is reliably heard. Such an office should not be understood as something which has power over God's word, as a place at which, so to speak, this word is administered. It is characterized by the fact that the Holy Spirit, promised and sent by the risen Christ, the Spirit who represents the life-power of the Church, who is present in the Church and acts through it, works in a special way through those entrusted with this office. The office guarantees that it is really God's word and not human imagining which is proclaimed. Its significance lies in the fact that it is an institution of Christ by which God's word is actualized again and again. Actualism and dynamism are therefore not legitimate alternatives to the notion of office, they do not stand in contrast to it—it cannot be understood in a purely objectivistic fashion, as if it lacked the element of the actualistic and dynamic. Office in the Church is rooted in the word—that is, in a dynamic reality. As God produces the world and keeps it in existence by an uninterrupted act of creation, in the same way the dynamism of Jesus Christ's word streams continuously into the Church, keeping it in being and activating it. Thus we can say that the office in the Church is continuously nourished and activated by the dynamism of God's word. It lives from the word of Jesus Christ, while on the other hand this word needs the office in order to be presented to men in a form which is audible and visible to them (1 Cor. 12,27f.).

A more exact presentation of these problems will be offered in the section on the Church. Leo Scheffczyk rightly says:

Thus it is the Spirit-filled word itself which establishes order and law in the Church. It produces out of itself services and offices, at the same time requiring that these external structures be enlivened and supported by the inner meaning of the spiritual word; i.e., that they do not harden into external laws existing for their own sake, but serve as aids for the correct proclamation and for the sincere acceptance of the word. We may thus say that the Church of the word necessarily possesses services and offices, but that these are not the Church, but only organs of it. (Acts 6,1–7; 1 Cor. 12,27f.).[2]

The First Epistle of John bears witness to the presence of God's word in the word of the Church in the following manner (see also Gal. 1,11):

It was there from the beginning; we have heard it; we have seen it with our own eyes; we looked upon it, and felt it with our own hands; and it is of this we tell. Our theme is the word of life. This life was made visible; we have seen it and bear our testimony; we here declare to you the eternal life which dwelt with the Father and was made visible to us. What we have seen and heard we declare to you, so that you and we together may share in a common life, that life which we share with the Father and his Son Jesus Christ. (1 Jn. 1,1ff.,*NEB*)

The Second Vatican Council was well aware of this task. In the Dogmatic Constitution on Divine Revelation it states (#7):

In his gracious goodness, God has seen to it that what He had revealed for the salvation of all nations would abide perpetually in its full integrity and be handed on to all generations. Therefore Christ the Lord, in whom the full revelation of the supreme God is brought to completion (cf.2 Cor. 1:20; 3:16; 4:6), commissioned the apostles to preach to all men that gospel which is the source of all saving truth and moral teaching, and thus to impart to them divine gifts. This gospel had been promised in former times through the prophets, and Christ Himself fulfilled it and promulgated it with His own lips. This commission was faithfully fulfilled by the apostles who, by their oral preaching, by example, and by ordinances, handed on what they had received from the lips of Christ, from living with Him, and from what He did, or what they had learned through the prompting of the Holy Spirit.

The commission was fulfilled too by those apostles and apostolic men who under the inspiration of the same Holy Spirit committed the message of salvation to writing.

But in order to keep the gospel forever whole and alive within the Church, the apostles left bishops as their successors, "handing over their own teaching role" to them. This sacred tradition, therefore, and sacred Scripture of both the Old and the New Testaments are like a mirror in which the pilgrim Church on earth looks at God, from whom she has received everything, until she is brought finally to see Him as He is face to face (cf.1 Jn. 3:2).

THE APOSTLES AS THE ORIGINAL
WITNESSES TO CHRIST

When Christ left this earth and entrusted to his disciples the mission he had received from his Father, his work expanded beyond the narrow horizons of the Jewish people into the broader dimensions of the world. He had to leave, as John said, so that this transformation could take place, for the Holy Spirit could appear only in consequence of his departure. The Holy Spirit was needed if the apostles were to come to a genuine understanding of Jesus Christ. Only through the understanding of Christ made accessible to them by the Holy Spirit were they able to proclaim the salvific Christ-event beyond the boundaries of their own people, to the "heathen" —i.e., to the entire world (Jn. 14,16ff.; 16,7; 2 Cor. 5,16f.). The Holy Spirit interpreted Jesus of Nazareth to them (see Mt. 10,19f.). The Second Vatican Council rightly stresses that the apostles were the first witnesses of Christ: they had been set a task by him which was both difficult and far-reaching. Their closeness to Christ profoundly illuminated their lives, but at the same time placed on them a burden human beings were scarcely capable of bearing. They had to remain in the world, to stand their ground before it and, sent by him and empowered by him, to proclaim in his name something which would mean salvation, but which the world was not willing to hear because it was alien to its own spirit.

The apostles were equipped for their task in a twofold way—in the first place, by the mission itself with which they were entrusted. When he left the world, Christ did not give back to his Father the

task which had been set him, but handed it on to the apostles
(Jn. 20,21). In Matthew's gospel a statement of Christ's is reported which can be considered his last will and testament: "Jesus
came up and spoke to them. He said: 'Full authority in heaven and
on earth has been committed to me. Go forth therefore and make
all nations my disciples; baptize men everywhere in the name of
the Father and the Son and the Holy Spirit, and teach them to observe all that I have commanded you. And be assured, I am with
you always, to the end of time.' " (Mt. 28,18–20, *NEB*) The
gospel of Mark gives the saying in somewhat different words
(Mk.16,15f.). The mission of the apostles was based on an indispensable precondition. This was the fact that they had been eyewitnesses (Acts 1,8. 21f.; 2,22. 32; 10,40f.; 13,31). It was above
all the resurrection of Jesus which the disciples as eyewitnesses of
the appearances of the Lord had to have experienced (Acts 1,21f.;
10,39–41). The apostle Paul, although he did not see Jesus during
his earthly life, is no exception to this rule.

The apostles did not take up the task of proclamation immediately after Christ had gone. They had to go through another inner
crisis and transformation. It was when the Spirit came to them and
interpreted Jesus to them that they were capable of executing their
missionary task. From that moment on their word became a testimony to Jesus—such testimony as the Holy Spirit himself gave to
Jesus. The Holy Spirit and the disciples are not two series of
witnesses but only one, because the Spirit gives witness through the
disciples, and as Christ is active in the Holy Spirit, the testimony of
the Spirit is Christ's testimony to himself. As Jesus in his time did
not speak of himself but of the Father, so that the Father himself
spoke through Jesus, so the Spirit does not speak of himself but of
Christ, so that Christ speaks through him. In the word inspired by
the Spirit, which the apostles proclaim, it is the risen Christ himself who is acting. He makes his word audible in the word of his
witnesses.

Thus there is a certain, though not total, identity between the
word of the apostles and the word of Jesus Christ. Jesus Christ's
word always transcends the word of men, but it is present and
effective in the word of the apostles. The apostles, in their turn,

assume responsibility for the fact that through them Christ's word
reaches men (1 Cor. 1,17; 4,15; Acts 6,4). Not only *what* they
say guarantees the dynamism of salvation, but also the fact *that*
they say it. But again, in the activity of the apostles Christ becomes
present as the acting subject, through the Holy Spirit. He enters
the word of the apostles in such a manner that he becomes the
speaker: so that what the apostles proclaim is attested out of the
Holy Spirit's own salvific dynamism. The apostles are thus from
the very beginning a part of the empirical and historical process of
the Church's founding (Scheffczyk). After the conclusion of Jesus'
life on earth, they became, through the Holy Spirit, the builders
of the Church, they erected its structure according to God's plan.
Therefore the word entrusted to them by Christ belongs intrinsically to the act by which the Church was founded. It is the constructive (Acts 20,32) and strengthening (1 Thess. 3,2) force in
the historical process by which the Church came into being.

THE SUCCESSORS OF THE APOSTLES

Even if no one actually questions the fact that Christ gave the
apostles a mandate to preach in his name, as soon as we look beyond the apostolic era a problem arises: the question of succession.
Was not the apostolic period unique, so that what was true of it
cannot be expected to be true of the age that followed it?

After all, the apostolic era was the time of revelation. We cannot say the same of the post-apostolic epoch: God's revelation
came to an end with the apostolic period. However, we cannot
conclude from the uniqueness of the apostolic situation that the
structures of the initial period had no significance for the time
which followed and were not intended to be preserved in the future. If we consider the mandate given by Christ, and the picture
which the early Church presents to us, it is unambiguously clear
that those structures were intended to be lasting. If Christ promised his followers that he would stay with them until the end of
time, that meant he would be present in history beyond the
apostolic period, and would execute his instructions in historical

forms. Nevertheless the difference between the apostolic and the post-apostolic time must not be overlooked.

According to the sixth chapter of Acts, the first Christian congregation chose out certain men who were filled with the Holy Spirit, and the apostles entrusted them with permanent tasks by the imposition of hands. Timothy, for example, received his charism of office through imposition of hands by the group of presbyters (1 Tim. 4,14). He and Titus were to appoint other suitable officials (1 Tim. 3, 1ff.; Tit. 1,5ff.). The exact designations of these office-bearers developed only later. In the post-apostolic time the conviction arose that the Church was apostolic because of its succession from the apostles. The institutionalization of the tasks left by Christ by no means meant their mechanization. For the institutional element is borne by the living successors of the apostles and is effective in the living voice of its bearers.

A special role was played by the notion of "recalling" or "remembrance," because the testimony of the post-apostolic witnesses of Christ was basically a Christ-testimony, derived from that of the apostles. One needed only to look back to what had been "transmitted" by the apostles in order to be able to proclaim the absolute future. The apostolic word, taken over, testified to, and handed on by the disciples of the apostles, had an absolute, normative character. The preaching of the disciples was nothing other than the word of the apostles in a new form. In this word, too, the Holy Spirit, and in him Christ himself, is present and effective (2 Cor. 3,17; 2 Tim.2,7.14; 4,4.17; Tit. 3,1.8). Heinrich Schlier writes in this connection:

But if there is no doubt that the proclamation continued in the Church (Acts 20,32), in what way is God's word as such continued in it? For the direct self-revelation of Jesus Christ which formed the basis of the gospel and the apostolate is finished and unrepeatable. (Cf.1 Cor. 15,8; see also 3,5ff.: Eph. 2.20.) The pastoral letters give one answer. In any event, the "tradition" of the free and the formulated, of the oral and the written, word streams into the Church. And in any event this "tradition" is intended to be "preserved"; and the Lord will "preserve" it, as a "prototype" and "model" of the authentic word, as an apostolic legacy (see 2 Tim. 1,12–14). This tradition then is meant to be handed on further. In such a connection we find, for example: "What you have heard from me before many witnesses entrust to faithful men who will be able to teach others also" (2 Tim. 2,2; see 1 Tim. 1,3f.; 4,6; 6,3; 2 Tim. 3,10.14; Tit. 1,9). In point of fact this handing on by the disciples of the apostolic word once given to them was already taking place during the lifetime of the apostles on occasions when they themselves were absent. The proclamation of the disciple is then designated as a "recalling" of the ways and the doctrine of the apostle (1 Cor. 4,17; see 1 Cor. 11,2; 1 Thess. 4,18). The pastoral letters, however, speak of this in a programmatic fashion: "Command this and teach it" (1 Tim. 4,11; see 1 Tim. 5,7; 6,3). "Remind of that" (2 Tim. 2,14; 3,1; see 1 Tim.3,15; Tit.2,1; 3,8,etc.). Such recalling means on the one hand that the disciple and successor takes up and passes on the apostolic word and no other (1 Tim.4,16; 6,14.20). On the other hand, it means that he does not repeat it mechanically but unfolds it with comprehension in various ways in concrete situations. Timothy proved himself a good servant of Jesus Christ when he nourished himself on "the words of the faith and of good doctrine" which he followed (1 Tim. 4,6) and allowed himself to be helped to full understanding by the Lord in all things (2 Tim. 2,7). However, this process of development of the once-transmitted word of God in the proclamation of the apostles' successors took place in the power of the Spirit, who is already given potentially with the office itself (1 Tim.4,14; 2 Tim. 1,6f. 14), and in the context of a life which is a genuine following of Jesus Christ and the apostle (1 Tim. 1,18ff.; 4,14f.; 6,11ff.; 2 Tim. 3,10, etc.). It is true also for the continuation of God's word in the proclamation of the Church, that it is a matter of God's word as the foundation, that this word is understood and spoken as being present, that in the power of the Spirit and in personal surrender it proves its openness and preserves it. With this word of God it is no longer a question of the word of revelation as such, but of the word of revelation which has entered into the apostolic tradition, a word which has remained relevant in the manner described above. In it God's word reaches its goal as a historical word (tradition).[3]

THE MEDIATING FUNCTION OF THE ECCLESIAL WORD

The preaching of the Church has the power of making present. It makes Christ himself present to those who listen. Firstly, there takes place in the act of proclamation an encounter between speaker and listener; and in this encounter Jesus Christ, who is being proclaimed, is himself present. He is at the same time the one about whom the proclamation is made and the one who speaks. Here the statement applies which is reported by Matthew (Mt. 18,20): "For where two or three are gathered in my name, there am I in the midst of them." This proclamation, which makes Christ salvifically present, presupposes his resurrection and his glorification. The word of proclamation does not produce Christ's glorified life but makes him present in it. The ecclesial proclamation brings about an encounter with Christ. The relationship of the listener to Christ is that of mediated immediacy. As John the Baptist pointed to the coming Lord, so the Church, in its proclamation, points to the present Lord who, at the same time, is the coming one. Therefore the word of proclamation has essential significance for the encounter with Christ. In the word, the epiphany of Christ takes place, not in a general manner, but concretely, so that the listener is affected in his own personal situation. Jesus Christ encounters man salvifically in the kerygma, in the word of proclamation. The past history of salvation in Christ becomes the living present for the listener in the Church's word of proclamation. This, however, means that the act of proclamation not only teaches and informs man but is itself a salvific event. By it the Christ-event is made dynamic, is actualized for that particular time. When the past thus becomes the present, it becomes so only for the sake of the absolute future. In the fact that the Christ of the historical past is proclaimed, the Christ to come is proclaimed, the return of the glorified Lord.

If the representative function of proclamation is stressed, it must be added that while the risen Jesus certainly becomes present through the word of the Church, he can only become present because he also lives outside, and apart from, the Church's word. The risen Lord reaches men salvifically through the word of the Church. But he does not live simply in this word. His resurrection is not merely an event in the word of the Church, but is a reality before this and apart from it. It is in the word of the Church, however, that it gains salvific dynamism. It is the merit of Rudolf Bultmann to have emphasized this.

We must, however, go behind the word of proclamation and look for the objective reality and significance of Jesus Christ. It is a fatal weakness in Bultmann's theology to have overlooked this. Otherwise the word of proclamation is merely an empty appeal and does not differ from a summons belonging to the psychological or philosophical dimension. The idea that Christ lives only in the word of proclamation because it is only in this word that he is salvific and dynamic reduces the Church's proclamation to something purely existential. Let us remember our former distinction between "historical" (*geschichtlich*) and "existing in the course of history" (*historisch*). According to this distinction introduced by Bultmann, the word "historical" designates Jesus' significance for salvation, while "existing in the course of history" indicates simply the fact of his existence. Jesus both "exists in the course of history" and is "historical." We would not do justice to the Christ-event if we understood it only objectively as a series of things that happened. That would be to overlook the decisive fact that it took place for the salvation of men. To interpret the figure of Jesus in a purely existential fashion, however, would be to deprive the Church's proclamation of its objective foundation.

PREACHING AND DOCTRINE

If we inquire beyond the act of proclamation for the occurrence which preceded it and which it makes present, we obtain a doctrine concerning Jesus. This is something distinct from proclamation. But it must be seen by the Church as a necessary part of its task. Doctrine and proclamation are most closely connected, for it is doctrine which decides what is to be preached, and on the other hand it is only for the sake of preaching that doctrine exists. This connection can be seen clearly from the history of the Church. The councils of the first millennium were generally teaching councils; they made statements about objective matters. Also, those councils which are called reform councils, such as the general councils of the first half of the second millennium, have doctrinal elements.

It is of fundamental importance for the significance and the effectiveness of the Church's preaching that it rest on and make present objective events, which it has not itself created, but which it transmits and faithfully affirms. Because the statements of the Church stand in the service of proclamation, they do not carry their meaning and their value in themselves, and therefore are not truths "in themselves"; they are rather truths "for us."

The connection between doctrine and proclamation strikes us from another point of view when we consider the difference between *fides quae* and *fides qua*. In the act of proclamation the Church announces the absolute future opened up to us in Jesus Christ. In it the Church calls for the faith of the listener as *fides qua,* faith as the impetus and the intensity of belief, the act of faith as an act. However, by offering the proclaimed content in the act of proclamation, it calls forth the *fides qua* in order to realize the *fides quae*. The act of faith and the affirmation of the contents of that faith are a unity, just as the act of proclamation and the offering of its contents are the one thing. We cannot isolate the two elements, the act and its content, from one another. It would not be an ecclesial, but a philosophical or scholarly, activity simply to make known the content of the faith. In the same way a knowledge of the content of the Christian faith without the personal involvement of the act of faith would not be Christian faith but simply an intellectual enrichment. This process would remain within the dimension of the history of religions. The act of faith is intentionally oriented: it is tied to its content, Christ, whose word and work call for the act of faith. It is in fact the living Christ who speaks in the word of the Church, who calls the listener to himself, who both brings about the movement forward and orients this movement towards himself. This problem of "doctrine" will be discussed in greater detail when we present the individual contents of the Christian faith, especially that concerning the Trinity and Christology.

A completely new situation developed through an event which was to alter the entire future of the Church, namely, the proclamation in the form of Scripture. The formation of the Canon of Sacred Scripture and the relationship between Scripture and the Church will be the subject of the next chapter.

Readings

Congar, Yves. *Power and Poverty in the Church*. Baltimore, Helicon, 1965.

Küng, Hans. *The Church*. New York, Sheed and Ward, 1968.

Notes

[1] E. M. Nielen, *Leben Ausdem Glauben* (Dusseldorf, 1963), 10.

[2] *Von der Heilsmacht des Wortes*, p.178.

[3] "Wort" in H. Fries, *Handbuch Theologischer Grundbegriffe*, II (1963) 863f.

◂ 10

The Sacred Scriptures

Sacred books are not a phenomenon peculiar to Christianity. They are a constitutive element of existential significance for the great world religions, appearing wherever a religion has a prophetic character. If we understand the world religions as a general way of salvation in which God's universal will to save is objectified, we may assume that in the sacred books of these religions God's grace-full will to save is also expressed, even though the truth is distorted in them through human shortcomings and errors.

THE BOOKS OF THE OLD TESTAMENT

In the beginning of Christianity there was no scripture concerning Jesus Christ. This does not mean that there was no scriptural theology with regard to his person: it was a matter of using the scriptures of the Old Testament which the early Church quoted to establish scriptural support for Jesus. The self-revelation of God in the Old Testament had been written down at God's command (Ex. 32,16; Dt. 22,22). The written word was to keep alive the memory of the revelation and to actualize God's word to the people of Israel so that they might receive, on the one hand, a confirmation of the divine reason for their existence and a summons to live accordingly, and on the other hand, in times of defection, testimony against themselves (Dt. 30,16ff.).

From the Old Testament a written theology was developed in the apostolic period according to which Jesus is the promised Messiah (see Acts 2, 14–36; 2 Cor. 3,6–18; 1 Cor. 15,1–5; Acts 13, 18–41). The meaning of the Old Testament remained an open question until Christ appeared; only through him did it become clear what goal it was directed towards. It was Jesus himself who revealed its ultimate meaning. The first witnesses of Christ presented this meaning theologically in terms of Jesus' own statements about himself.

The Second Vatican Council, in the Dogmatic Constitution on Divine Revelation (#14–16), made the following official statement regarding the Scriptures of the Old Testament:

14. In carefully planning and preparing the salvation of the whole human race, the God of supreme love, by a special dispensation, chose for Himself a people to whom He might entrust His promises. First He entered into a covenant with Abraham (cf. Gen. 15:18) and, through Moses, with the people of Israel (cf. Ex. 24:28). To this people which He had acquired for Himself, He so manifested Himself through words and deeds as the one true and living God that Israel came to know by experience the ways of God with men, and with God Himself speaking to them through the mouth of the prophets, Israel daily gained a deeper and clearer understanding of His ways and made them more widely known among the nations (cf. Ps. 21:28–29; 95:1–3; Is. 2:1–4; Jer. 3:17). The plan of salvation, foretold by the sacred authors, recounted and explained by them, is found as the true word of God in the books of the Old Testament: these books, therefore, written under divine inspiration, remain permanently valuable. "For whatever things have been written have been written for our instruction, that through the patience and the consolation afforded by the Scriptures we may have hope" (Rom 15:4).

15. The principal purpose to which the plan of the Old Covenant was directed was to prepare for the coming both of Christ, the universal Redeemer, and of the messianic kingdom, to announce this coming by prophecy (cf. Lk. 24:44; Jn. 5:39; 1 Pet. 1:10), and to indicate its meaning through various types (cf. 1 Cor. 10:11). Now the books of the Old Testament, in accordance with the state of mankind before the time of salvation established by Christ, reveal to all men the knowledge of God and of man and the ways in which God, just and merciful,

deals with men. These books, though they also contain some things which are incomplete and temporary, nevertheless show us true divine pedagogy. These same books, then, give expression to a lively sense of God, contain a store of sublime teachings about God, sound wisdom about human life, and a wonderful treasury of prayers, and in them the mystery of our salvation is present in a hidden way. Christians should receive them with reverence.

16. God, the inspirer and author of both testaments, wisely arranged that the New Testament be hidden in the Old and the Old be made manifest in the New. For, though Christ established the New Covenant in His blood (cf. Lk. 22:20; 1 Cor. 11:25), still the books of the Old Testament with all their parts, caught up into the proclamation of the gospel, acquire and show forth their full meaning in the New Testament (cf. Mt. 5:17; Lk. 24:27; Rom. 16:25–26; 2 Cor. 3:14–16) and in turn shed light on it and explain it.

For the exegete, who works with the critical-historical method, the question now arises whether the original historical meaning of the texts of the Old Testament is identical with the meaning given them by Christian theology. He must inquire whether in the Christian interpretation of Jesus, of the apostles and, in the further course of events, of the Church, Christian theology has not imposed on the Old Testament a meaning foreign to it, whose strangeness we do not feel only because we have become accustomed to it. This question will be felt to be all the more urgent if we consider that the core of the revelation in the New Testament is the resurrection of Jesus and the promise of our own resurrection. The Old Testament on the other hand, except for its last books, thinks in terms of this life rather than a future one, and sees its salvation in the presence of God in his people, in peace on earth, in a great number of children, in the blessings of the harvest and in a long life.

The solution of this problem is extremely difficult and cannot be completely successful in the present state of our exegesis. It might, however, lie in the following direction: the Old Testament must be understood in the light of the Christian faith, that is to say, in the light of the glorified Jesus, in its totality as a promise. The content of the promise is God's gracious presence and a life in peace.

How God's dynamic presence will affect his people in the future and how life in peace will be given remain unsaid. This was only clarified through the Christ-event. Each of the individual books and particular texts belongs to a general context which is the totality of the promise of the Old Testament. They certainly must be interpreted according to their literal meaning, but they obtain their ultimate meaning only in the comprehensive historical whole of which they are a part—i.e., only from the goal of the history itself. We would miss the salvific meaning of a text of the Old Testament if we stopped at the sense in which it was understood when it was written. We would, however, also miss its literal meaning if we interpreted it only Christologically, by the use of allegory. We reach the ultimate meaning only if we understand the individual part in the light of the total tradition. On the horizon of such an interpretation there stands always the absolute promise which God has made of himself for man's salvation, in whatever form it may come.

THE CANON OF THE NEW TESTAMENT

During the course of the apostolic period there began a considerable writing activity. We find the result in the collection of twenty-seven individual writings which compose the canon of the New Testament. It is surprising that it is not until the year 367 A.D. that we find the canon of these twenty-seven books for the first time in its entirety in the history of the Church—namely, in Alexandria. In the West it took even longer before the canon was complete, till the end of the fourth or the beginning of the fifth century. This was due to the fact that some books dating from the time immediately after the apostles enjoyed canonical authority for a long time, but were later removed from the canon, while others—e.g., the Apocalypse in the East or the Epistle to the Hebrews in the West—seem to have been almost unknown for a long time but later were received into the canon. The definitive clarification was given only by the Council of Trent.

We can explain this development in the following way: it is difficult, if not impossible, to prove, as some theologians once main-

tained, that a particular revelation was given concerning the
books which were to belong to the canon. The history of the growth
of the canon seems to run counter to such an assertion. This is
especially true of the thesis that there was an oral tradition concerning the contents of the canon. We are obliged to say that the
Church, by the authority conferred on it by Christ and exercised
in the Holy Spirit present in it, itself determined the canon, not
arbitrarily but on the basis of definite criteria. The following
quotation from B. Brinkmann is useful here for its clarity and
accuracy:

Which of the apostolic, and therefore inspired and canonical, writings
belong to the canon cannot be traced back to a revelation, but only to
the fact that these writings of the Church were transmitted as written
by apostles or disciples of apostles in exercising their apostolic mission.
Others, on the other hand, which were apostolic, occasional writings
from the time when the Church began to collect the apostolic writings,
either were no longer available, or treated such concrete questions of a
particular congregation (e.g., a pre-canonical epistle of Paul to Corinth),
that the Church did not receive them among its writings, which were
intended to be canonical for the entire Church. Thus it can be easily
understood that it accepted the letter to Philemon because here basic
questions on the position of baptized slaves are discussed. If it did not
ultimately accept the first epistle of Clement, although according to
what we have said above it should be considered as inspired and therefore canonical—i.e., as normative—since it was an apostolic letter of a
disciple of the apostles, the reason may have been that in the beginning
it only accepted works written by the apostles themselves, or at least
works ascribed to them; the only addition being the Gospels of Mark
and Luke and the Acts, which on account of their special significance
were accepted because they were backed by the authority of Peter and
Paul. The reason why it hesitated for a time in accepting Hebrews,
Revelation, James, 2 Peter, 2 and 3 John, and Jude lies in the fact that
their authorship was doubtful. Yet even by the ultimate acceptance of
these writings into the canon the question of authorship was only decided insofar as according to the conviction of the Church, the authors
were apostles or, at least, disciples of the apostles. It restricted its selection to the writings from the apostolic period, without implying that
nothing was inspired among the later writings. It would be quite con-

ceivable in principle that the writings of a disciple of an apostle would be accepted which had been written only after the death of the last apostle; for the question is not whether revelation was completed with the apostles, but which inspired books the Church incorporated into the canon; that is, by means of its infallibility, declared to be unquestionably inspired and therefore canonical for the entire Church. Only if such a book contained new revelations, which had not been contained in earlier documents of the faith, or if the fact of its belonging to the canon resulted from a distinct revelation, would it not be possible for it to have been written after the death of the last Apostle.[1]

We can also say: through its conviction of the normative character of the faith and preaching of the early Church, the Church has a means of recognizing and declaring which writings are inspired and canonical—namely, those which, on the basis of its experience of the faith and its ever deepening reflection on that experience, it finds an accurate objectivization of the faith of the original Church (Rahner).

THE INSPIRATION OF SACRED
SCRIPTURE

The Scriptures declared canonical were declared such only because they were inspired by the Holy Spirit. There is no other inner reason for a book being accepted into the canon than its inspiration by the Holy Spirit. The fact of this process will be established first, then its meaning and implications will be explained. The Church has commented frequently on both questions. The decisive text is the statement of the First Vatican Council: "The Church receives these books as sacred and canonical not as if they were written by merely human effort and then subsequently were approved by her authority, nor simply because they contain revelation without error, but because, having been inspired by the Holy Spirit, they have God for their author and were handed on to the Church as such";[2] similarly Leo XIII, *Providentissimus Deus* (1893),[3] Benedict XV, *Spiritus Paraclitus* (1920);[4] Pius XII, *Divino afflante Spiritu* (1943).[5] In considerable detail and in agreement with the results of contemporary theology the Second Vatican Council commented on the problem of inspiration (Dogmatic Constitution on Divine Revelation, #11–12):

Those divinely revealed realities which are contained and presented in sacred Scripture have been committed to writing under the inspiration of the Holy Spirit. Holy Mother Church, relying on the belief of the apostles, holds that the books of both the Old and New Testament in their entirety, with all their parts, are sacred and canonical because, having been written under the inspiration of the Holy Spirit (cf. Jn. 20:31; 2 Tim. 3:16; 2 Pet. 1:19–21; 3:15–16), they have God as their author and have been handed on as such to the Church herself. In composing the sacred books, God chose men and while employed by Him they made use of their powers and abilities, so that with Him acting in them and through them, they, as true authors, consigned to writing everything and only those things which He wanted.

Therefore, since everything asserted by the inspired authors or sacred writers must be held to be asserted by the Holy Spirit, it follows that the books of Scripture must be acknowledged as teaching firmly, faithfully, and without error that truth which God wanted put into the sacred writings for the sake of our salvation. Therefore "all Scripture is inspired by God and useful for teaching, for reproving, for correcting, for instruction in justice; that the man of God may be perfect, equipped for every good work" (2 Tim. 3:16–17, Greek text).

12. However, since God speaks in sacred Scripture through men in human fashion, the interpreter of sacred Scripture, in order to see clearly what God wanted to communicate to us, should carefully investigate what meaning the sacred writers really intended, and what God wanted to manifest by means of their words.

Those who search out the intention of the sacred writers must, among other things, have regard for "literary forms." For truth is proposed and expressed in a variety of ways, depending on whether a text is history of one kind or another, or whether its form is that of prophecy, poetry, or some other type of speech. The interpreter must investigate what meaning the sacred writer intended to express and actually expressed in particular circumstances as he used contemporary literary forms in accordance with the situation of his own time and culture. For the correct understanding of what the sacred author wanted to assert, due attention must be paid to the customary and characteristic styles of perceiving, speaking, and narrating which prevailed at the time of the sacred writer, and to the customs men normally followed at that period in their everyday dealings with one another.

But, since holy Scripture must be read and interpreted according to the same Spirit by whom it was written, no less serious attention must be given to the content and unity of the whole of Scripture, if the meaning of the sacred texts is to be correctly brought to light. The living tradition of the whole Church must be taken into account along with the harmony which exists between elements of the faith. It is the task of exegetes to work according to these rules toward a better understanding and explanation of the meaning of sacred Scripture, so that through preparatory study the judgment of the Church may mature. For all of what has been said about the way of interpreting Scripture is subject finally to the judgment of the Church, which carries out the divine commission and ministry of guarding and interpreting the word of God.

It is important to realize that according to the teaching of the Church inspiration extends not only to religious truth in the narrower sense but also to everything which the human author really wanted to say.

Inspiration not only affects the writer personally but also influences what he writes. As far as the inspired writer is concerned, he need not be directly conscious of the fact that he is being inspired. We would, however, reduce inspiration to an empty word if we did not see that it causes a change in his mental activity. It produces in him a new horizon of consciousness, opens new perspectives and associations of knowledge, shows him the place of the individual in the whole, and stimulates him to decide to communicate these findings of his to others by means of the written word.

In view of the manner in which the sacred books took their origin we may ask, Who is inspired? all those who take part in the composition of the work, or only the final editor? One might venture the opinion that all the cooperators, even the authors of the small units inserted into the final text, are inspired. In any case the author of the last and definitive edition is inspired. There are, however, no grounds for supposing such a thing as a collective inspiration of the Christian communities where the books came into existence. As proof for the fact of inspiration we can, to be sure,

point to some individual texts of Scripture which allude to instruction given by the Spirit in connection with the authorship of written testmonies to Christ. There is a difference in this case between
the perceptibility of inspiration in the Old and in the New Testament. We may assume that the verbal inspiration which was
granted to the prophets called by God was also extended to their
written formulations, in particular where God himself commanded
the writing. We can also refer to the utterances of Christ according
to which the prophets wrote in the Spirit. But we cannot in this
way gain a knowledge of inspiration for the totality of the Old
Testament. There was no authority in the Old Testament that
might have given a binding declaration on this question. Nor was
there a canon of inspired books.

We can gain knowledge of the inspiration of the writings and the
precise extent of the canon of the Old Testament with certainty
only from the New Testament. We can only judge from the character of a book of the Old Testament insofar as it represents a
preparation for the Christ-event or, as Luther puts it, insofar as it
"carries on the cause of" (*treibt*) Christ. Jesus Christ is the standard for measuring the sacred books of the Old Testament. At the
same time, however, it is Christ and his apostolic witnesses who
determine to what extent the books of the Old Testament are directed towards him as their fulfillment. In this view, ecclesiastical
teaching can establish the Christ-quality of the writings of the Old
Testament, but not without using exegetical scholarship. Within
this framework, and with the assistance of scholarly exegesis, the
teaching Church can determine the Christ-quality of the writings
of the Old Testament.

Neither for the Old nor for the New Testament can we take it as
a rule that the inspired character of a writing can be deduced from
its religious efficacy alone, although this will not be missing. The
living teaching tradition of the Church will always be decisive.

It is an important element of the entire process that the Church
itself is filled with the Holy Spirit and is led by him into the true understanding of Jesus Christ. He is the hidden interpreter of Jesus
Christ. What he accomplishes in this interpretative function receives its tangible, historical form in the word of proclamation. It
would be most strange if he were not also, and in a special way,

effective in the written word of this proclamation. Though the word aims at the encounter between the proclaimer and the listener and therein finds its fulfillment, the written word, all the same, has a high rank, which is even to a certain extent superior to that of the spoken word. In the written word, the original word of the apostolic proclamation, forever authoritative, is reliably preserved, so that it can no longer escape from memory and can be actualized for each succeeding generation in its original normative meaning.

If the Holy Spirit was the authentic interpreter of Christ in the preaching of the apostolic Church, then given the decisive significance of the commitment of this to writing, his interpretative function must remain particularly effective precisely in this act of committing the Christ-testimony to writing. The early Church is intended, according to God's will, to remain the source and norm of the proclamation of the Christian faith for the entire course of human history. The medium for this is the written deposition of the faith-consciousness of the apostolic Church. The written objectivization was willed by God himself as the authentic norm for and decisive aid in the later proclamation of the faith.

The sacred books therefore originated as a divinely-willed, constitutive element of the Church which was established by God through Christ; they are the objectivization of the apostolic Church's awareness of its own faith, and the lasting foundation of the subsequent Church's life and belief. These written objectivizations of the Christ-message are the enduring focal points of the kerygma in the Church. We must advert to the fact that the authors of such written formulations certainly wrote as individuals, but also that the congregation itself was represented in them. One may say that every Christian represents the Church, but not that each one does so in the same way. Those carriers of the Christ-message in the apostolic age who deposited in writing what they proclaimed must be counted among the authentic representatives of the Church. Behind them stands the congregation to which they belong, with the vitality and involvement of its faith in Christ. Thus we can understand the work of the individual as the objectivization of the faith of the congregation without its ceasing to be the creation of the individual himself.

There is another aspect of the matter to remember. What we

encounter in the Sacred Scriptures is first of all the objectivization of the belief in and understanding of Christ which was possessed by the Church or the local congregation. In other words, it is the answer to the revelation of God. In this answer, however, the word of God itself is expressed, for this word has entered into the answer of the Church and is effective in it. On the other hand we must not forget (we will come back to this later and in more detail) that God's word, which enters into men's answer of faith, nevertheless always transcends it.

In the early Church the proof of the fact of inspiration was summed up in the formula that the authors of the Scriptures possessed the gift of prophecy. According to Thomas Aquinas inspiration is also an element of prophecy. There is, certainly, the difficulty that some authors of the Scriptures of the New Testament do not belong to the circle of the apostles proper. Paul belonged to it, but Mark and Luke did not. Theologians of the ancient Church such as Irenaeus, Clement of Alexandria, and Tertullian refer, for the authority of Mark and Luke, to their dependence on Peter and Paul, and their close personal connection with them. Thus we reach the result that it was in exercising the office conferred upon them directly or indirectly by Jesus, even if not upon his formal command, that the authors wrote. The normative character of the sacred writers can thus, in the last analysis, be traced back to Christ.

From the fourth century on, principally in order to defend the Old Testament against the Manichean heresy of the demonic origin of the Old Testament, it became customary to refer to the Holy Spirit as the author of Scripture. The human writer is viewed, in this terminology, as a "tool" of the Holy Spirit. Thus the same relationship is seen to obtain between the divine and the human author which is expressed in scholastic philosophy by the distinction between principal and secondary cause. In this case, if we are to obtain an accurate understanding of inspiration, it is very necessary to interpret correctly the concept of secondary or instrumental cause. If this terminology is used, attention must be paid to the fact that the terms "principal cause" and "instrumental cause" are to be understood analogously; that, in particular, the human author does not operate like a secretary taking divine dictation. Such an idea leads, as can be seen from the theology of the Reformation, to an almost mechanistic concept of verbal inspiration. Even though the Council of Trent speaks of "dictating," [6] an understanding of the analogous sense of the term is not lacking. Both from analysis of the human instrumental cause precisely as a human one, and from the results of the historical-critical method of investigation, it is possible to see to what a high degree the human author participated in the creation of Scripture, so much so that some investigators were mistakenly led to equate the Sacred Scriptures with the other religious literature of antiquity as merely documents of an unusual religious quality.

In order to understand rightly what is meant here by the term "instrumental cause," we must note that the human author brings to the work his own initiative, his personality, his linguistic talents and limitations, his social background, his entire cultural horizon, to such an extent that what he writes is really his own work and shows all the peculiarities of his individuality. An inspired book is wholly God's work and wholly that of the human author. Each of them acts in his own manner, God as God, man as a creature. It would be naive to characterize such a work as a common achievement of God and man. In the last analysis we face here the impenetrable mystery which lies in the cooperation of God and man.

For the interpretation of the canonical writings it is therefore important not only to know that the Holy Spirit stands in the background, but also which man is the human author. This makes it necessary to determine with some exactitude the special literary characteristics of each canonical writing. The first official statement to this effect was made by Pope Piux XII in his encyclical ("Divino afflante Spiritu" #35):

Frequently the literal sense is not so obvious in the words and writings of ancient oriental authors as it is with the writers of today. For what they intended to signify by their words is not determined only by the laws of grammar or philology, nor merely by the context; it is absolutely necessary for the interpreter to go back in spirit to those remote centuries of the East, and make proper use of the aids afforded by history, archaeology, ethnology, and other sciences, in order to discover what literary forms the writers of that early age intended to use, and did in fact employ. For to express what they had in mind the ancients of the East did not always use the same forms and expressions as we use today; they used those which were current among the people of their own time and place; and what these were the exegete cannot determine *a priori,* but only from a careful study of ancient oriental literature.[7]

The Pope points out that unless we pay attention to these literary forms the Sacred Scriptures cannot be correctly interpreted ("Divino afflante Spiritu," #28):

If the Catholic exegete is to meet fully the requirements of modern biblical study he must, in expounding Sacred Scripture and vindicating its immunity from all error, make prudent use also of this further aid: he must, that is, ask himself how far the form of expression or literary idiom employed by the sacred writer may contribute to the true and genuine interpretation; and he may be sure that this part of his task cannot be neglected without great detriment to Catholic exegesis.[8]

SACRED SCRIPTURE AND THE WORD OF GOD

The dialectic between divine and human authorship leads us to the problem whether or not, things being what they are, Sacred Scripture may still be called the word of God. The answer can only be given in a differentiated fashion. The Second Vatican Council offers an answer on two levels. In one instance it says that Sacred Scripture *contains* God's word. This clearly means that God's word is not simply identical with Scripture. On the other hand, however, the same council declares that Sacred Scripture *is* God's word. Obviously different points of view are responsible for these contrasting statements. It must be said that Scripture cannot simply be identified with God's word, for it contains passages which cannot be called God's word, but which, for example, rather serve to make the narrative more easily imaginable, to establish the revelation in a certain cultural context or describe personal conditions of the author. We need only recall Paul's epistle to Philemon, or the personal advice which he gives in other epistles, or the statement of Luke that he used all the sources within his reach in order to write his gospel.

The inspired word of Scripture, then, includes more than the word of revelation. Add to this that, as we emphasized before, Scripture is the written testimony of the apostles and the apostolic Church to God's word. God's word itself is therefore the high authority to which Scripture continually refers. It does so, as Scheffczyk points out, not in the manner of a merely formal testimony, but after the manner of a sacrament, to make present the one to whom witness is borne. It contains the word attested to, although the latter is always greater than the testimony itself. The written form of the kerygma is similar to the oral kerygma, the self-revelation of the glorified Christ, which entered into the testimony of his witnesses. Thus revelation is contained within human written testimony, and yet God's word transcends the written word.

That is why the fear expressed by some Protestant theologians that the presence of God's word in the written word might lead to the work of man dominating the word of God is goundless. This can be said as little of the written as of the oral proclamation. In the former also God remains master of his word. The written word serves God's word. Let us quote further from Scheffczyk's instructive statement:

As regards the reality of the relationship between God's word and man's word, we can conclude that neither the individual nor the Church can dispose of the true power of God's word when they have this word in the finite form of a human word. God's word, although really present in human words, always remains the unreachable, the inexhaustible, which we must enter into as if into an immeasurable space, even though we already stand in it and possess a section of it. . . . This incommensurability is not due only to the imperfection and weakness of human testimony and expression. It lies in the nature of God and of his perfect word of revelation, which can be given expression only inadequately even by the most perfect of human words.[9]

On the other hand we can rightly maintain that Scripture is God's word because it is inspired by the Holy Spirit, so that the

Holy Spirit expresses himself or makes himself present in the human word of Scripture. This thesis has no suggestion in it of the Protestant concept of verbal inspiration. The Holy Spirit gives himself as uncreated grace to the human mind, and thus opens up new insights and perceptions which are expressed in the word of Scripture. Since the Holy Spirit himself asserts and expresses himself in the human words, which preserve their fully human character, he is at the same time the speaking subject.

We can go further: the Holy Spirit was sent by Jesus Christ. Paul occasionally gives the impression that the Holy Spirit sent by Jesus is identical with the risen Lord himself. Although such an identification is not complete in the apostle's doctrine, it nevertheless serves to demonstrate that Christ himself is active in the Spirit. Thus we arrive at the conclusion that Scripture is not only a word about Christ, but the word of the risen Christ about himself, so that, in the human author-subject, he himself is the speaking-subject. Thus it is comprehensible that in Sacred Scripture we find ourselves asked to read to the congregation the written words or the written kerygma (e.g., 1 Thess. 5,27; Col. 4,16; 2 Thess. 2,2.14; 2 Cor. 10,11f.; 1 Tim. 3,14f.; 1 Pet. 5,12; Heb. 13,22; Jn. 20,30f; 21,24f.; Apoc. 1,3; 22,7.9f.18f.).

THE INERRANCY OF SCRIPTURE

The human participation in its composition leads us to the difficult problem of error in Scripture. It would be possible to put forward the view that the human author, chosen by God, participates with the whole of his limited mentality—erroneous ideas included—in the authorship, except insofar as the question of divine revelation itself is involved. This thesis is, in fact, maintained by Protestant theology. In official Catholic utterances it was, until lately, always denied. But in the statements of the Second Vatican Council we see, so to speak, a compromise, insofar as it is stressed that the Sacred Scriptures indeed teach truth with certainty, faithfully and without error, but this truth is characterized in a subsequent relative clause as that which God wished to be included in Sacred Scripture for the sake of our salvation. Therefore we should, as the Second Vatican Council declares, carefully investigate what the sacred writers really wished to say, and what God wished to reveal in their words. We should remember particularly in this context that the Second Vatican Council takes account of the differences between literary *genres*.

We probably do justice to the situation created by Pope Pius XII and the Second Vatican Council if we distinguish between the form and the content of revelation. In view of the importance of the matter and of a still widespread confusion, it might be in order to go into the question at some depth. The whole problem, however, goes so deep into questions of linguistic logic and philosophy that to solve it completely an investigation into the philosophy of language would be required. Martin Buber, to whom we must at least concede an especially close contact with the Old Testament, offers a contribution to the clarification of the problem. He maintains that people of former times, when they were confronted by events which were deeply impressive, unexpected, and of such a nature as to change their historical situation at one stroke, reacted by accepting what had happened, but in a condition of intense excitement, which affected their whole being.

A man seized by such enthusiasm exists in a state of astonishment which affects all the imaginative powers of his soul. What takes place in all this is not a perversion of what he originally saw, not a creation of his fancy, but a picturesque representation of the event in its historic potency. This distinction is of the greatest significance, as we can see in the case of several fateful historical events—e.g., the Galileo trial, or the supposed contradiction between theology and the theory of evolution in the nineteenth century. It is, to be sure, not so simple as it might seem at first. The linguistic form is not just a dress which the content puts on, or a vessel into which the spirit flows; rather, it has in relation to the content a function similar to that which the body performs for the spirit. Consequently the form reacts on the meaning of the content: the content and the form of a statement are one indivisible whole. Yet it must be possible to make not only a distinction but a separation, so that we can say, though with many reservations and

some vagueness, what belongs to the content of the statement and
what to its form.

It would be extremely useful if we could find a norm for this distinction. How difficult it is to do so is demonstrated by the century-
old argument between the Church's preaching and theology on the
one hand, and science with its various branches on the other. Both
theologians and scientists were generally convinced that this was
an either-or issue. But the theologians did restrict themselves to
the abstract and formal statement that there can be, in reality, no
contradiction, because there can be only one source both for faith
and science, namely God. But such a thesis attained no concrete
effectiveness, because it was confined to the realm of abstract
assertion. If in our days the situation has changed, we may ask
whether or not the victorious advance of science has caused the
theologians to abandon positions which obviously had become un-
tenable and to withdraw resignedly before the victor. We would
indeed have to assume something of this kind if there were no
norm by which to distinguish between the content and the form of
statement.

It is, however, the convincing conclusion of all our previous considerations, and it is also suggested by the texts of the Second Vatican Council, that there is in fact such a distinction. If God
communicates with man in his self-revelation, he intends to enable
him to have the right, salvific relationship to himself; or, more
exactly, to call him into the absolute future of his own immediate
self-communication. What serves this goal must be counted among
the contents of the revelation testified to in Scripture. The way in
which the world or man was created is not immediately affected by
this finality of divine self-revelation unless man's nature must be
so defined that his position of pre-eminence over all other creatures
becomes evident. On the other hand it is true that in the apostolic
era the special history of salvation was announced by proclaiming
Jesus as the promised Messiah and testifying to his resurrection.
This is without doubt fundamental for the absolute future of man.

Considering the resurrection of our Lord as a form of myth
would thus mean abandoning the biblical faith. The content of
revelation in Scripture is frequently offered in mythical images;

but they are still not myths, for a myth is the representation of a dramatic event. It is not yet certain whether Scripture also uses myths as well as mythical images for presenting the content of revelation. However this question may eventually be answered, we must, for the understanding of Scripture, distinguish between the probably mythical element and the content of revelation. This means that Scripture must be demythologized. It has fundamentally demythologized itself by bearing witness to the one living God and dethroning the gods immanent in the world. The demythologization of the word of Scripture is therefore an interpretation of the demythologization already carried out by Scripture itself. The criterion mentioned above for the theological differentiation offers a useful principle for distinguishing the content from the form of scriptural statement. It will, however, frequently be very difficult to apply this principle. For the moment let it suffice to point out that ultimate competence in the matter rests with the teaching authority of the Church, which in its turn is assisted by theology.

A more detailed and exact insight into the problem can be gained by examining the way in which the New Testament, especially the gospels, came into existence. We can quote in this connection the Second Vatican Council, as also the *Instructio de historica Evangeliorum veritate* ("On the Historical Truth of the Gospels") of the Papal Biblical Commission of April 21, 1964. The statement of the Council on the matter is a turning point for the whole of theology and therefore deserves verbal citation (Dogmatic Constitution on Divine Revelation, #17–20):

17.   The word of God, which is the power of God for the salvation of all who believe (cf. Rom. 1:16), is set forth and shows its power in a most excellent way in the writings of the New Testament. For when the fullness of time arrived (cf. Gal. 4:4), the Word was made flesh and dwelt among us in the fullness of grace and truth (cf. Jn. 1:14). Christ established the Kingdom of God on earth, manifested His Father and Himself by deeds and words, and completed His work by His death, resurrection, and glorious ascension and by the sending of the Holy Spirit. Having been lifted up from the earth, He draws all men to Himself (cf. Jn. 12:32, Greek text), He who alone has the words of eternal life (cf. Jn. 6:68). This mystery had not been manifested to other

generations as it was now revealed to His holy apostles and prophets in the Holy Spirit (cf. Eph. 3: 4–6, Greek text), so that they might preach the gospel, stir up faith in Jesus, Christ and Lord, and gather the Church together. To these realities, the writings of the New Testament stand as a perpetual and divine witness.

18. It is common knowledge that among all the Scriptures, even those of the New Testament, the Gospels have a special pre-eminence, and rightly so, for they are the principal witness of the life and teaching of the incarnate Word, our Savior.

The Church has always and everywhere held and continues to hold that the four Gospels are of apostolic origin. For what the apostles preached in fulfillment of the commission of Christ, afterwards they themselves and apostolic men, under the inspiration of the divine Spirit, handed on to us in writing: the foundation of faith, namely, the fourfold Gospel, according to Matthew, Mark, Luke, and John.

19. Holy Mother Church has firmly and with absolute constancy held, and continues to hold, that the four Gospels just named, whose historical character the Church unhesitatingly asserts, faithfully hand on what Jesus Christ, while living among men, really did and taught for their eternal salvation until the day He was taken up into heaven (see Acts 1:1–2). Indeed, after the ascension of the Lord the apostles handed on to their hearers what He had said and done. This they did with that clearer understanding which they enjoyed after they had been instructed by the events of Christ's risen life and taught by the light of the Spirit of truth. The sacred authors wrote the four Gospels, selecting some things from the many which had been handed on by word of mouth or in writing, reducing some of them to a synthesis, explicating some things in view of the situation of their churches, and preserving the form of proclamation but always in such fashion that they told us the honest truth about Jesus. For their intention in writing was that either from their own memory and recollections, or from the witness of those who themselves "from the beginning were eye-witnesses and ministers of the word" we might know "the truth" concerning those matters about which we have been instructed (cf. Lk. 1:2–4).

20. Besides the four Gospels, the canon of the New Testament also contains the Epistles of St. Paul and other apostolic writings, composed under the inspiration of the Holy Spirit. In these writings, by the wise plan of God, those matters which concern Christ the Lord are confirmed, His true teaching is more and more fully stated, the saving

power of the divine work of Christ is preached, the story is told of the beginnings of the Church and her marvelous growth, and her glorious fulfillment is foretold.

For the Lord Jesus was with His apostles as He had promised (cf. Mt. 28:20) and sent to them as Paraclete the Spirit who would lead them into the fullness of truth (cf. Jn. 16:13).

In agreement with the statements of the council and the Instruction mentioned above, in which the reliable results of present exegetical scholarship are used, we must maintain that the books of the canon cannot be understood as literary works of certain authors in our modern sense—they are testimonies of faith on a historical foundation; that is to say, they are reports based on and characterized by theological reflection. Christ is seen and presented in them in the light of the Easter mystery. The doctrine and life of Jesus are not simply handed down so that their memory should not be lost. They are proclaimed, so that they can be for the Church the foundation of faith and life, as the Instruction says of the gospels. The Instruction makes it clear that the truth of the gospels is not reached by committing ourselves to a fundamentalist, purely literal understanding of the text (J. A. Fitzmayr).

The council and the foregoing instruction indicate, in agreement with present exegesis, that the most important canonical Scriptures originated in three steps. The first step concerns the relationship of the disciples to Jesus. In this phase lie the words immediately spoken by Jesus ("verba ipsissima"). The second phase lies between the ascension of Jesus and the writing of the canonical Scriptures, above all the gospels. It is the time when Jesus was proclaimed in the light of the resurrection before the written formulations of our canonical texts.

This proclamation is still preserved to some extent in abbreviated kerygmatic formulas in the gospels and also occasionally in the epistles. We find it in catechetic and homiletic summaries— for example, in Acts or 1 Cor. 15,3b–5—in missionary sermons, in baptismal professions of faith, in prayers, hymns and some other forms. It would be natural to look for the authors of these among the original apostles. However, these texts are not connected with a particular name, they are anonymous. They are characterized by the fact that they interpret Christ on the basis of his resurrection from the dead. They choose from the life and the doctrine of Jesus what is important for a congregation or for a particular audience. According to the needs of their listeners, they arrange the chosen pieces in a definite way. For most of these texts we can designate the liturgy—i.e., the celebration of divine service—as their *Sitz im Leben.*

The divine service with its preaching and its worship, with its baptisms and celebrations of the Eucharist, with apostolic instruction and prophetic sermon (see 1 Cor. 14), offered plenty of opportunity to establish and to deepen the congregation's faith in Christ, but also from the side of the congregation, to strengthen it by profession of faith and song, by acclamations (Amen) and doxologies. In these partly oral, partly written, abbreviated formulas we may see the first theology, the theology of the early Church. It would be an exaggeration and a denial of the truth, to assert that the faith represented in such formulas had no connection with the historical life of Jesus, but was a pure creation of the congregation. Although the congregation, with the special needs caused by their situation, did have a decisive influence on the formulation of this original theology, the authors of it were nevertheless individual believers. It does not contradict truth to hold that the authors of such single texts transmitted what Jesus really said and did, in a fuller understanding which they themselves reached only through the Easter experiences and the illumination of Pentecost (see, e.g., Jn. 2,22; 12,16; 11,51f.; Acts 10,36–41).[10]

The third phase is represented by the writing of the texts of the New Testament, above all the gospels. In these the abbreviated formulations already available are collected together and arranged. Of the gospels we must say, and with even greater emphasis, that they testify to Jesus Christ on the basis of the new understanding brought by Easter. This consists above all in the fact that they bear witness to Jesus as the Christ. Under the influence of the illuminating Spirit the authors offer a selection, a synthesis, and an interpretation of the life, the sayings, and the deeds of the historical Jesus. Their work is determined by the goal they set for themselves. They adapted themselves to their expected readers. They often transposed episodes from one context into another. They also made the words and deeds of Jesus actual and relevant to the particular pastoral situation they were concerned with. In the gospels, then, we encounter Jesus' words to a large extent in a theological interpretation.

Further we can distinguish between the theologies of the individual gospels. In spite of their unity in faith they differ so much from each other in their testimony to the faith that we must assume a different *Sitz im Leben* for each gospel. We may assume that Matthew's gospel with its systematic division of material was intended mainly to serve catechetic purposes; that Luke's was above all an attempt to win over pagans and assist Christians converted from paganism, to preserve and to present what had once happened in order to make clearer to the Christians their situation in salvation history, and to attract to faith in Christ those who still stood aloof. Of Mark's gospel, too, we may conclude that it was directed to one particular congregation. We do justice to the situation of the gospel of John if we state that it proclaims the transmitted contents of the story of Jesus in a particularly developed theological reflection, and with great concern for pastoral relevance.

The investigation of Jesus' words and deeds before their written formulation in the gospels has been called form-criticism (*formgeschichtliche Methode*). The bulk of the work in this field was done in Germany after the First World War, and its results have since been widely acknowledged. After the Second World War form-criticism was joined by the investigation of the history of the editing process, redaction-criticism (*redaktionsgeschichtliche Methode*). The purpose of this is to discover the role of the individual authors in the creation of their gospels despite their collective character.

It is of greatest importance not to view the early Christian testimonies of faith as creations of the local congregations. The Christ of faith is not the result of faith. The historical Jesus was understood as the Messiah because of his resurrection. The apostles are very much concerned with the historical Jesus. He has become for them the glorified Lord. Their intention is to proclaim the salvifically significant fact of Jesus as the Christ. On the one hand, the apostles wanted to transmit the words and deeds of Jesus; on the other hand, they had a new understanding of the entire Christ-revelation as a result of the Easter event. This tension between the immediate experience of Jesus and the interpretation of his significance in the Holy Spirit is characteristic of the gospels. This is also true of John's gospel. Even though it is difficult to determine the *Sitz im Leben* of this gospel, because it incorporates many spiritual movements of its time, we may say that it is recognized more and more strongly that its roots lie in Jewish thought and in the convictions of the early Church, and that the extreme existential interpretation of it is more and more vigorously criticized. Even John's Christology is concerned most intensely with the historical Jesus of Nazareth. It contains the germ of the development of Christology in the Church which later took place under the influence of Greek thought.

THE TRUTH OF THE GOSPELS

In view of this situation difficult questions arise for the theologian. Can we trust the gospels, seeing that they transmit to us the words of Jesus not in their literal original shape, but in a form altered in consequence of the historical situation of the Church? Can we still speak of their "truth"? In the Instruction of the Biblical Commission already mentioned we find it stated calmly and without anxiety that the gospels as we now have them do not contain the words and deeds of Jesus from the first phase of tradition. Frequently they are not even in the shape in which they were proclaimed in the second phase; rather they present the words and deeds of Jesus in the form in which the evangelists assembled and edited them. This final phase reflects, to be sure, the two preceding ones, the second more than the first. But it might be a fruitless effort to try to attain through this to the actual words uttered originally by Jesus himself. We shall return to this question in the section dealing with Christology.

We can overcome the first shock of this discovery if we realize that it is precisely this state of affairs which shows the dynamism of the word of Jesus. What matters is not the letter, but the meaning and the power of Jesus' words. They have such a wealth of meaning and such a power for salvation that they are applicable to any situation. They are of such profundity that they need to be interpreted, commented on, explained and made accessible to the listener in order to be comprehended in their entire significance; and yet, at the same time, they are accessible to listeners of the most varied receptivity. Above all, we must not overlook the fact that the very form of the sayings and deeds of Jesus which issued from the editing activity of the writers of the gospels is inspired. The authors of the gospels were led by the Holy Spirit, whom Jesus himself sent, to put together and to formulate their contents in the way they did. Their inspiration guarantees the "truth" of the gospels and their protection from error. Their truth, however, is not a truth of the letter, but one of meaning and of facts.

Precisely in order to understand the truth revealed to them by Christ, the first witnesses of Christ had to detach themselves from the letter of the word in order to be able to lead their readers and listeners to its substance; namely, to the salvation offered by God— that is, to the absolute future. Since Jesus Christ himself in the Holy Spirit acts in his Church, it is he who interprets his original words in the gospels. Perhaps here, too, we can gain some measure of understanding from our experience of interpersonal relationships. We can compare the self-interpretation of Jesus Christ in the New Testament with the development which a lover may subsequently give to his simple and short sentence: I love you.

The difference between the formulas in which Christ was borne witness to in the second phase, and even more so the different formulations in Sacred Scripture, lead to the question whether there was in the original Church a uniform doctrine on Christ. Form- and redaction-criticism have come to the conclusion that there were certain tensions or contrasts in the Christ-interpretation of the original Church. Protestant theology occasionally speaks explicitly of a decay of the unity of doctrine. But Catholic theologians, too, speak of a plurality of theologies, especially Christologies, in the New Testament. Yet we can and must speak of a unity. The unity of Scripture is found in the unity of the Christ-

event testified to in its different texts. This thesis presupposes that
we can distinguish between the event itself and the proclamation
of the event. The Christ-event is not created by the proclamation of
Christ, it carries its salvific significance in itself. It is thus a matter
of comprehending this Christ-event as the reality standing behind
all the differences in the various testimonies to Christ, and effective throughout the different doctrines. The testimonies collected
in the New Testament and recognized by the Church in the canon
harmonize in fact in the profession of the one Lord, the one baptism,
the one God and Father of all (Ep. 4,5f.). In order to recognize
this unity in variety, we certainly need the theological insight that
the individual witnesses to Christ are conscious of being committed to a common understanding of Christ. We can call this the
formal principle of unity. Beyond this we can also, as far as content
is concerned, see a number of elements which, in spite of all differences, belong together in a unity rich in variety. Otto Kuss says in
this connection:

If we try, with all due reservations . . . briefly and in the broadest of
outlines to characterize the most important elements which went to
make up the faith of the earliest congregations of the disciples, we
might point out the following. First of all, the small group of believers
in Jesus take their first steps entirely within the sphere of Judaism. In
the second place it has an altogether simple Christology which is attached to the manifold appearances of the Resurrected One: "This Jesus
God raised up, and of that we are all witnesses" (Acts 2,32); "Let all
the house of Israel therefore know assuredly that God has made him
both Lord and Christ, this Jesus whom you crucified" (Acts 2,36). A
prayer of the congregation is rendered: "Sovereign Lord, who didst
make the heaven and the earth and the sea and everything in them (Ex.
20, 11), who by the mouth of our father David, thy servant, didst say
by the Holy Spirit, 'Why did the Gentiles rage, and the peoples imagine
vain things? The kings of the earth set themselves in array, and the
rulers were gathered together, against the Lord and against his
Anointed' (Ps. 2,1.2)—for truly in this city there were gathered together against thy holy servant Jesus, whom thou didst anoint, both
Herod and Pontius Pilate, with the Gentiles and the peoples of Israel,
to do whatever thy hand and thy plan had predestined to take place.

And now, Lord, look upon their threats, and grant to thy servants to speak thy word with all boldness, while thou stretchest out thy hand to heal, and signs and wonders are performed through the name of thy holy servant Jesus." (Acts 4,24–30) In the third place the salvation which the first proclamation promises consists in the forgiveness of sins, the gift of the Spirit, and salvation from this perverted generation. Fourthly, baptism is granted as a special sign of salvation, and at the same time as a rite of acceptance into the new eschatological congregation of salvation. Fifthly, the congregation assembles for common prayer in the temple and for common meals: with one mind they kept up their daily attendance at the temple, and breaking bread in private houses, shared their meals with unaffected joy (Acts 2,46). Sixthly, the community affirms itself in far-reaching mutual assistance. Seventhly, it is understandable that the congregation soon seeks justification for its existence in Scripture. Eighthly, the faith in the salvation wrought by God through Jesus Christ seems in the beginning to have found quite a number of forms of expression; there is no unity of doctrine at first, but a variety of forms of comprehension.[11]

As far as the Hellenistic congregations are concerned, which were constituted soon after and alongside these forms of the new faith which emerge from Jewish thinking, we can, in Kuss's view, only say that they were in possession of that central reality which can be expressed by the words: Salvation has come.

THE MUTUAL RELATIONSHIP OF SCRIPTURE AND THE CHURCH

The New Testament originated when the congregation of Jesus' disciples, the Church, already existed. We may assume with Heinrich Schlier that there were preliminary symbols, pieces of proclamation, in a certain sense a rule of faith (e.g., 1 Cor. 15, 1–36) which was set down in writing as a normative apostolic kerygma, and around which the Sacred Scripture was formed, as around a kerygmatic core. This assumption makes the birth of the Scriptures out of the womb of the apostolic community of faith particularly comprehensible. Thus the Church is not the product of Scripture. It is rather the other way around: Scripture is the product of the

Church. It comes from the sphere of the Church—i.e., from the community of the believers in Christ. It makes the proclamation of Christ and the faith in him something objective, and thus testifies to the Christ-event which is itself present both in the proclamation and in the faith. This results in a reciprocal relation between the Church and Scripture. On the one hand Scripture expresses the faith of the Church; on the other hand the Church is ruled by Scripture.

The origin of Sacred Scripture from the faith of the Church can be viewed under a double aspect. Those formulas of faith were received into Scripture in which faith presented itself before the written formulation. Thus Scripture is an element of tradition in the apostolic era. It is the expression of the oldest proclamation and the oldest faith, in which historical tradition was conscientiously and responsibly preserved. In addition the Church is the author of the Sacred Scriptures inasmuch as the individual representative believers whose names give their titles to the gospels wrote not as private citizens but as representatives of the community. Thus in spite of the individuality of the authors, the congregation, their faith, the situation within which they believed, their difficulties and problems as believers, their controversies with contemporary tendencies—all stand behind the gospels. Sacred Scripture contains an ecclesial element. It bears the imprint of the Church.

On the other hand, however, we must stress with all possible emphasis that the Church has borne the imprint of Scripture ever since a Scripture has existed. Just as Scripture is ecclesially constituted, so the Church is scripturally constituted. The Church is the community of believers which brought forth the Scriptures as the expression of itself. If it wishes to preserve its original self-understanding, it must consult Scripture as the expression of its own existence. It becomes conscious of its identity with itself in all generations, in being aware of its identity with its original form, which it finds in Scripture. The Church must therefore constantly listen to the word expressed and preserved in the Scriptures. It is always a listening Church. By listening to Scripture it listens to Christ, testified to and present in Scripture, and to the Holy Spirit who bears witness to Jesus. If the Church were to abandon Scripture, it would abandon Christ and the Spirit himself. Thus Scripture always remains the norm of true self-understanding for the Church. Scripture itself, however, is no longer subject to another norm. It is, as we say, the *norma normans non normata*. Fundamentally this thesis means simply that Christ, present in Holy Scripture, is the norm of the Church, a norm not subject to any other norm. In this conviction Protestant and Catholic theology agree.

Because the Church is subject to the norm of Scripture, it can never treat Scripture, or Christ, to whom Scripture testifies, as though they were at its disposal. The Church always remains subject to Jesus Christ. Although he has entered into Scripture, he is greater than Scripture. As far, however, as he is present in it and works in it, he does so as the head of his body, the Church. It will shortly become clear what shades of meaning must be given to the principle that Scripture is the *norma non normata* of the Church if it is not to be understood in too mechanical a fashion or be raised to the status of an idol.

The proclamation, interpretation, and explanation of Sacred Scripture are entrusted to the Church. If the Church objectifies its faith in, and understanding of, Christ in Scripture, this necessarily leads to the thesis that it understands Scripture. Its understanding of Scripture results from its understanding of itself, just as Scripture in its turn is the objectivization of the Church's original understanding of itself.

This active relationship of the Church to Scripture has the consequence that Christianity, though bound to a book, does not become a bookish religion, and that Christians in their faith in Christ do not become simply a community of readers. Christianity remains a community of listeners.[12]

Faith comes, as Paul stresses (Rom. 10,14f.), from what is heard. Listening, however, presupposes the spoken word. Nonetheless the written form of the apostolic proclamation is neither superfluous nor meaningless. We may assume that the reason for the writing of the Scriptures lay in the guarantee it gave that no human omissions or additions, no inventions of an imaginary sort, will interfere in the transmission of the apostolic words. Furthermore it is possible for the written word, even if only as a makeshift, to reach people whom the Church's preaching cannot reach. Scripture is thus a medium through which the Church's proclamation preserves its reliability. The first step which the Church undertakes here is to bear witness to Scripture as the written word of God. Without the Church's testimony we could not know that Scripture is fundamentally different from other religious writings which have come down to us from antiquity. It is through the Church that Scripture comes to us as God's word.

The most important step, however, is the proclamation of the word of God objectified in Scripture. Without proclamation Scripture would remain a dead letter. It is not sufficient to investigate it like an ancient manuscript or a historical document. Such a procedure would not make it speak. If the Holy Spirit is objectified in Scripture, it was not for the purpose of merely being present there, but in order to speak to men through the words of men from a tangible and visible place. If the Church does not proclaim Christ through some other medium—through the firmament of heaven, or the blue ocean, or the bright colors of flowers—but through the medium of Scripture, it is precisely because the Holy Spirit is present in Scripture as the one who speaks through the Church. Scripture is actualized by the word of the Church.

With these theses the Catholic idea of Scripture differs considerably from the Protestant. It appears to be a generally accepted thesis in Protestant theology that Scripture becomes God's word on each occasion when God, by means of Scripture, touches the individual man in the illumination of the Holy Spirit. This thesis could be accepted by Catholic theology if it was not intended to describe the nature, but only the function, of Sacred Scripture. For this is actually true: even though Scripture is God's word expressed in human words by the Holy Spirit, it becomes effective as God's word only in the person of the believer. For the unbeliever it is no more than religious literature. That it can be effective in the believer as God's word derives from the fact that it has previously been God's word or contains God's word. The action of a thing derives from its being, and its being manifests itself in action. Protestant theology since Luther has argued that the Holy Spirit himself through his own efficacy testifies to the reader that Scripture is

God's word. This thesis need not be completely rejected by the Catholic theologian. It has rather considerable theological and religious significance, insofar as the Holy Spirit is indeed efficacious in Scripture. The thesis only becomes erroneous if it isolates the inner testimony of the Holy Spirit from the ecclesial proclamation.

Some differences between the Churches rest on misunderstandings. The decisive point at issue here is that Protestant theology considers that the Catholic Church usurps authority over Scripture itself when it claims authority to proclaim and to interpret it. Protestant theology fears that the way in which the Catholic Church conceives of Scripture leads to a situation in which the believer's dialogue with God slips imperceptibly into a pure monologue on the part of the Church—i.e., that the Church reads into Scripture its own intentions and desires. But this immediately calls forth from the Catholic theologian the counter-objection that the concept of the word of God as simply an event taking place in the believer involves the danger that the word will fall prey to the limitations and preconceptions of the individual.

According to Protestant theology, Scripture itself has a formal authority over the reader. This thesis is transformed by the Catholic Church as follows: formal authority belongs to the Church, as the community of believers in Christ, characterized in a special way in that it has persons who hold the office of teaching but that material authority is due to Scripture. The Church does not determine the content of Scripture, much less create it. Its task is exclusively to proclaim it and to help it be effective. If that is what the Church does, it simply expresses the ecclesial character of Scripture. The latter is not directed to the individual as an individual, it is the book of the community, since the common faith of the original Church is objictified in it. Therefore it is the community which bears the responsibility for the content of the book reaching mankind. If the community as such is burdened with this responsibility, let us stress again that within the community a special task has been given, according to Christ's commission, to some members— namely, those who hold the office of teaching in the Church. The fulfillment of this task, however, is and must be viewed as service to the community.

The Church can fulfill its task of proclamation only if it interprets Scripture and at the same time explains it. The question is whether Scripture needs an interpretation or whether it is not rather self-explanatory by its own lucidity. It would in any event be strange and scarcely comprehensible if Scripture were so obscure that its central testimony remained inaccessible to the ordinary believer. It could then be only a mystical cryptograph. It is well known that Luther distinguished between that inner lucidity which the reader experiences as an assurance of his salvation and the external clarity which belongs to the text itself; the latter, he declared, made it possible for the official preaching office of the Church to proclaim Christ's message for the strengthening of those weak in faith and the refutation of adversaries. He enumerated the doctrines which made up the subject matter of this external clarity: the Incarnation, vicarious suffering, heavenly kingship, and the resurrection of Jesus Christ illuminating all; and, over and above them, the Trinitarian and Christological dogma in its fullness. The center of these realities, which in his opinion appear clearly in Scripture, is Jesus Christ. His doctrine of the external clarity of Scripture did not, of course, lead Luther to deny that there are sentences in Scripture whose meaning is not clear.

It cannot be maintained that there is a genuine difference between Luther's understanding of the "external clarity" of Scripture and the Catholic position. For according to the latter also, the Bible is not a "book with seven seals." In the Catholic conception, too, the doctrines concerning Christ's salvific death and resurrection, the forgiveness of sins, and the call of men to eternal glory are clearly to be found in Scripture. If the question of the clarity or obscurity of Scripture involved only the meaning attached to it by Luther, the intervention of an ecclesiastical teaching office would not be required. The purpose for which this exists is to proclaim the testimony of Scripture in living words and to defend it against rationalistic objections.

Even though the written word may be superior to the spoken word in permanence, in independence, and in fulfilling the functions of a norm, yet the written formulation has only the significance of a transitory stage; it does not exist for itself, but to lead us on to the vitality of the spoken word—a vitality which, in the long run, is of more lasting significance. As Leo Scheffczyk points out, if a script exists only as a work in a library, it has largely lost its character as word, for however much it may have the furthering of knowledge as its reason for existence, it is not in actual fact doing this. Sacred Scripture, having been born of the living proclamation of the Church, has from the beginning, as its reason for existence, only the purpose of serving the living, spoken word.

It is the object of proclamation, then, to release that vitality which characterizes the spoken word and which originally belonged to those words now written down in Scripture. That Scripture should achieve this goal in its speech to men and in the claim which it makes on them is guaranteed by the fact that it is entrusted to the Church. As far as the interpretation of Sacred Scripture is concerned—without which its proclamation is not possible —this may be said: interpretation is necessitated by the historical character of Scripture and of the Church. As we have noted, the word of God as it is set down in Scripture already represents a translation from its original form. If God's word reaches men only through the words of men, this has consequences of immense significance for the Church. The human words in which God's word appears are naturally determined by the linguistic development, by the entire cultural situation of the time, and by the individuality of God's messenger. The trends of thought among men, their forms of culture, their educational levels, vary continually according to mysterious laws. As a result, what is readily comprehensible to one generation seems obscure and remote, like something belonging to the past, to another.

God's word itself is always young, but the language in which it reaches men participates in the laws affecting every human cultural form: it can become so out-of-date that the divine content of which it is the bearer is no longer accessible to a whole generation, since in the meantime new thought forms and cultural images have developed. The Church would no longer fulfill its task if it were to proclaim divine revelation in signs which belong to the past and seem like hieroglyphs to the present. It must carry out a translation, which means that it must move away from the earlier form of God's word in order to preserve it. Just as the writers of

Sacred Scripture had to some extent to abandon the original words of the kerygma in order to make their subject matter accessible to their new readers and listeners, so the Church must always be prepared to sacrifice the letter of a formulation for the sake of its spirit and its content.

The new way of thinking which characterizes a new generation may be brought about by the spread of new pre-philosophical, philosophical, cosmological or other ideas, or simply by a new feeling for life, inexplicable in its origins. Thus, when the message concerning Jesus, the Messiah, left the narrow Jewish domain and entered into the broader sphere of Hellenistic culture, the Church was faced with the task of proclaiming its message of salvation against a horizon widened by this more universal culture and in constant dialogue with it. In modern times, when the universal-cosmic way of thinking which had, consciously or unconsciously, been so widely adopted was radically altered by a new sense of history, the Church found itself obliged to interpret the unchangeable revelation of Jesus Christ against this universal-historical horizon or background of thought. In our own times it must interpret and formulate the unique divine self-revelation, given once for all, against the background of the radical secularization which has taken place and in view of the radical hope for the future of mankind which has come to characterize our society. The purpose of this interpretation is to present an answer deriving from the faith to the questions which human thought and feeling pose to the Church. Interpretation always includes an explanation, an unfolding; we shall discuss this later in the analysis of dogma and its development. First let us treat another problem which is as oppressive as it is decisive for the ecumenical dialogue—the question of the Church's infallibility.

INFALLIBILITY

It is in precisely this claim to announce the word of God infallibly that Protestant theology sees the setting up of an authority over God's word. Here, in the Protestant view, a human authority is exalted over God's word and even over Jesus Christ. It was in this theological dimension, and not in the emotional sphere, that the notion of the pope as the antichrist had its origin. This is an idea based on a fateful misinterpretation of the concept of infallibility as Catholics understand it. Since the Catholic claim that in particular situations and under specific conditions the teaching office of the Church possesses infallibility separated the Churches more than all other differences during the Reformation, it requires carefull analysis. We shall begin with the analysis of what infallibility does *not* involve.

The concept of "infallibility" must be clearly distinguished from the concepts of perfection and sinlessness and also removed from any connection with a desire for security with regard to salvation. Omniscience or divine illumination is not claimed for those who exercise infallibility. What is maintained is this—that those to whom the office of teaching is committed in the Church, when they interpret authoritatively for the whole people of God a particular matter of revelation attested in Scripture, are prevented from error in this procedure; they state accurately what is revealed, so that we can rely on their interpretation. In the thesis of infallibility nothing is stated as to how the bearer of infallibility acquires the knowledge of what is revealed. Both the Second Vatican Council and the Instruction of the Biblical Commission mentioned above indicate that theological scholarship can and will assist the teaching office by means of the results it obtains. Nor does the thesis of infallibility mean to assert that what is being proclaimed is expressed in the best possible manner. It is compatible with this thesis that what is being proclaimed may be stated imperfectly and even one-sidedly; that it may be overemphasized in such a way as to disarrange the order of the whole.

Although the First Vatican Council did not say it in so many words, it nevertheless belongs to the sense of faith of the Church that her preaching, infallible doctrinal decisions included, is subject to that law which Paul expressed in the First Epistle to the Corinthians: "For our knowledge and our prophecy alike are partial, and the partial vanishes when wholeness comes. When I was a child, my speech, my outlook, and my thoughts were all childish. When I grew up, I had finished with childish things. Now we see only puzzling reflections in a mirror, but then we shall see face to face. My knowledge now is partial; then it will be whole, like God's knowledge of me." (1 Cor. 13,9–12, *NEB*) Nor is the dogma of infallibility intended to serve man's desire for security in regard to salvation. Its purpose is to preserve and to hand on God's word, safeguarding it against all the dangers which threaten it from human liability to error, presumption, and hybris. God has entrusted his word to fallible men; at the same time, by the charism of infallibility, he has guaranteed that it will not be lost, perverted, or deprived of meaning.

It may be useful here to point out again that in interpreting the word of God, the Church fulfills a mediating task in which it is bound by, and subject to, the word of Scripture. This relationship to Scripture is not changed by the Church's claim to trustworthy interpretation of the text of Sacred Scripture. The Church's infallibility guarantees that violence is not done to the text but that its true sense is revealed. Infallibility must be understood as the Church understands it—that is, as the God-given ability to comprehend Scripture in the sense intended by the writers and by the Holy Spirit himself. It guarantees that in every generation we can hear God's word in its original meaning. The question of the Church's actual possession of the gift of infallibility and who are its bearers will be discussed later, in the analysis of the Church itself.

The charism of infallibility comes into operation when the Church finds herself at a crossroads in the understanding of God's word, so that a decision is necessary for further progress in man's pilgrimage towards the absolute future—for instance, when a false understanding of Christ places the Christian community in jeopardy. In such a time of danger the Holy Spirit brings it about that a reliable word is spoken which will indicate the right path. What brings such a word to life is obedience to God himself. When God presents men with his word, it is not for them to do anything they please with it. In the face of the inconstancy of all that is human, God has created an institution through Christ in the Holy Spirit which is intended to keep the pure word of God intact. Men have a right to hear the pure gospel, and not human inventions which contradict God's meaning. It cannot be validly objected that God's word is capable of securing itself, by its own power, against all human distortions. The experience of the chaotic interpretations of God's word which have taken place outside the sphere of belief in infallibility shows clearly that this is not true. Assuredly, God has sent his word into the mouth of men. Infallibility, therefore, is a disposition of divine providence, ensuring that God's word, entrusted to men, will be transmitted in its original sense down to the end of time—i.e., till the beginning of the absolute future. Hence infallibility does not mean a claim which a man makes for himself against God but a help which God gives to man, whom he has called to salvation. It is not the product of an anti-Christian will to power, but a gift which serves the preaching of the gospel and is subordinate to it; and like every divine gift it carries with it an obligation which can grow into a heavy burden.

Readings

Eissfeldt, Otto. *The Old Testament: An Introduction.* New York, Harper, 1965.

Levie, G. *The Bible, Word of God in Words of Men.* Translated by S. H. Treman. New York. P. J. Kenedy and Sons, 1961.

Rahner, Karl. *Inspiration in the Bible.* Translated by Charles Henkey. New York, Herder and Herder, 1961.

Wikenhauser, A. *Introduction to the New Testament.* New York, Herder and Herder, 1958.

Notes

[1] "Inspiration und Kanonizität der hl. Schrift in ihrem Verhältnis zur Kirche," in *Scholastik* 33 (1958), 218–221.

[2] Denz., 3006, 3029.

[3] Denz., 3293.

[4] Denz., 3652.

[5] Denz., 3825.

[6] Denz., 1501.

[7] *Selected Documents of His Holiness, Pope Pius XII* (Washington, D.C.: NCWC, N.D.).

[8] *Ibid.*

⁹ *Von der Heilsmacht des Wortes.*

¹⁰ Rudolf Schnackenburg, *Neutestamentliche Theologie* (Munich, 1961), 49ff.

¹¹ "Die Rolle des Apostels Paulus in der theologischen Entwicklung der Urkirche," in *Münchener Theologische Zeitschrift* 14 (1963), 110-112.

¹² See H. Schürmann, "Lukanische Reflexionen über die Wortverkundigung in Luk. 8, 4–20" in *Wahrheit und Verkundigung* (Paderborn, 1967), 213–228.

◄ 11

Scripture and Tradition

The concepts of Scripture and tradition are closely connected. Scripture, as we have seen, is the written expression of tradition; we can call it the original witness of tradition. The relation between Scripture and tradition has been the object of much theological analysis, and more than once it has given rise to doctrinal statements in the Church. Owing to the Second Vatican Council, the problem has recently been treated in a manner full of implications for future theology.

The concept of tradition plays a decisive part in the history of religion, although it is interpreted in very different ways. From the point of view of the history of religion, it means what is very old, what was taken over from prehistoric times and handed on down through the ages. This is true both for the so-called civilized religions and for the so-called nature religions. It does not matter for the definition whether the transmission is carried out in writing or orally.

In the Jewish and Christian sphere the concept of tradition is determined by the historical character of revelation. In the Old Covenant the revelation that had occurred in historical processes was written down. The written formulation gradually received the title of Torah. In the so-called "Traditions of the Fathers" the decrees of the Torah were preserved, interpreted, and applied to definite situations.

215

Christianity is characterized by the fact that the Christ-event took place only once. Since mankind's salvation depended upon it, it was not permitted to be forgotten, but was transmitted to later generations through the proclamation of the word and the enacting of the signs of salvation. When the original eyewitnesses had died and heresies arose through which the meaning of Christ and his work was falsified or altogether denied, tradition assumed a special importance. In this situation it was necessary that the Church should transmit intact the faith which it had from Christ, which had been attested by eyewitnesses, in such a way that its historical identity with its origin should not be destroyed by fanaticism or gnostic speculation. As F. Mussmer has emphasized, we see this concern particularly in Mark's gospel, in the writings of Luke, in the pastoral epistles (2 Tim. 1,13f.; 2,2; 4,1f.), in the second epistle of Peter and in that of Jude, and in the epistles of John. Out of this abundance of material let us stress here only that according to the pastoral epistles the true tradition of the Christ-event is bound to the *successio apostolica,* the apostolic succession maintained by the laying on of hands, and to an understanding of the apostolic proclamation which is implied in a clearly defined doctrine. Paul, too, attached decisive importance to the identity of his message with tradition (1 Cor. 11,2; 15,1–5).

Of its very nature, Sacred Scripture is the authoritative medium for the preservation and development of sound doctrine. By the durability, clarity and fullness peculiar to it, it provides the objective condition for the preservation and proclamation of the message of salvation until the arrival of the absolute future. The authors of the Sacred Scriptures, of course, proclaimed God's word even aside from their literary activity. What they said took root in the congregations and was told to others. Human habits in passing on information to others being what they are, however, it must be presumed that some foreign elements slipped into the contents communicated by the apostles. Therefore it is difficult to discover in its pure form what was handed on apart from Scripture. In any case it is subject to Scripture as its norm, which in its turn is presented and interpreted by the Church. Furthermore the bishops, as successors of the apostles, have the task of distinguishing between genuine apostolic traditions and those which are simply human customs.

UNWRITTEN TRADITIONS

In recent years the question of whether there is an unwritten tradition which contains more than Scripture has been the subject of long discussion in the Catholic Church. The discussion took as its point of departure the definition of the Council of Trent concerning unwritten tradition. The council declared in 1546 (distinguishing traditions in matters of faith from other traditions of practice, such as fasting, the discipline of penance, liturgical rites, etc.):

The sacred, ecumenical and general council of Trent . . . has as its intention the preservation of the purity of the gospel in the Church, and the removal of error. This gospel, promised beforehand by the prophets in Holy Scripture, was first promulgated by our Lord Jesus Christ, the Son of God, himself, who then commanded his apostles to preach it to every creature, as the source of all salvific truth and moral order.

The sacred synod knows that this truth and order is contained in written books and unwritten traditions (*contineri in libris scriptis et sine scripto traditionibus*), which the apostles received from Christ, or which the apostles, inspired by the Holy Spirit, handed on, and which in this manner have come down to us, as it were from hand to hand.

Following the example of the orthodox Fathers, it receives and venerates with a like piety and reverence (*pari pietatis affectu ac reverentia*) all the books of the Old and New Testaments, since the one God is the author of both, together with the traditions themselves pertaining both to faith and to morals, as having themselves been received either verbally from Christ, or dictated by the Holy Spirit and preserved in unbroken continuity in the Catholic Church.[1]

The First Vatican Council speaks in the same vein. These texts of the councils were, until a short while ago, understood in Catholic theology in the sense of the Two Sources theory. According to this we can prove from unwritten tradition those truths taught by the

Church which cannot be demonstrated to be in Scripture. Therefore it does not matter too much if a dogma does not appear implicitly or explicitly in Scripture, since in any case the unwritten
tradition is available.

Theologian J. H. Geiselmann, with other scholars, has shown
that the Two Sources theory does not correspond to the intention of
the Council of Trent. According to his account of the proceedings,
two drafts were presented to the council fathers concerning the relationship between Scripture and tradition. The first stated that the
truth of the gospel is contained *partim in libris scriptis, partim in
sine scripto traditionibus*—that is, partly in the books of Scripture,
partly in unwritten traditions. This draft encountered vigorous
opposition. Therefore in a second text, the one accepted by the
council, the expressions "partim . . . partim" were eliminated
and replaced by an "et"—indicating, as Geiselmann points out,
that God's word is contained both in Sacred Scripture and in the
oral tradition. According to Geiselmann, the intention of the council was to a great extent misunderstood in the theology which followed the council, because the first draft had not been published,
and the change made by the council went unnoticed. Geiselmann's
opinions met with widespread agreement, although they did not
remain unopposed.

VATICAN II ON SCRIPTURE AND
TRADITION

The Second Vatican Council took the new problem very much
into account. It abandoned the Two Sources theory, which
conceives of Scripture and tradition as two possible sources of
knowledge running alongside each other without any necessary connection. The Dogmatic Constitution on Divine Revelation, #8–
10, says:

8. And so the apostolic preaching, which is expressed in a special
way (*speciali modo exprimitur*) in the inspired books, was to be preserved by a continuous succession of preachers until the end of time.
Therefore the apostles, handing on what they themselves had received,

warn the faithful to hold fast to the traditions which they have learned either by word of mouth or by letter (cf. 2 Th. 2:15), and to fight in defense of the faith handed on once and for all (cf. Jude 3). Now what was handed on by the apostles includes everything which contributes to the holiness of life, and the increase in faith of the People of God; and so the Church, in her teaching, life, and worship, perpetuates and hands on to all generations all that she herself is, all that she believes.

This tradition which comes from the apostles develops in the Church with the help of the Holy Spirit. For there is a growth in the understanding of the realities and the words which have been handed down. This happens through the contemplation and study made by believers, who treasure these things in their hearts (cf. Lk. 2:19, 51), through the intimate understanding of spiritual things they experience, and through the preaching of those who have received through episcopal succession the sure gift of truth. For, as the centuries succeed one another, the Church constantly moves forward toward the fullness of divine truth until the words of God reach their complete fulfillment in her.

The words of the holy Fathers witness to the living presence of this tradition, whose wealth is poured into the practice and life of the believing and praying Church. Through the same tradition the Church's full canon of the sacred books is known, and the sacred writings themselves are more profoundly understood and unceasingly made active in her; and thus God, who spoke of old, uninterruptedly converses with the Bride of His beloved Son; and the Holy Spirit, through whom the living voice of the gospel resounds in the Church, and through her, in the world, leads unto all truth those who believe and makes the word of Christ dwell abundantly in them (cf. Col. 3:16).

9. Hence there exist a close connection and communication between sacred tradition and sacred Scripture. For both of them, flowing from the same divine wellspring, in a certain way merge into a unity and tend toward the same end. For sacred Scripture is the word of God inasmuch as it is consigned to writing under the inspiration of the divine Spirit. To the successors of the apostles, sacred tradition hands on in its full purity God's word, which was entrusted to the apostles by Christ the Lord and the Holy Spirit. Thus, led by the light of the Spirit of truth, these successors can in their preaching preserve this word of God faithfully, explain it, and make it more widely known. Consequently, it is not from sacred Scripture alone that the Church draws

her certainty about everything which has been revealed. Therefore both sacred tradition and sacred Scripture are to be accepted and venerated with the same sense of devotion and reverence.

10. Sacred tradition and sacred Scripture form one sacred deposit of the word of God, which is committed to the Church. Holding fast to this deposit, the entire holy people united with their shepherds remain always steadfast in the teaching of the apostles, in the common life, in the breaking of the bread, and in prayers (cf. Acts 2,42, Greek text), so that in holding to, practicing, and professing the heritage of the faith, there results on the part of the bishops and faithful a remarkable common effort.

The task of authentically interpreting the word of God, whether written or handed on, has been entrusted exclusively to the living teaching office of the Church, whose authority is exercised in the name of Jesus Christ. This teaching office is not above the word of God, but serves it, teaching only what has been handed on, listening to it devoutly, guarding it scrupulously, and explaining it faithfully by divine commission and with the help of the Holy Spirit; it draws from this one deposit of faith everything which it presents for belief as divinely revealed.

It is clear, therefore, that sacred tradition, sacred Scripture, and the teaching authority of the Church, in accord with God's most wise design, are so linked and joined together that one cannot stand without the others, and that all together and each in its own way under the action of the one Holy Spirit contribute effectively to the salvation of souls.

With these statements the council did not answer all the relevant questions, but has rather left a number open. It is, however, of the greatest significance that it characterizes Sacred Scripture as the apostolic proclamation through which God's word is transmitted in a "special way." The formula "in a special way" does not refer to the contents but to the mode of tradition—i.e., the fact of its being written. The question of the content, on the other hand, was deliberately left open. The formula used presupposes that there is a mode of tradition to which the predicate of a "special way" does not apply. The council, with this thesis on Scripture, goes back to the apostolic proclamation. That means to him from whom everything comes: Jesus Christ. Furthermore, the tradition set down in a "special way" in Scripture is understood as embracing both the matter which is handed on and the act of handing it on. As regards the contents handed on, the council does not consider this restricted to doctrine: it embraces the whole life of faith. The act of handing it on—that is, the act of proclaiming Jesus Christ—awakens and promotes the living of the faith in daily life and in liturgical worship. It is the task of the whole people of God to deepen their faith and their life in the faith which they have received through the preaching of the word, and to hand it on to the next generation. The preaching of the official successors of the apostles plays a special role in this, which becomes clearer when we examine the connection between Scripture and tradition as set forth in the conciliar text.

Particular attention must be paid to the fact that the council puts Scripture and tradition in a twofold time relationship: in the past, the apostolic sermon; and in the future, the proclamation of the Church's teaching office. Scripture and tradition are not static and do not exist in their own right, but only in relation to their past and their future. It is said of sacred tradition that it transmits God's word intact to the successors of the apostles. "Tradition" here can only refer to the act of transmitting. This statement establishes an indissoluble connection between tradition and apostolic succession. We have already discussed this unity in the pastoral epistles. It was stressed later with the greatest emphasis by Irenaeus of Lyons against gnosticism, with its belief in secret traditions. Tradition, as we see here, is tied to the apostolic office. But the task did not end with the apostolic era, or when the canon was created—as if, from then on, Scripture interpreted itself. The task of handing on the tradition will continue until the return of Christ. In the meantime it is the writings collected together to form the canon which constitute the principal basis of the Church's preaching.

It is worthy of note that the council states that tradition has the function of deepening our understanding of Scripture and helping us to put its teaching into practice; that is to say, the act of handing on the tradition involves interpretation and explication of Scripture. We shall not err if we designate the function of the Church in handing on the tradition as one of interpreting and, even further, of explicating—i.e., of unfolding—Scripture.

This thesis can be understood more easily if we remember that it is the Church which has objectified its faith in writing the Scriptures; therefore it is also competent to interpret them. It thus continues on a new level what was already taking place in apostolic times, and before the word became Scripture: the interpretation of the Christ-event in such a way as to lead to a deeper and more adequate understanding of it. The difference lies in the fact that the interpretation which took place during the apostolic period has itself the character of revelation, while the post-apostolic interpretation does not serve to increase the scope of revelation itself, but only to interpret it. If the conviction expressed above is correct, that the original rule of faith was the core around which Scripture was fashioned, then the interpretation of Scripture by the Church is in a certain sense Scripture's interpretation of itself (F. Ratzinger), since the original rule of faith, as the objectivization of the kerygma and faith of the early Church, is the measuring rod for our understanding of Scripture. As the original rule of faith is sustained by the Church, the Church and Scripture mutually sustain each other. It is true that the Church can by no means decide what God should reveal; but it knows what it believes and can, therefore, say what its own Scripture means.

PROTESTANT AND CATHOLIC VIEWS

This statement is all the more important since it has now come to be accepted in Protestant theology that tradition is indispensable for explaining Scripture. Thus T. Althaus, for example, declares that there is no direct access to Scripture which could overlook or by-pass the history of the adoption of the gospel by the Church, and E. Kinder and H. Rueckert make similar statements. Admittedly they understand tradition more as the actual process of transmission than as the unfolding of the content of Sacred Scripture. But the latter idea also is advanced by several Protestant theologians of our time. Thus, for example, H. Diem asserts that there is such a thing as an authentic development of the teachings of Scripture. W. Pannenberg declares that there is an unfolding of the significance of the transmitted events by dogmatic doctrine.

The Catholic understanding of tradition, however, differs from these views in considering tradition to be binding on belief. The Church's interpretation creates something new—not a new revelation but a new understanding of revelation. The Church's interpretation is a kind of commentary on Sacred Scripture, so that Scripture comes to us in the interpretative form given it by the Church. This ecclesial interpretation is binding for the Catholic faithful. It can reach a greater degree of depth and lead to results of a kind which could not otherwise be attained. This may be said, for example, of the dogma of Mary's assumption. In such a case tradition, in the form of interpretation and thus having a declarative character, is in effect constitutive of our knowledge of this datum of revelation.

Catholic theology must come to grips with the question of how the development of Sacred Scripture by the tradition of the Church occurred; or rather, what inner connection there is between the knowledge of revelation gained through the Church's activity in handing on the tradition and the form of revelation in Scripture on which it is founded. This problem is among the most important and most difficult in Catholic theology. We will be confronted with it again in investigating the question of the development of dogma, and it is more convenient to postpone consideration of it till then. But let us emphasize at this point that the Church in the apostolic age accomplished its function of interpreting and developing tradition above all in the liturgy—that is, in prayer and in faithful association with its Lord.

The role of tradition was most closely connected with the celebration of baptism and the Lord's Supper. It was the expression of that experience of faith which the Church underwent in its religious services. Also, the text of the Second Vatican Council quoted above points to the efficaciousness of experienced faith for a deeper understanding of the Christ-event testified to in Scripture. Faith here is understood not simply as believing something to be true, a truth objectivized in statements, but as an encounter with Christ which takes place in religious, spiritual experiences. This view of it is the result of influences not only from the theology of Augustine and of the Franciscan school but also from the theology of Thomas Aquinas. To the latter we owe the phrase: "Ubi amor, ibi oculus." [2] Love, that is, gives us the power to see, even in the realm of faith. This no doubt leads to the conclusion that he who lacks love will not be able to see things which he who possesses the vision given by love sees. A reality which is visible only to the eyes of love therefore cannot be proved to him. Likewise, speaking purely logically, the connection between the original and the developed forms of revelation is not always strict. It need not be so. Thomas Aquinas expressed the same thought when he says that we need a certain *connaturalitas*—that is, an inner likeness between the knower and the thing known—for the knowledge of all human things, but that this applies particularly to religious realities.[3]

If we explain the relationship in this way, we must nevertheless keep in mind that it is always Scripture which is the object of the interpretation, and hence Scripture acts as a norm or criterion in relation to all religious experiences.

THE QUESTION OF THE SUFFICIENCY OF SCRIPTURE

Such reflections enable us to answer the question of the sufficiency of Sacred Scripture. If we mean by this phrase that Scripture offers us God's word in a plenitude sufficient for salvation, then we must ascribe sufficiency to it. Tradition does not contain any part of the contents of revelation which is not to be found in Scripture in one way or another. After all, tradition is only the unfolding of Scripture. Certainly tradition builds on the literal sense of Scripture and can only do so. The literal sense of Scripture is the indispensable foundation for the Church's development, interpretation, and explanation of Scripture. Scripture is sufficient in its literal sense. This thesis remains true even if, in the explication of Scripture by the Church on the basis of its spiritual authority, insights into the mystery of Christ can be achieved which are not to be found as such in the literal sense.

If we mean the word sufficiency to refer to the attainment of salvation, we must speak not of Scripture but of Christ. It is not faith in the word of Scripture, but only faith in Christ who acts through Scripture, which makes man blessed. Faith is not a nominal but a real process. It is not the affirmation of the credo, but the affirmation of the reality proclaimed by the credo.

Let us stress again that Scripture contains the whole of revelation. The sacred writers, above all the evangelists, were governed by the intention of writing down the whole content of God's word intact, to communicate it to their readers. Some of the contents of revelation, however, have been put down in writing only so far as the essentials are concerned, so that they can be clearly perceived in all their elements only through the Church's work of explication. Thus some of the content of revelation is contained, as regards the form of its expression, only in "tradition," while Scripture furnishes the foundation. This is true, once again, of the dogma of the assumption of Mary.

THE BEARER OF TRADITION

Who is the bearer of the Christian tradition? The Second Vatican Council provides a clear answer to this question: the entire people of God is its bearer. The faithful possess an instinct of faith—as it were, a spiritual sixth sense—by which they are able to judge whether or not a statement or an attitude is compatible with the mystery of Christ. It is true that the Church as a whole can determine the extent to which this sense of faith should be active in tradition only by coordinating and subordinating it to the teaching office within the Church. Thus, whereas it does not by any means play a merely passive role in the handling on of the tradition, it is not independent of the teaching office in the Church, to which the final decision is reserved.

In the course of post-Tridentine theology the opinion arose that a thesis universally held to be a truth of revelation by the people of the Church is demonstrated to be a truth of revelation by this very fact, and that such a general conviction can and must be looked upon as a source of tradition. But however active the part in religious tradition attributed to the whole body of believers, this activity of tradition nevertheless stands subject to a superior norm, namely Sacred Scripture. As examples from history show, we must reckon with the possibility that un-Christian, even anti-Christian, elements may enter into the Church and attempt to establish themselves with the power of authentic faith in Christ. Unless Sacred Scripture functions as a superior norm and the faith of the Church is subject to criticism by it, not only confusion of faith but human disaster results. This can be sufficiently illustrated from the superstitions which grew up among Christian peoples concerning witches, especially from the trials and executions which the unfortunate suspects were made to undergo.

Readings

Congar Yves, *The Meaning of Tradition*. Translated by A. N. Woodrow. New York, Hawthorn Books, 1964.

Geiselmann, J. R. *The Meaning of Tradition*. New York, Herder and Herder, 1967.

Notes

[1] Denz., 1501.
[2] *In Quattuor Sententiarum P. Lombardi Libros* III, 35, 1, 2.
[3] *Summa Theologica* II–II, q. 45, a. 2.

◄ 12

Dogma

Through the interpretation of Sacred Scripture which takes place in the process of handing on the Christian tradition (*traditio activa*) the historical continuity between the original source and the present is maintained. On the basis of Scripture a continuum of tradition is created; yet, at the same time the path into the future remains open, for God's revelation of himself can never be explained exhaustively in human terms. The Church will never complete this task; in carrying it out, she lives as a pilgrim on the way to the absolute future. Her explicatory role will be fulfilled only when Christ gives himself to man directly and in person and the need for the medium of Scripture and its explanation exists no longer. We encounter the climax of the Church's activity in the interpretation and explication of Scripture in what is termed dogma.

THE CONCEPT OF DOGMA

The word "dogma" in the sense in which we now use it has been current only since the eighteenth century. In the pre-Christian era the Greek word "dogma" was employed with a variety of meanings. It was used to designate a philosophical opinion, a rule—in particular a religious doctrine—God's decrees or simply the deci-

227

sion of an individual or of an assembly. In the New Testament the decisions of the so-called apostolic council (Acts 16,4) are called "dogma"; furthermore the laws of the Torah of the Old Testament abolished by Christ (Eph. 2,15; Col. 2,16, Rom. 14,20f.) as well as edicts of the state (Lk. 2,1; Heb. 11,23; Acts 17,7) are referred to by this term. In the time of the fathers, too, the word was used with various meanings. By the apostolic fathers the expression was employed in the sense of a statement or an authoritative declaration of the doctrine of the faith. According to Ignatius of Antioch the preservation and transmission of dogmas of the Lord and of the apostles are bound to the offices established in the Church. According to the *Epistle to Diognetes* the dogmas are not human wisdom but God's revelation. Vincent of Lérins is of particular importance in the history of this concept. For him dogma is a divine doctrine which is revealed once for all, and which was given as part of the deposit of faith to the entire Church, or the body of office-holders in the Church, to be guarded and preserved. Understanding of the dogma must grow; the dogma itself, however, remains unchangeable. Vincent of Lérins thus established a concept of dogma which we find recurring in the texts of the First Vatican Council—though not as a technical term. For the council states: "With divine and Catholic faith, therefore, all should be believed which is contained in God's written or transmitted word and which is presented by the Church in solemn decree or through common general proclamation to be believed as God's revelation." [1]

In the twelfth and thirteenth centuries the expression *articulus fidei,* article of faith, is used in the same sense as the word dogma. According to Thomas Aquinas, the one revealed truth must be divided into *articuli fidei,* articles of faith, for the sake of better understanding. Such an *articulus* contains three elements: the character of truth, salvific significance, and reference to the community—this last because it is put forward by the Church. An individual truth is an article of faith only if it is important for the whole of revelation. Thomas particularly stresses the meaning for salvation inherent in an article of faith. The assent in faith to such an article creates, he says, a resemblance in the believer to the First Truth himself; hence it is a step on the way to the direct vision of him.

According to present usage we understand by the term dogma a saving truth of revelation presented as binding on the belief of all, either by the regular and general teaching of the Church or by a solemn definition of the pope or a general council. This concept presupposes that a doctrine or doctrines are contained in God's historical revelation of himself. Behind the individual dogmas, however, stands the whole of revelation. To this the concept of dogma applies which we find in the apostolic fathers. The individual dogmas are particular articulations of this total dogma for teaching purposes.

Such a truth expounded out of the whole must, like the whole, be accepted on the authority of God revealing himself, and at the same time on the authority of the Church established by Christ —that is, with *fides divina* and *fides catholica*. A dogma represents an individual portion of revelation in a special form for teaching which the Church has given it. We can say: Dogma, in this sense, is the explication of Sacred Scripture in a special form of statement proper to the teaching office in the Church.

Let us not forget that the whole of revelation, of the Church's preaching, and of our faith constitutes the "dogma" of Christianity; that individual dogmas are only like certain mountain peaks standing out from the immense massif of the faith—often very important, but not always the most important. Christianity in any case is more than the sum of its individual dogmas. These have their significance only as members of the whole, and their place within the whole.

In Protestantism the term "dogma" has various meanings attached to it. In early Protestantism, when no teaching office in the Church was acknowledged, the self-sufficient Scripture became the foundation and norm of faith as far as content was concerned. Nevertheless the Trinitarian and Christological dogmas of the ancient Church were acknowledged as a binding testimony to the message of salvation. They distinguished between fundamental and non-fundamental dogmatic statements. Knowledge and acceptance of the former are necessary for salvation, but not of the latter. In the eighteenth and nineteenth centuries the concept of dogma was abandoned, only to enjoy a renaissance in the twentieth century in various forms. According to Karl Barth, dogma is the

agreement of the preaching of the Church at a particular time
with the revelation testified to in Scripture—that is, the preaching of
the Church insofar as it agrees with the Bible as the word of God.
The investigation of dogma thus has the task of examining the
conformity of the Church's preaching with Scripture, without,
however, reaching or being able to reach a result beyond the question of this conformity. Emil Brunner identifies dogma with the
Church's profession of faith and designates it as the norm of correct faith and correct doctrine. But in his view doctrine has no
obligatory force: it is only a finger that points towards Christ. According to Rudolf Bultmann every dogma is a metaphysical statement, and for that reason must be rejected. He includes the
Christological dogmas of the ancient Church, seeing them as "impossible" forms of expression for our modern way of thinking. The
Christian kerygma should be interpreted in each age in such a way
as to shed light on man's understanding of himself according to the
historical situation of his time, so that it assists man to achieve
authentic existence.

According to present-day Lutherans, dogma is a binding interpretation of the knowledge which is derived from faith, an interpretation gained from the message of Sacred Scripture. As regards its origin, dogma exists only in relation to the profession of
faith which is the Christian's answer to the preaching of the gospel.
As regards its essence, dogma is the ecclesiastical basis of Christian
doctrine. It is binding on all Christians in regard to their faith and
their life.

Paul Tillich's concept of dogma is farthest removed from the
thought of the original Reformers. "Dogma" is understood by him
as the Church's historical profession of faith, but he does not at-
tribute to it an obligatory character. The expressions "dogma" and
"dogmatics" are to be avoided because historically they are laden
with the idea of "dogmatic coercion" and "constraint of conscience"; they should be replaced by the term "systematic
theology." This, however, is to be restricted to existential interpretation of the meaning of being, and it should occupy itself only
with what concerns us unconditionally. It thus comes close to
philosophy, from which it is distinguished only by the fact that

whereas philosophy investigates reality in itself, theology investigates the meaning of being for man. In this theology the word or divine revelation hardly plays any part.

THE PROPERTIES OF DOGMA

From this description of the essence of dogma we can see its most important properties. The fundamental thing is its agreement with Scripture. It is the witness of Scripture in a later, more explicit form. It contains one aspect of the revelation of himself which God made once for all in Christ, and is therefore of divine origin as far as its content is concerned. If we say that the Church "makes" or "creates" dogma, this is an expression open to misunderstanding. The Church creates the form. The content is given to it in advance and is not at the Church's disposal. It is in creating the right form, however, that the task of the Church lies, because it must transmit the content in a comprehensible manner.

God's communication of himself to man was first made in a form comprehensible to its original recipients. But this form must be translated into new forms for men of other times, other cultures, other educational levels, and other ways of thinking. This presupposes that the content of God's self-revelation can be distinguished from its form. Without this presupposition, either there would have to be constantly new revelations, or else the word of Scripture would simply have to be repeated literally. Preaching and theology could only be either archaic or revolutionary. This presupposition is therefore fundamental if the identity of revelation is to be preserved during its development, and if genuine development is to take place within that identity. When the proclamation of Jesus Christ as the Messiah penetrated into the sphere of Hellenistic culture, it had to be made comprehensible to the men living in that region. After a long struggle decisive steps were taken in this direction at the councils of Nicaea, Ephesus, and Constantinople. In these centuries the Christian message encountered gnostic syncretism or syncretistic gnosticism, and Greek philosophy with its rationalism. A completely different type of thought prevailed in these movements from that in the Scriptures of the Old and New Testaments. In the Scriptures God's actions, his salvific presence in his people, were central. The question of his being belonged to the background. It was certainly an important question for the faithful, as we see particularly in Paul's writings. But it became urgent and a source of danger only when Greek ontology appeared on the horizon. Then the problem arose as to whether, perhaps, this Greek ontology could be of assistance in answering the question of who this Jesus was, to whose salvific action Scripture testified. As we shall see in considering the doctrine of the Trinity, the first attempts to convert the biblical testimony of Jesus' salvific function into ontological statements in terms of Greek thought led to serious errors. The most fateful of these was Arianism, which represented an almost complete Hellenization of Christianity. This danger of Hellenization was eventually overcome in Christianity out of the resources of the biblical faith, and yet without rejecting Greek ontology. The latter was taken instead into the service of the faith, and the question posed by Scripture and by the dynamics of the human spirit of who this One was whose saving power was affirmed by the faithful was answered by means of Greek ontology at the councils we have mentioned above.

The answer, it may be noted, was intended only to state who Jesus is, and in what relationship he stands to God and to us. A truth already contained basically in Scripture was expressed according to the modes of thought prevailing in the Hellenistic world. Subsequently many attempts were made to bring into a scholarly system the projection onto the ontological level of the statements in Scripture concerning Jesus's salvific action; the first to achieve this successfully was Thomas Aquinas.

When in the sixteenth century a new era began, marked by a new ferment in history, many questions had to be answered which until then had presented no problem for believers in God. At the present time reflection on the Church's dogmas is being integrated for theology through confrontation with the natural sciences and sociology, without neglecting the integrating function of philosophy and history. Ultimately it is not a matter of choice for the theologian whether he enters into these confrontations. They are essential for theology.

Just as the pre-existing eternal Word of God himself became incarnate in human nature, so the word of divine revelation has
translated itself again and again into new human ways of thinking
and forms of speaking. The explication of Scripture which occurs in
dogma takes place through that role of the Church which we call
active tradition. The result of this tradition is tradition in the objective sense of the word. Thus dogma is linked with Scripture by
means of the *traditio activa et objectiva*.

Since dogma is the expression of divine revelation, it is also the
expression of the faith of the whole people of God, of their response
to the divine self-revelation. In every dogma the entire people of
God professes its belief in Christ. It is a trans-subjective confession
of Christ, and thus also a Christ-doxology. One who rejects it rejects not only Christ but also the community of believers in Christ.

Dogma, as the objectivized form given in a particular culture to
the scriptural witness to Christ, participates in the uniqueness,
definitiveness, and universality of God's revelation of himself in
Christ. A dogma is an unconditional statement of truth and a definitive explanation of the faith. It is unchangeable as far as its content is concerned. This does not mean that dogmas are rigidly
static. In spite of their unchangeable core, they are in constant
need of new interpretation by the Church, and in this process they
are always in movement. In a dogma an individual truth of faith is
taken out of the whole and emphasized. The consequence of this
may be that it leaves its due place in the ordered whole of revelation, attaining a pre-eminence over other truths of revelation to
which it is not entitled and being seen in a distorted perspective.
When the gaze of the faithful is directed one-sidedly to an individual truth thus precisely formulated and stressed, a narrowing
and impoverishment of the faith can occur in which one particular
aspect absorbs all the attention. Furthermore, rationalism becomes
a danger, insofar as the believer can fall prey to the misapprehen-
sion that the element of faith in question has been fully clarified
for human reason by the formulation of the dogma. He may quite
forget what Paul wrote to the Corinthians on this subject (1 Cor.
13).

Dogma must not be removed from its personal connection with

Jesus Christ, for then it loses its meaning. Its purpose is to bring Jesus Christ to the attention of the faithful from a particular point of view. Since it always aims at Jesus Christ and demands surrender to him, it is not something which gives man the power to dispose as he likes of revelation. Therefore also dogma must be examined critically again and again from the point of view of Sacred Scripture, not as regards its core of truth, but as regards the position due to it in the whole, the weight it should carry, and the form in which it is expressed.

How important this can be both for doctrine and for piety we can see from the dogma which the Council of Nicaea defined concerning the metaphysical divinity of Jesus Christ, and also from the dogma which the Council of Trent defined concerning the (special) priesthood. In the first case the creation of the dogma, necessary as it was for the faith, led in practice to a view which suppressed the human element in Jesus Christ, so that the structure of Christian faith and prayer represented by the formula *"per Christum in Spiritu Sancto"* has suffered diminution (except in the Roman liturgy).

In the second case the strong emphasis on the special priesthood led to the neglect, even frequently to the forgetting, of the priesthood which has been entrusted to everyone who is baptized, and which was emphasized by Luther. Only at the Second Vatican Council, with its statement concerning the role of the laity, has this state of affairs been corrected. These examples could easily be multiplied. Thus every dogma, as time progresses, is newly comprehended, insofar as it is newly inserted into the general context of revelation. The individual dogma, in spite of its unchangeability, always stands in the critical light of the whole of revelation.

Very often the concept of dogma is associated with something rigid and immovable which rationalizes faith, imposes a burden on the faithful that is borne more or less reluctantly or at best indifferently ("coercion by dogma"), and threatens the freedom of the Christian. Let us make the following observations regarding these difficulties. Dogma gives a reliable orientation in a situation where faith is threatened; it sets up a boundary against error—i.e., against misinterpretations of the way to salvation. It shows the right way, and at the same time demands adherence to it. By its origin it represents in every case the end of a discussion which was frequently carried on passionately. What remained an open question in the Church until the dogma was established, although it was accepted without reflection as part of the substance of revelation, is brought to a definitive elucidation. At the same time, however, dogma is a beginning. If we remain with the metaphor of the road, we can say: It is like a map which enables us to plan the next stage of the journey. The statement of a truth of revelation in the shape of a dogma does not prevent us from giving to the statement an even more distinct and more intelligible form at a later time. Such an action, to be sure, can be undertaken only with great caution; but it is not simply impossible. On the contrary, it is a matter of necessity that the truths of revelation be embodied in a new way in new cultural epochs.

The defining of a dogma by no means ends discussion of the contents of the dogma. It does have the result that what has once been defined as true cannot later be declared untrue. But it also brings about a deeper and more comprehensive understanding of the reality presented in the dogma and of the whole area of faith surrounding the dogma. Usually it means that a new effort must be made to understand the entire foundation of the faith, Scripture, tradition, and the relationship of Scripture and tradition to the Church. The dogma of the bodily glorification of Mary, for example, made it clear that the relationship between the resurrection from the dead, which is the main promise of the New Testament, and the Beatific Vision needed to be examined more closely. Since this can only be done on the basis of the history of the problem, the dogma has led to the investigation of many questions concerning the history of theology which till then had claimed little attention. Further, it raised again the question of the relationship of body to soul. The dogma thus brought into being many questions outside its own immediate dimension—and not only marginal problems but questions central for theology and the kerygma. Ultimately it is the central kerygma, namely the Christological, on which the dogma has cast new light.

The formulation of a dogma is not a brake on the dynamics of

Christianity. It releases new currents and often intensive investigations. It brings about progress; yet it does not provide carefree certainty or fulfill a false desire for security; it leads to new efforts towards the goal of the future which is glimpsed on the horizon. For example, much that had been peacefully taken for granted concerning the doctrine mentioned above before it was defined as a dogma was shown to be open to question, and it is likely to be a long time before the stirrings which the definition produced come to an end.

Because of this dynamism dogma is not inimical to human freedom. First of all, it is obvious that it can be accepted only in freedom. True, it carries with it a demand for acceptance; but on the other hand, it would contradict the point of the demand if it did not challenge man's freedom and spur it to action. Principally, however, dogma is an aid to the right use of freedom. Freedom is, in the first instance, man's psychological and metaphysical capacity for responsible self-determination. This is a capacity not for acting arbitrarily but for acting correctly. If the right thing is not done with this freedom, it will issue in either useless or destructive activity. Freedom cannot exist without an object. It is of course a serious question—What is the right thing whose accomplishment justifies the free act and makes it worthwhile? If there is no unified opinion on this subject in our time, it is still obvious to the Christian that the right thing is whatever God wants done. That, however, is always what is worthy of man, both collectively and individually. The meaningful realization of freedom, therefore, is man's meaningful realization of himself. Dogma is God's communication of himself to man, as this is formulated by the Church, and therefore it makes a decisive contribution to man's realization of himself in his life in the world and for the world. Thus dogma, contrary to first appearances, has a fully human significance. It is an integral element of true humanism and of the humanistic unity of men. It helps to liberate man from the forces of egotism and hatred, which are hostile to freedom, so that he can work for the humanization of the world.

The linguistic formulation of dogma is conditioned by time, and therefore not unchangeable. It always takes place within a particular culture. As we mentioned above, the Councils of Nicaea, Ephesus, and Constantinople on the one hand, and the Council of Trent, on the other hand, drew up their statements in the conceptual world and the linguistic usages of Greek philosophy. The time-bound formulation can be supplemented or replaced by a new and better one. Since every conceptual and linguistic form of expression is naturally inadequate to express the content of revelation, every linguistic form can be replaced by a more perfect one. For the scholarly, theological explanation of a dogma, it is of the greatest importance to investigate the culture, and particularly the language, of the time in which the dogma took its origin.

In the translation of the linguistic expression into a new form, great prudence is always required. On the one hand we must observe the fact that the community of faith is always represented in a common form of language. A true community cannot endure a Babel-like confusion of languages. The common form of language is of great significance for the faith-community's sense of solidarity. On the other hand we must not forget that linguistic forms are transformed imperceptibly both outside and inside the Church in a mysterious process, and eventually to such a degree that what was formerly comprehensible to all becomes incomprehensible while the new language cannot yet express the old contents. The Church can guide this process to a certain extent, but the current of change is so strong that she cannot, in the long run, oppose it and must therefore seek new forms of expression for dogma if it is to continue to serve the preaching of the gospel. In addition it must be noted that owing to the way the attitude towards life varies among human groups, not all share the same kind of linguistic mentality. Pope Pius XII has touched on this problem with his statement concerning the "literary forms" which are in use with the Orientals. It is practically certain that for the people of the Far East, particularly the Indians, formulations of revelation in the conceptual language of Aristotelian philosophy are well-nigh useless. *Vice versa,* it would appear that not a few of the images in Scripture are readily intelligible to them without the type of reflection which we require.

A second point should be noted with regard to the process of change in language. As we have already said, the content and form of language should not be understood as separate entities; the relation between them is living and organic. A change in the form of language affects the content expressed, the ideas in the first place, but then what is meant by the ideas. Hence modifying the language can lead to altering the content of meaning, and an acute sensitivity is required if this is to be avoided. Nevertheless the Church may not evade the task of repeatedly translating Christian dogma simply because it contains this element of risk, for then it would be unfaithful to its mission.

THE ORIGIN OF DOGMA

A glance at the origin of dogma can help us to a deeper understanding of it. Dogma has its origin not in whims or imperialistic inclinations of the Church or Church authorities, but in a strong desire to protect and preserve God's revelation of himself and man's faith in it. When the preaching of the faith encounters the intellectual forces of the world, with its own cultures and forms of education, the result will always be a struggle. In the process, the danger is great that the faith may be radically misunderstood, even by persons of good will, because of their cultural and philosophical a prioris. History shows us how, from particular cultural spheres —for example, from the Hellenistic or the Germanic—intellectual forces issued which twisted and distorted the faith of the Church as it is expressed in Scripture. Such an occurrence is almost inevitable because of the one-sidedness of human nature. The word of Scripture is true, that there must be heresies (1 Cor. 11,19). J. S. von Drey, of the theological faculty of Tübingen, has said that it is a general human law that truth is completely known only through the conflict of opposites. In this view dogma, in comparison with other truths of revelation, is the final phase of a dialectic process caused by the conflicting movements of orthodoxy and heresy. J. A. Moehler has maintained that it is only against the background of the movements of error in history that full insight into divine revelation is obtained. Thus we owe to the unenlightened zeal for the law of the Jewish Christians the apostle Paul's presentation of the faith and power of the gospel. Likewise it is to the divisions in the Church in Corinth that we owe his important statements on the structure and the life of the Church; and to the Pelagian controversy, Augustine's doctrine of grace and subsequently that of the Church. These analyses show that heresy, too, has its significance, its place in God's salvific plan. Augustine declares: "Much indeed that belongs to the Catholic faith, when it is attacked by the passionate unrest of heretics, is more carefully considered, more clearly understood and more emphatically proclaimed, and so a question raised by an adversary becomes an opportunity for learning." [2]

In dogma the Church presents itself as a community in Christ. It pronounces, in a confession of faith in Christ, what all have always affirmed, either after reflection, or without reflection and unconsciously. In the transition from unreflected to conscious faith, dogma originates. Those who hold the office of teaching in the Church, in pronouncing a dogma of the faith, do not force on the Church a view which is accepted more or less willingly or reluctantly; as the representatives of the people of God, appointed by Christ, they announce that which the Church as a whole already believes. They do not stand above God's people in an attitude of command, but express the faith of the community within the community as members of it who officially represent it. Thus in its dogma the Church is reconstituted ever anew as God's people and as the body of Christ. In confessing Christ, the Church reaches its climax as event and as act. At the same time in a certain dimension, it binds itself anew to Christ. On the one hand dogma is the expression of the Church, on the other hand it constitutes the Church by giving explicit expression to an element of it which, though it existed before, now for the first time becomes clearly visible.

We see, then, that dogma is the result of a historical dialectic in belief. In dogma the Church, as the community of the faithful, asserts its faith in Christ in face of threats and dangers in a new formulation.

The formulation is done in a language which is removed from

that of error and shows the truth as contrasting with error. It is proclaimed by those who hold the office of teaching in the Church, but it expresses the faith of the entire people of God. The latter react against the dangers threatening faith with their own sense of the faith. Although the bearers of the teaching office in the Church are the divinely-appointed guardians of the faith, they do not proclaim a new faith, but that faith which has been lived, reflectively or unreflectively, by the entire people. They do not say anything different from what has already been believed, but they say it in a different way.

Since dogma is an expression of faith, and so of surrender to Christ, a salvific dynamism must be attributed to it. It is the Church's answer, an answer which possesses the power of salvation, to the Lord who is present in her and speaks uninterruptedly to her. We arrive, then, at the thesis that it is God himself who is at work in the declaration of a dogma. In dogma God, at a particular period of history, promises himself to man in a form comprehensible to him. The God who has given himself to man once for all and irrevocably in Christ affirms that gift again and again to the Church and her members in a new form. In dogma, then, the gift of himself which God has made once for all in Christ takes effect in the concrete, here and now. Dogma thus has an existential significance for man's salvation.

Although a dogma singles out a particular truth of faith from the whole, so that it can be seen clearly like a lofty peak jutting out from an extensive mountain range, still we must never isolate it from the whole. It is so closely connected with the whole of revelation that frequently we cannot delimit it with strict precision. It is living only as a part of the whole of revelation and can only be understood, in its meaning and importance, within the whole. Consequently we do not always know exactly whether or not a particular thesis should be considered a dogma. But this does not make any great difference, since faith is always a question of the whole of revelation. In addition it may be pointed out that according to the Code of Canon Law only those statements are to be considered dogmas whose dogmatic character is unambiguously certain.

Sometimes other motives than danger to the faith have led to the proclamation of a dogma. This is particularly true of the two most recent dogmas concerning Mary. Their *Sitz im Leben* is the liturgical worship of the Church, and they are an expression of piety. Even of these, however, the dogma of her freedom from original sin and that of her bodily glorification, it can be said that they are the result of a general situation dangerous to the faith. We might see in the first, in face of the growing secularization of the age, a proclamation of the primacy of the ethical and religious; in the second, in face of modern materialism, a proclamation concerning matter in its relation to spirit—namely, that the goal and destiny of matter lie in an absolute future which transcends this world.

THE ANALOGICAL CHARACTER
OF DOGMA

Although dogmas are statements of truth, they have value only as analogues of the reality itself. The meaning of this is that the ideas concerning God which we have developed out of our experience of life are much more unlike him than they are like him. The declaration of faith made in the dogma always remains inadequate to the richness of the kerygma, and even more so to that of the reality the kerygma proclaims. From this has been derived the so-called negative theology which asserts that we can say of God only what he is not, and not what he is; that into the structure of every one of our statements about God a negation must enter, inasmuch as he is not what we say of him in the same way that earthly things and circumstances are what we say of them. We shall see more of this in the section dealing with the Christian concept of God. At the beginning of our century Modernism tried to evade these problems by taking dogmas to be only symbols—so to speak, mere ciphers.

We need not totally exclude this understanding of dogma as a symbol of divine truth. For if it is rightly understood, such a description can make the analogical character of dogma more intelligible. The meaningfulness immanent in a symbol indicates a unity of spirit and form, and so it is possible to distinguish, in terms of the contemporary philosophy of language, between the meaning inherent in the symbol itself and the significance which is given to it. Human words are symbols insofar as man, as *animal symbolicum,* expresses and communicates spiritual content in words. As the physical objectivization of a spiritual insight, a word will to a greater or lesser extent, but always and necessarily, fall short of this insight. We would be missing the symbol-function of words if we saw only the words themselves and failed to consider them as inadequate expressions of something which can never be adequately expressed. The manner of thinking which makes absolutes of what are not absolutes is the mother of all false ideologies. On the other hand, a symbol would become empty of content if we saw in it only a cipher for something totally unknown, a statement with no concrete meaning whatever. It depends on the freedom of the concrete man what symbols—that is, what words—he chooses as forms of expression and communication. It may be that the chosen symbol (word) represents and communicates the spiritual content with a particular transparency, serving as a powerful vehicle which yet is never wholly adequate to the content.

Human imperfection enters into any expression of spiritual insight: poverty of language; one-sidedness; laziness; the desire always to be in the right; philosophical, theological, or other prejudices, etc. These considerations apply particularly in the case of the dogma of the Christ-event. In the first place we must say that the dogma of the Logos become man and of his salvific actions and words is the only valid expression of that inexpressible mystery, lying in the background of all that is, which we call God; but we must also say that the aforesaid imperfections enter even into this statement. That does not mean that there is a formal error in the dogma. Rather, the dogma is a protection against error; but it is so in the way of all that is human. For this reason dogma, as the human expression of divine truth, is subject to criticism and to alteration of form; and yet what is stated in the dogma is not by that fact simply caught up in the whirlpool of historical change.[3]

We can classify dogmas according to their importance, their contents, their formal or informal proclamation by the Church, and their relationship to human reason. The most important classification is the first mentioned. It is true that all dogmas are guaranteed by the authority of the Church. Formally speaking, they are all equally certain as far as their truth is concerned. But some are more significant for the whole of revelation and of salvation than others, just as one member is more important than another for an organism, although all are important. The truth concerning Christ stands at the center of revelation. The proclamation of the absolute future opened up by him is the most decisive. There is certainly no element in God's revelation of himself which is without significance for human salvation. However, in accordance with his creative love, God has taken abundant pains in his design for our salvation. We are therefore able to distinguish between those revealed truths whose affirmation in faith is necessary for salvation and those truths whose implicit affirmation is sufficient for salvation (*dogmata fundamentalia seu generalia* and *dogmata specialia*).

As regards the distinction from the viewpoint of relationship to reason, there are mysteries in the strict sense of the word and mysteries in the broad sense. The former cannot be known in any way by human reason through its own efforts. The latter, whose contents can be known by reason, are distinguished from mere truths of reason by the fact that their content is connected with revelation; and hence it is seen in a perspective different from that of a purely rational truth and affirmed by the Christian believer on another level.

THE PROBLEM OF THE DEVELOPMENT OF DOGMA

The question has arisen again with a new urgency: What is the relationship between the form of revelation presented in dogma and that given in Scripture? Protestant theology, unfamiliar with dogma in the sense of the foregoing discussion, views Catholic dogma with misgivings, fearing that it is a falsification of Scripture, an innovation in contradiction to Scripture.

It cannot be doubted that there is a development of dogma in the sense that both the Church's faith and its preaching have a history. For there are things now recognized as truths of faith which formerly were not explicitly proclaimed by the Church, or were differently conceived, or were not known at all. We must admit with regard to all the dogmas accepted by the Church, including those which Protestantism also acknowledges, that they cannot be found in Sacred Scripture in the shape in which we know them. This is true even for the ancient dogmas of Nicaea, Chalcedon, and Ephesus—a fact which is particularly significant for the ecumenical dialogue, because these councils are also largely accepted by Protestants. What, then, is the relation between the later faith and the earlier faith? Does the later only offer a new knowledge of truth, or does it offer a new truth; only a new form of the old truth, or the discovery of a new one? The distinction is by no means always easy to make.

In the background of these problems stands the much larger one concerning the knowledge of truth in general in relation to its history. Even universally valid principles are discovered at a particular time in history. Their content therefore carries the imprint of the understanding of life and the world, of being itself, which prevailed at that time, and the same thing is even truer of their formulations. Does the validity of a truth stand or fall with the act of discovering or forgetting it? Although the question of when and by whom it was first stated may be irrelevant to the validity of a truth, the knowledge of truth nevertheless has its own *kairos*. Not the validity but the recognition—the power of the truth to assert itself—is conditioned by history. Not every truth can be recognized and expressed at every time. This problem, which plays a role in historicism as well as in the present problem of the nature of history, will not be further developed here. It is only mentioned as the background of our theological question. It is evident from this background that it is a problem for theology, though within the larger context of cultural and intellectual history, and that the two are not without influence on each other.

In the first place it is the conviction of the Church that the development of dogma cannot be identified with the development of revelation. The Church not only makes no claim to receive new revelations, it explicitly rejects the idea. All opinions to that effect in the course of history have been repudiated by the Church: the views of the gnostics, of certain unbalanced enthusiasts of the Middle Ages, of the spiritualists and the theosophists. In the Middle

Ages, Joachim of Fiore (died 1202) proclaimed the beginning of a new epoch. His *Evangelium Aeternum* ("Eternal Gospel") divided history into three ages, corresponding to the persons of the Trinity: the epoch of the Father (the Old Testament), which had been the age of married and lay people; the epoch of the Son (the New Testament), which was the age of the clergy and that of monasticism in which Joachim was himself living; the new epoch of the Holy Spirit, which would bring a higher, spiritual understanding of the two Testaments.

Of considerable significance in this connection is the phenomenon of Modernism, which is still an issue at the present time. The word was first used in the sense of attempts to take the results of science and culture into account in theology without in any way damaging the faith. From the beginning of the twentieth century it has been used in ecclesiastical documents in a narrower sense, as a collective term for explanations of Christianity which contradict its true nature, especially those which understand dogma as the expression of man's religious experience of himself. According to the chief representatives of Modernism, Christian dogma began with the religious experience of Jesus. This gave inspiration to the religious sense of his disciples. Dogmas are later intellectual interpretations of man's natural religious sense, which arises from the depths of his subconscious. These interpretations were then approved by the Church and presented to the congregations. Dogmas in this view are in constant flux, like the experiences underlying them. Their function is to arouse the religious emotions which Jesus and his apostles had and which they communicated to others. If, owing to changed cultural conditions, they are no longer capable of that task, they have lost the reason for their existence. Dogma says nothing about God. God is completely unknowable by us. In support of this latter thesis well-known representatives of the Modernist movement refer in a rather biased way to the "negative theology" of the Fathers of the Church.

Against such views the Church emphasizes that there is something which remains constant in the development of dogma; namely, God's revelation of himself once for all in Christ, which is present in every generation. Yet something changes; namely, the mentality of the believer, in terms of which the unchangeable and the unique become present to him.

Just as the development of dogma must be distinguished from the development of revelation, it must also be distinguished from the development and history of theology. True, it is most closely connected with the history of theology, for the latter is its trail-blazer, and often its traveling companion. In theology, dogma is, so to speak, always ahead of itself. For there is no deeper insight into what has been revealed, no growth in the understanding of the faith, without that intellectual and spiritual effort which we call theology, since the Holy Spirit who is at work in the Church gives no illuminations regarding revelation. The difference between the history of theology and the development of dogma lies in this, that while theology makes dogma possible by deepening our under-standing of the faith, dogma itself is binding on the universal Church and is an obligatory norm for preaching and for faith—which cannot be said of theology. We must find an explanation, then, for the development of dogma which does not allow it to ap-pear either as history of revelation or as history of theology. It is less than revelation and more than theology, though both are essen-tially bound up with it. Dogma can only claim to represent revela-tion if it is nothing more than a new way of expressing God's revelation of himself in Christ. It differs from theology only in the fact that it gives a universal binding force to an understanding of the faith which has been developed through theological reflection and is expressed in theological concepts.

These statements mean that a dogma must be contained in that which was always believed and taught, even if it was not believed explicitly. This raises the double question: how it was contained in what was believed previously, and how it can be known to have been contained in it. Both questions are really different aspects of one basic problem.

When we looked at the process by which a dogma comes into being, we saw that there are two driving forces at work in it: on the one hand the dialectic in the understanding of the faith during the course of the Church's history, and on the other hand the forms of piety which develop likewise in the course of the Church's history.

As far as the first is concerned, the Church can only proclaim the word of God through an encounter in history with the world. This necessarily leads to intellectual difficulties. The world is not a vacuum into which God's word can flow without resistance, but an intellectual force with definite religious, social, philosophical, anthropological, and cultural conceptions. Frequently these will have a positive inner relationship to the Christian message, but more frequently there will be tension and antagonism between the two, and a struggle will then ensue which may last for centuries, and is often marked by violence. J. Metz has shown that there are, above all, two great universal horizons of human self-understanding which the Christian message encountered and which it had to deal with in order to be able effectively to proclaim Christ and the absolute future opened up by him. The first of these encounters took place, as we indicated above, when Christianity emerged from the cultural backwater of Judaism into the breadth and universality of Greek philosophy and education, where it met a highly developed culture. The encounter was all the more difficult as the Christian message was, structurally, a historical movement above all, while Greek thought centered on the essence of things and took upon itself every effort of conceptual thinking in order to penetrate this essence. Whereas the book of Genesis, in order to help solve the problems of life, told the story of God's dealings with men, the Greeks tried to penetrate into the meaning of the world and of human life through abstract thought. Therefore the Christian message had, so to speak, to be transformed from history into metaphysics. In this way there came into being a universal theology, which took account of the entirety of the world, and which both in Origen and in Augustine contained existential elements (*existential* and *existentiell*). The possibility of such a metaphysical theology was given with the fact that metaphysical questions were in the background of the historical events in which God revealed himself to man. Perhaps we may repeat an example we have already given several times—that of Paul, who, out of his experience of God's saving action, asked with passionate concern who this God was. He was in fact groping his way from the realm of history into that of metaphysics.

However important the theological process arising out of the encounter between the Old Testament experience of God and Greek
philosophy was for the universality of Christianity, it was at the
same time costly: the idea of history and what it implies lost its
force; history was reduced to a set of pictures used as examples of
abstract truths and principles. In the course of this process, many
objections, questions and contradictions arose against the Christian
message out of the intellectual milieu into which Christianity had
entered. We need only recall the situation in Corinth as described
in Paul's First Epistle to the Corinthians. Centuries of struggle
were required, before even the principal questions received a binding answer—namely, the relationship of the Old to the New Covenant, the being of Jesus Christ, and his relation to God and to men.
It was reached not through quiet organic growth, but by nothing
less than battle for the faith. Nor was it by any means clear from
the beginning what the result would be. The revelation present in
the consciousness of the Church—or rather, the Holy Spirit working in it—asserted itself through the free decisions of men. Thus the
decisions of the councils are forms of the biblical faith called for
by the times and conditioned by the times, arrived at by God's
grace in free human deliberation, even though they differ in no
small measure from the letter of the original faith.

Quite different was the intellectual horizon confronting the
Christian message at the beginning of the modern era, when the
consciousness of history and the natural sciences awoke. The
world was no longer understood as a static totality of relationships,
to be penetrated and clarified philosophically, but as a process of
development which extended both forwards and backwards in
time with an effect of staggering immensity. Luther himself in the
beginning felt history as a burden and attempted to shake it off by
dismissing as rank growth all that had developed in the Church between gospel times and his own—though he accepted the authority
of the ancient councils. Subsequently, however, the development
of historical and critical methods of investigation, to which Christianity was also subjected—above all, Sacred Scripture—resulted
in severe shocks which the Christian message and the Christian
faith had to withstand. The real significance of the situation which

was in fact characteristic of the whole of the modern era was not recognized by theologians until the nineteenth century, and full recognition has come only in the twentieth. In this process of historicization Christianity recovered an element of decisive significance for itself, since the whole character of the Christian revelation is historical. But outside the Church the rediscovery of history resulted in the loss of many elements from the content of the Christian faith which had been preserved till then. The Church tried to save these in a series of dogmas.

Although the main stimulation for the creation of dogma comes from such confrontations with the broad horizons of man's understanding of reality, we must not underestimate the motives deriving from piety. The life of devotion does not move in a timeless sphere of mystic interiority; meditation, as well as the exterior life of the Christian, derives its character from the attitude towards life which marks a period of history. As there are no ahistorical men, neither is there an ahistorical piety. Furthermore, although it is as the consequence of human freedom and not of an irruption of the divine that dogmas are drawn from the liturgical life of the Church, nevertheless even here the Holy Spirit lets his voice be heard.

Let it be added here in passing that it is not within the province of theological speculation as such to establish dogma. It does not have the inner dynamism for that purpose.

DEVELOPMENT AND IDENTITY

How should we explain the connection between dogma and the faith that preceded it? Theologians try to answer this question in various ways. Working with the concepts of the explicit and the implicit, they explain dogma as the making explicit of what is already present implicitly. Again there are different opinions about this. Most of them are concerned with the intellectual level only, while others take into account the entire man with all his powers. Some of the most important attempts will be mentioned here. According to one opinion dogma is always contained formally, even if not explicitly, in Scripture. It is the conclusion, defined by the Church, of a logical deduction in which both premises are truths of revelation. Those who hold this view maintain that the conclusion must also be acknowledged as having been formally revealed. A second opinion states that a truth may be defined as belonging to revelation if it can be arrived at by a syllogism in which the major premise is to be found formally in Scripture while the minor premise is a natural truth—i.e., one known by reason or experience. The natural knowledge expressed in the minor premise has the sole purpose of unfolding the content of the major premise drawn directly from revelation. Therefore the conclusion also must belong to the content of revelation. The truth expressed in the conclusion is said to be virtually revealed.

These theses find their supplement nowadays in the observation that in Sacred Scripture God wishes to reveal not only what is directly expressed (*das unmittelbar Gesagte*) but also what is said indirectly (*das Mitgesagte*). Every statement, it is said, has an inherent dynamics which contains not only what is formally expressed but also what lies within the sphere of what is expressly said. Whereas we human beings can never anticipate the consequences of our speech, God himself deliberately wills to communicate the totality of that which lies within the sphere of what is expressly said in Scripture. The connection between what is directly stated and what is indirectly stated need not be strictly logical. Yet it may be seen so clearly—for example, in the case of statements expressing a personal relationship—through the eyes of love that he who sees it has no doubt about it.

Against this explanation the objection has been raised that while such indirect statements are no doubt closely connected with revelation, they cannot be called revelation itself, because they are only derived from revelation. However, let us not overlook the fact that human thinking only serves to develop more fully the truth which God has communicated to us. The result is not a human but a divine truth which has simply been singled out of the totality. We can make the point clearer perhaps through the following reflection. Divine revelation can only reach us, as we saw, by asserting itself in our consciousness. It aims at becoming present in our consciousness. It is by no means identical with our consciousness of it, but without human consciousness revelation can have no existence.

Thus it is only through our understanding of the faith that divine revelation, in spite of its uniqueness, can be present and effective in mankind.

Our natural human knowledge offers a parallel to this phenomenon. As we know from the endeavors of centuries of philosophy, reality in itself is inaccessible to us. That objectivism which assumes that we can know truth in itself, as if it were static reality, is no longer tenable even outside the sphere of theology. The world in which we live is always a synthesis of what is objectively given and our own act of knowledge. Likewise revelation is accessible to us only in our understanding of it, in the faith which is born of proclamation and makes profession of itself in proclamation. This is all the more true because even after his revelation of himself God remains for us an impenetrable mystery. He always remains greater than our knowledge of him. We can know him only by means of analogous ideas and concepts. The more man opens himself to God, the more intensive and extensive can be the unfolding of his analogous knowledge of him; and so man's consciousness can increasingly be filled with God's communication of himself and stamped with the divine imprint.

There is no essential difference between these processes and the knowledge which we obtain when something implicit in revelation is stated explicitly—that is, when new elements are perceived in the inexhaustible complex of God's self-communication. As long as this is done only by an intellectual process, we lack, it is true, the ultimate certainty which faith needs. Something must be added to the purely logical function of explication. This is to be found in the vital experience which man can have in the encounter with revelation, whereby he is given a power of vision by which he sees more than another person; through it he can gain a conviction which is unshakable, even though it is not reached by a logical process.

To this must be added as a decisive factor the preaching of the Church. Although it does not explain the kind of connection that exists between dogma and the form of faith which preceded it, it nevertheless testifies to the reality of such a connection.

We must beware of understanding the idea of explication as simply the elaboration of the literal meaning of Scripture, so that exegesis could or must offer a genuine proof for a dogma. Explication can lie beyond the results achieved by exegetical scholarship. Exegesis would become unfaithful to its scholarly methods if it tried to say more than it can attain by philological and historical means. Pope Pius XII has stated that it is the primary duty of biblical scholars to establish the literal meaning of Sacred Scripture. Leo Scheffczyk rightly says: "In many cases it will only be possible to demonstrate in Scripture the starting-points, the traces, and the organic seeds out of which the dogma slowly developed. However, we must always bear in mind that often the way in which these truths are found in their scriptural context is quite different from that in which they have developed in the soil of systematic thinking, so that they may be difficult to recognize in the later dogma." [4]

It would be of little avail to refer, for an explanation of the connection between dogma and Scripture, to the *sensus plenior* which is often mentioned in biblical scholarship. The term *sensus plenior* means a sense of the Scriptures which contains more than is expressed by the simple literal meaning. The reason adduced for the assumption of such a fuller sense of Scripture is that the Holy Spirit in inspiring the sacred writers was able to say more through their words than they themselves knew. That is incontestable, but the question remains of how this "more" can be known. Obviously only by progress in man's understanding of the faith. That is to say, however, through the Church's or the individual's work of explication. We know that the Church's word of explication is nothing but its activity as the voice of tradition. In this form of Sacred Scripture explicated by the Church, we no longer have the original statement. So we are still left with the same question, how to explain the connection between the explicated form of Scripture and its original form. It is precisely this question which needs to be answered. The assumption of a *sensus plenior* poses the question but cannot answer it. We cannot overlook the fact that none of the theories put forward so far suffices to prove a strictly logical connection. But that seems to be unnecessary. Both the inner illumination of the Holy Spirit—i.e., the a priori of grace—and the testimony of the teaching office of the Church guarantee the connection. We would not be doing justice to the Church's intention in defining a dogma if we understood her decision as a purely ecclesiastical decree concerning a truth, and not as the proclamation of a truth of revelation binding on belief. For the implication of ecclesiastical positivism contained in the former view would be scarcely defensible.

In the last analysis the problem of the transition of revelation—without being changed in itself—from the form of Sacred Scripture to that of a new understanding of the faith for which scholarship cannot satisfactorily account exists in the same chiaroscuro which environs the problem commonly called that of the analysis of faith.

When the Church is confronted with the complex of problems concerning the development of dogma, what it is really faced with is the broader context of human cultural and intellectual history. We can call it the contrast between relativistic historicism on the one hand and metaphysical objectivism on the other, or between anti-philosophical biblicism on the one hand and evolutionary progressivism on the other.

In explaining the development of dogma we must not forget that behind the human struggle stands the magisterium of the Holy Spirit. It is he who invisibly sustains the process by which the understanding of revelation continues to deepen in the Church. It is he who brings it about that the understanding of the faith develops to a definitive truth and clarity by wrestling with contradictory views.

Since the Church has to proclaim the message of salvation until the end of time, and the absolute future until its arrival, she will never cease to wrestle intellectually with the challenge presented by the world; and so likewise the Church will never cease to create dogma. In this respect also the Church must remain open to whatever the future may bring. She is the pilgrim people of God, who in the course of her wanderings unceasingly hears the voice of Christ, present within her, and yet calling to her from the future; and in refusing to listen to other voices, she gives answer out of her own faith, an answer which to all her children is clear, instructive, and binding.

Notes

1 Denz., 3011.
2 Sermon 51, 11.
3 Cf. L. Bejerholm—G. Horning, *Wort und Handlung* (Gütersloh, 1966);
J. Splett, "Glaube und Dogma," in *Stimmen der Zeit,* 92 (1967), 182–190;
R. Guardini, *The Life of Faith* (1963).
4 In E. Neuhäusler—E. Gösmann, *Was ist Theologie?* (Munich, 1966),
202.

‹ IV

Theology in the Church
and for the Church

‹ 13

The Necessity and Nature of Theology

FAITH AS THE ENTELECHY OF ANY THEOLOGY

We turn to the last complex of problems in this first part, intended as it is principally to lay the foundation for what follows: namely, to the explanation of theology—that is, the scholarly endeavor to understand what is communicated through God's revelation of himself, the Church's proclamation of it, and its acceptance and affirmation in faith, an endeavor not devoid of salvific significance in itself. The necessity of theology derives from the nature of revelation, from the nature of faith, and from the nature of the human mind. Revelation, as God's communication of himself, contains in itself an inexhaustible dynamism whereby it asserts itself increasingly in human consciousness. Faith, for its part, is not simply an act, it is concerned with a particular content which must be understood. Faith has genuine value only insofar as it is related to reality. As regards the human mind, it is constructed dynamically insofar as it has a natural tendency to penetrate more deeply into reality. This tendency does not depend on man's free choice; it is part of his nature and belongs to his self-realization. Add to this that the human mind, although capable of dealing with a multitude of different things, and of acting on different levels, nevertheless

257

has a need for unity and order which urges man to link up his faith with the rest of his experience of life and the world.

Faith and reason, then, go together. Faith is impossible without some measure of understanding and of experience, and so understanding is a necessary part of its existential structure. Understanding is not something incidental added to faith from outside. It belongs at the heart of faith.

It can exist in different degrees. Paul boasts of his understanding of Christ (Eph. 3,1–5), a type of understanding which can be called charismatic theology. This kind of theology did not die out with Paul, any more than charisms ended with the apostolic age. The Holy Spirit, the foundation of charismatic gifts, is always active in the Church. The permanent importance of the charisms is brought out by a sentence of Paul's to the Thessalonians (1 Thess. 5,19): "Do not quench the Spirit."

The word theology means, according to its etymology, *logos*— that is, speech about God. Speech about God only exists, however, as an answer to God. Therefore, in theology God is subject in the first place, and only secondarily object.

The acceptance of God's word to man takes place in faith. Theology, as the understanding of God's word or as an understanding answer to God's word, must first of all try to explain what it understands by "faith." We do not wish to go into that in detail now. It will be discussed in theological anthropology. We are concerned here with faith insofar as it is the foundation of theology.

What is called faith in the New Testament appears in the Old Testament under various names; as the acceptance of God's revelation of himself to the people of Israel, as the affirmation of the covenant with God in thought and deed by obedience, confidence, and faithfulness. In the New Testament faith means both assent to truths in the sense of statements and confidence in and obedience to the God who revealed himself definitively in Jesus—the acceptance of God's unique salvific action in Jesus. In this sense faith is a unity of act and content. This fuller form of faith as the act of accepting the kerygma could, of course, only develop after the resurrection of Jesus Christ and the sending of the Holy Spirit. For only then was the message of Jesus' life, death, and resurrection understood as a message concerning events decisive for salvation. Only then was the original bearer of the message recognized as the substance of the message itself, the revealer as the revelation, the one who preached as the one to be preached. We cannot analyze in any detail here the differences between the various writings of the New Testament in their understanding of faith, except for a word about Paul and John. For Paul faith means obedience, but also knowledge of the new situation which has developed in human history. It includes a new understanding of man, insofar as he understands man in terms of Christ. Faith means therefore: to know God, to know the truth, to obey God and so come to share the salvation brought by Christ; to have hope, as a result, in the absolute future. For John faith means: to come to Jesus. Thus it is a living union with Jesus. It enables one to see, to hear, to recognize. In faith man passes over from the sphere of death to that of life. According to John also, faith has an eschatological orientation towards the future.

During the period of the fathers, faith was frequently interpreted as true gnosis, the true philosophy; that is, principally as an intellectual process. Augustine's ideas on faith cover a broad field. Of significance for our purpose here is his conception of the personal character of faith, in the sense of an encounter with God, and also as a means of arriving at deeper knowledge. As we will shortly need Augustine's concept of faith in another connection, let us quote an important text from his sermons on the gospel of John:

Therefore, do not seek to understand in order that you may believe, but believe, in order that you may understand. For "unless you believe, you will not understand." If you wish to have the possibility of understanding, it is my advice that you must first have the obedience which consists in believing. And we find the Lord saying: "Whoever has the will to do the will of God will know my teaching." What does it mean, "he will know"? It means, he will understand. But what is the meaning of "Whoever has the will to do the will of God"? It means, to believe. That he will know, or have understanding, is something all will understand. But what he says about "Whoever has the will to do the will of God," that this refers to believing, so that it will be possible to understand better—we need the Lord himself to tell us whether doing his will means believing. . . .

But the Lord himself says clearly elsewhere: "This is the work of

God, that you believe in him whom he has sent" (Jn. 6, 29). "That you believe in him," not "that you believe him." But if you believe in him, you do believe him; on the other hand the fact that you may believe him does not necessarily mean you will believe in him. For even the devils believe, and yet they do not believe in him. . . .

What does it mean then, to believe in him? By faith to love him, by faith to commit yourself to him, by faith to enter into him and be incorporated in his body. This is the faith which God demands of us.[1]

These distinctions pointed out by Augustine have largely become an established part of theology.

During the age of scholasticism the attempt was made to carry out a psychological analysis of faith. According to Thomas Aquinas faith is a graced participation in God's own knowledge. Man is called to the vision of God. Faith is the way to this goal, and must therefore in principle be of the same nature as the vision of God. Thomas therefore sees it as that condition of the mind in which eternal life begins in us, an act by which the intellect gives its assent to him who is now invisible, but the direct vision of whom in the future constitutes the destiny for which man was created. Faith represents for man, then, an anticipation of his absolute future. Man believes on account of truth, and only on account of truth. But grace is the indispensable inner a priori of faith. Thomas describes it as "light" and "instinct." The light of faith creates certainty, a certainty founded not on evidence but on the experience of a value. Faith has a social structure: it is tied to a community. The Church itself is the transindividual subject of faith. The individual has faith insofar as he freely enters into the subjectivity of the Church and remains in it.

At the time of the Reformation, the elements of trust and surrender were emphasized by Luther, but it was not long before doctrine was stressed again. The Heidelberg Catechism explains faith as knowledge, assent, and trust.

In the period following the Council of Trent attention was given on the Catholic side chiefly to the objective aspect of faith, its content, particularly in defense against Descartes' thesis that assent can only be given to what is evident. Catholic theology therefore attempted to prove the evident character of God's truthfulness, the possibility and the fact of a supernatural revelation, the reliability of Sacred Scripture, and the establishment of the Church as the mediator of the divine message of salvation. On the Protestant side less attention was given to the object of faith than to its subjective side, its character of trust or confidence.

In modern theology discussion of the nature of faith occupies a central position. The problems connected with it have also received much attention from philosophy (Jaspers, and recently some of the analytic philosophers). The main question is whether faith has a truth-centered or a personal structure—i.e., whether it is an affirmation of certain statements or an affirmation of the "thou" of a fellow-human being. This distinction is not accidental. It has its roots deep in the historical soil from which Christianity took its origin. This is an instance of the problematic created when the biblical message with its I-Thou structure encountered Greek thinking with its object-subject structure, or in other words when the existential met the ontological, and had to fit itself into it.

We can distinguish these two forms of faith as "It" and "Thou" faith, or as "That" and "Thou" faith. At present the conviction is correctly maintained that faith should above all be interpreted as "Thou" faith. This kind of faith is preponderant by far in Scripture, although it is not the only form of faith to which Scripture testifies. In "Thou" faith man grounds his existence in the "Thou" of the person he encounters. This faith renders possible and produces that special form of human knowledge which surpasses the knowledge of things (H. Fries). As man is essentially fellow-man, and as his existence can only be understood and lived as coexistence, faith, in which he bases himself on his fellow-"thou," is the actualization of his own deepest existence as a person. (At the same time it cannot be denied that some understanding of being— that is, the relationship between subject and object—also belongs to man's nature. It would be one-sided to overlook this.) If he believes in Jesus in this way, and so grounds his existence in Jesus Christ, through the a priori of grace, he realizes himself in the manner demanded by the core of his personality. That form of existence then arises which Paul describes by the formula "to be in Christ." This faith is not only the expression of the personal structure of man but also reacts on him. What occurs here is what Augustine meant by the words: I believe "in" you. Christian faith is believing "in" God. However, since God has appeared in history in Christ, faith in God is also faith in Christ. The structure of faith in God is such that God is reached through faith in Christ. Faith in the "Thou" includes faith in the "It," insofar as it includes an affirmation of what the "Thou" says. In fact, without this affirmation, faith in the "Thou" can scarcely be said to exist.

In the present context one more problem remains to be discussed, the question of the so-called *analysis fidei*. The problem is as follows: Faith is founded on God's testimony to himself. From this fact comes its absolute certainty. The question, however, is how the believer can become certain that God is giving this testimony, this revelation of himself. If we say: because of its credibility—that is, by the demonstration of God's truthfulness and of the fact of divine revelation—the difficulty arises that by this method only a *fides scientifica* can be attained. This consists in reaching the conviction, on some good grounds, that the witness is reliable, and on the basis of this conviction accepting his judgment. This act of acceptance rests, then, on our own judgment about the reliability of the witness. If religious faith were sustained in the same way, solely on the judgment of the believer concerning grounds of credibility, it would be based not on God's authority but on human insight and would share in its weaknesses and deficiencies. We could attain the absolute certainty of faith only by means of an act of the will or the emotions. In its last phase faith would then be irrational. But if we believe by an act which omits reasons of credibility, and is thus based on God's authority alone, then again faith is an irrational act.

The attempts made so far to solve the problem can be divided into two groups. Within each group, again, the attempts at a solution show considerable variations. The first (Thomistic) group declares that God's authority, on which faith rests, is not obtained in support of an alleged revelation by proving its credibility, but enters the consciousness of man in the light of faith—i.e., in God's gift of himself to man—without the light of faith itself becoming an object of consciousness. In this light, it is claimed, the support of God's authority becomes immediately recognizable to the human mind. The second main view disregards the light of grace in the act of faith. It declares that logical or scientific faith—i.e., faith based on reasons of credibility—is a prerequisite which makes God's authority clear in regard to the matter in question; as soon as it is seen that the alleged revelation has God's authority, the logical basis is no longer needed. Faith is then founded directly on God's authority, not on our human knowledge of God's authority.

The problem is not likely to be satisfactorily solved as long as we understand faith exclusively as an "It" faith. The situation changes when faith is understood as "Thou" faith. In the latter, the believer is one with him in whom he believes. Faith in Christ is thus the expression of that existential structure which Paul speaks of as "being in Christ." This faith is ontogenetically founded on a decision for Christ occasioned by reasons of credibility. The reasons of credibility are not understood in this case as elements of proof, but as signs of a loving and effective presence. Logically the certainty of this faith is based on the believed "Thou," Jesus Christ, in whom God himself is present. This faith is an existential union with Christ, which can be considered under different aspects. One of its aspects is community of thought with Christ—community, that is, in regard to Christ's proclamation of salvation.

Finally it must be remembered that faith represents an altogether new beginning, which can neither be derived from previous premises nor accounted for in terms of purely rational elements (Seckler).

THE NATURE OF THEOLOGY

We said earlier that theology is faith insofar as it understands itself. It is understanding Christ, thereby understanding God, and thereby again human self-understanding. This very general description of theology is true for all theological disciplines, although it can take many different, even contradictory, forms. The subject matter of theology is full of tensions. If this has become more evident in modern times than it was formerly, it is not due to a regrettable decline in theology, but to a vital relationship of theology with reality and events.

To repeat something already said frequently, but which is still decisive: the self-understanding based on the understanding of God and Christ is not gained by a purely actualistic step into the transcendent, but only by looking to God's self-revelation, which reached its climax in Christ but will attain its definite fulfillment only at Christ's second coming; thus in looking forward to the absolute future which awaits us.

We find theology, in the sense of the attempt to understand and interpret revelation, already in Sacred Scripture—that is, in the apostolic era. It has therefore the warranty of Scripture that it is legitimate and cannot be touched by the allegation that it is an expression of human pride. Not only this, but both the theological interpretation of the Old Testament given by Jesus Christ and the theological interpretation of Jesus as the Messiah carried out by the apostles through the Holy Spirit belong to revelation itself. In this case, and only in this case, theology and revelation are identical. The Church also continues to develop theology in interpreting, explicating, and proclaiming Sacred Scripture. The Church's interpretation rests on divine self-revelation and its interpretation through the Holy Spirit within apostolic times: it is no longer revelation, but understanding of revelation.

We are concerned here with that form of theology in which an individual engages—not, to be sure, in isolated seclusion but as a member of the Church. We speak therefore of theology pursued by the individual within the Church and for the Church.

For a proper understanding of the matter, some knowledge about the term itself is needed. In Greek antiquity Plato and his disciples called "theologians," and criticized, those poets and philosophers who offered a mythical explanation of the world in sagas and stories about the gods. This criticism opened up the way from the world of myth to that of the logos. Aristotle developed this terminology beyond the application to myth and called metaphysics (the "first philosophy") "theology," to differentiate it from natural philosophy and mathematics. Thus ontological theology, in the Greek understanding of ontology, was introduced. Being (the God of the philosophers) became the end and goal of the "first philosophy," which has for its object Being from the point of view of its being, which makes statements on its original conditions and first causes, proceeding to the proof that there is a very first thing on which heaven and earth depend (G. Soehngen). The Stoics called every endeavor concerning God in the three dimensions of mythology, philosophy, and state cult "theology," and theologians "heralds of God."

Christian thinkers used the expression at first in a negative and critical sense to designate pre-Christian ideas about the gods. As was the case with other central expressions, this word had to go through profound transformations of meaning before it could find a home in Christianity. With Clement of Alexandria, and even more with Origen, the way was paved for the positive Christian use which we find fully developed with Eusebius of Caesaria in the fourth century. Theology, according to him, is the doctrine concerning the true God and his Christ. The fathers of the fourth century began the custom of calling the doctrine of the Trinity "theology," and that about Jesus' work of salvation "economy." But Theodoret of Cyr (fifth century) used the word also for the doctrine about salvation. In the regions of Latin language, it was not until the period of early scholasticism that the word received its Christian sense. Augustine speaks of the *sacra doctrina,* of *scientia, sapientia, ratio* or the *sermo de Deo.* In the Middle Ages theology is frequently called *sacra pagina* or *sacra scriptura.* The designation of theology in those terms was due to the fact that theological writings were, for a long time, explanations of Scripture. This manner of expression was still used when theology had long gone beyond the interpretation of Scripture and was attempting to do justice to its task by using philosophy.

For the acceptance of the word "theology" in the Latin world, the translations of the works of pseudo-Dionysius (the Areopagite) were of considerable influence. Particularly Abelard, with his *sic et non* method, made use of the expression. In the course of the twelfth and thirteenth centuries the word asserted itself more and more in the sense of "the science of the faith." The other designations used till then were replaced only in a slow process during the fourteenth and fifteenth centuries.

If we say that theology is a special manner of understanding the faith, we must add that it is distinguished from the understanding constitutive for "simple faith" not by greater rational insight but by methodical procedure—namely, by the application of those methods of research which are appropriate to its object. Such endeavors to understand the faith can lead to the development of *rationes necessariae,* as Anselm of Canterbury says—i.e., that the inner relationships of the elements of faith with each other and with the ultimate meaning of human existence are revealed. The First Vatican Council comments: "Reason enlightened by faith, when it searches with diligence, fervor and modesty, does indeed obtain a certain understanding of the mysteries (of faith), by the gift of God, and an understanding which is most fruitful, both by analogy with the things it knows naturally, and also from the connection of the mysteries with one another and with the last end of man." [2] As theology on the one hand is *understanding* of the faith, it is on the other hand understanding and knowledge of *faith.* Faith is a constitutive element of this discipline. In theology it is faith that seeks for understanding (*fides quaerens intellectum*). Faith is not only the point of departure but also the center and the goal of theology. The theologian consequently, in all his theological endeavors, is engaged in an activity which is salvific. Theology is an exercise of faith. It can, therefore, never be completely separated from proclamation, although the two are not identical. Faith can never be developed into a philosophical system by theology. However far believing reason can penetrate the contents of revelation, and however great its progress in knowledge may be, it cannot, either by acute investigations or by ingenious intuitions, be transformed into a set of rational truths. Let us quote the First Vatican Council again: "But it never becomes capable of seeing them directly, in the way it sees those truths which constitute its proper object. For the divine mysteries by their very nature so surpass the created intellect that even when they have been communicated in revelation and accepted in faith, they still remain veiled in the obscurity of faith, as it were in a mist, so long as we are in pilgrimage from the Lord in this mortal life; for 'we walk by faith and not by sight' (2 Cor. 5,6f.)." [3]

It is true that faith exists for the sake of future vision. But within history God, although he is the transcendent depth or the transcendent center of man, cannot be seen but can only be experienced as a reality which is hidden, yet present and powerful. (As we have already noted, Luther in his *theologia crucis* gives a strong expression to his sense of God's hiddenness.)

Faith exercises a double function in theology. First of all, it provides that inner relationship to the thing that theology is concerned with: God. Secondly, it chastens human knowledge. We must not forget that in his present condition man is always sinful, even when he is neither atheistic nor anti-theistic. His sinfulness also affects his relation to God in the sphere of knowledge. It is true that we cannot understand how a sinful attitude clouds man's vision of God. But we cannot doubt the fact. With Augustine, the whole of later theology assumes that faith exercises a chastening and cleansing function with regard to the knowledge of God.

It is implied in these reflections that theology is not only a matter of the interpretation and systematic co-ordination of concepts, but that it is a question of explaining reality—that is, God—with the help of concepts; that is, theology is not merely a nominal but a real science.

THE "OBJECT" OF THEOLOGY

The question has been frequently discussed: Under what aspect is the theologian concerned with God? Is it with God "in himself," or God "for us"? When Thomas Aquinas defends the thesis that God "in himself" is the object of theology, whereas earlier theology on the whole had treated God from the point of view of his salvific action in history, this is not a real but only an apparent transformation of theology into metaphysics. For Thomas takes into service for the explanation of revelation the neo-Platonic schema of the evolutionary origin of the world from God and its eschatological return to God. Thus it does not contradict the structure of his thought if God is considered in theology from the point of view of his salvific action, especially if he is considered as the always present One who, out of the future, calls us to himself. In trying to investigate what God is "in himself," Thomas is driven by the desire to obtain a deeper knowledge of his salvific action. The absolute future to which God calls man can be grasped more profoundly, the more deeply we understand the nature of him who calls and of him who is being called. Thomas is concerned with truth "in itself" because he is concerned with the truth which is "for us"—i.e., insofar as it affects us existentially. Like Paul, he is driven by the question: Who is this summoning and saving God? His answer takes a different form from Paul's, but he remains ultimately concerned with "God for us." Other great theologians—e.g., Bonaventure or Duns Scotus—give their attention more directly to God's salvific action, though without omitting the metaphysical questions. Every effort of theology concerning God bears a Christological stamp, because it is in Christ that God shows himself, it is through him that he calls man into the absolute future. If we call God the "object" of theology (using scholastic terminology), we must not forget that it is he who is at work in the elements of faith which are constitutive for theology, and that he therefore does not really have the character of an object at all, but of a subject.

HUMAN EFFORT IN THEOLOGY

The unbeliever cannot devote himself to theology in the true sense of the word because he lacks the necessary inner relationship to his subject matter. Through the analysis of concepts he may indeed arrive at much knowledge which he will have in common with a believing theologian, and he may even surpass the believer in this sense. Owing to the proficiency of his methods, he may, from his investigations in the field of philology or history or philosophy, offer the theologian valuable assistance. But he lacks the faculty needed to receive the truth expressed in the formulas; his theology is only nominal, not real. Theological truth lies at a deeper level than natural research can penetrate. We may recall the example of a physicist presented with a melody. He may investigate and describe all the physical phenomena most minutely; but if he has no appreciation of music, he misses the real meaning of the work.

On the other hand it should be stressed most emphatically that theology must use every means and instrument of knowledge that may be helpful for the understanding of the faith, and with a properly developed methodology. Piety does not dispense us from the need for philosophy, philology, history, and natural science. The theologian must refuse no effort of the mind, he must be ready to explore all the possibilities open for a deeper understanding. Important and indispensable aid is also offered by the experience, prior to all scholarship, which man has of God, of his fellow-men, and of the world. Since all statements of faith refer to human existence, analysis of human existence, too, is a basic means of theological knowledge. We may expect that the success of theological effort will be the greater, the more closely the light of reason is wedded to the light of faith, the more lively the faith and the keener the mind, and this both in the field of the historical and of the speculative.

THEOLOGY AS ECCLESIAL SCIENCE

Since faith is only really possible in the Church, a true understanding of faith will have an ecclesial character. Theology is a science of the Church in a twofold sense. It grows out of the Church, and it reacts upon the Church. Theology is not a private enterprise of the theologian but a life utterance of the community of the Church. The Second Vatican Council has summoned all the members of the Church to engage in the task of theology (Pastoral Constitution on the Church in the Modern World). If not every individual but only a few can follow this call, they do their work as representatives of the others.

Furthermore, theology receives from the Church Sacred Scripture, together with the form of interpretation which it has received in official professions of faith, the decrees of the councils, the decisions of the magisterium and the day-to-day preaching of the Church. The Church thus represents the transcendental possibilty for theology. Within the Church the theologian also meets those great men who in the past devoted themselves to the explanation of revelation. He can profit from their methods and the results of their thinking, and so he need not start from the beginning. This would be a hopeless endeavor, considering the shortness of our lives. Continuity of theology of course does not mean that we need only to copy out and repeat what great theologians have said in the past. Such a procedure would result in a barren, sterile, and ineffective theology, untroubled by problems and estranged from life. It would miss the enduring youthfulness which Pius XII saw guaranteed in continuous return to the sources. The study and the acceptance of theological knowledge gained in the past must rather be done with critical differentiation. This is required by the fact that theology in every age must be developed within the horizon of the basic understanding of being prevailing at the time. Therefore, what was said in the past must be recast in contemporary ideas and thought-forms if its real content is to be made accessible. New questions are always appearing which must be answered. The presupposition of such a critical function of the theology of an age is that all our statements about the God who appeared in Christ are fragmentary. The connection of theology with the Church preserves the true theologian from a supercilious alienation from his brothers and sisters; he can only exist within the community of faith as a member with a special task.

The Second Vatican Council considers it of great importance that theological research shall be done in freedom. The Pastoral Constitution on the Church in the Modern World promises freedom in theological investigation—formally, to be sure—to the lay person who pursues the study of theology. But it is of the nature of theology that the freedom proclaimed by the council belongs to every theologian. The council declares that in the study of theology truthfulness, courage, wisdom, reverence, and love must work together. We must, of course, be aware of the fact that the freedom promised to the theologian by the council is not to be confused with arbitrariness. It is rather a responsibility bound to truth and love. It may have a great effect on the future of theology that the council states, in the constitution mentioned (#62):

It is to be hoped that many laymen will receive an appropriate formation in the sacred sciences, and that some will develop and deepen these studies by their own labors. In order that such persons may fulfill their proper function, let it be recognized that all the faithful, clerical and lay, possess a lawful freedom of inquiry and of thought, and the freedom to express their minds humbly and courageously about those matters in which they enjoy competence.

The acceptance of revelation from the Church—that is, out of the sense of faith of God's people—does not mean submitting to a bond without reason. Rather the bond is inherent in the structure of revelation and its proclamation and is demanded by the matter investigated as a condition for correct methodological procedure. Through its preservation, the fragmentation of theology into a multitude of different explanations and a chaos of doctrines is avoided. In the case of the first centuries, with their doctrinal councils, this bond with the teaching authority of the Church is acknowledged even by Protestant theology.

If, on the one hand, the Church makes theology possible, theology, on the other, stands in the service of the Church. It cannot, and it does not want to, replace proclamation. It is not part of the theologian's task to share in the official teaching authority of the Church. As a theologian he does not, cannot, and does not want to, preach. A theological lecture is not a sermon. A work of theology is not a collection of sermons. Yet the theologian performs an important service for the preaching of the Church by deepening and broadening the understanding of the faith to be preached. Both the Second Vatican Council and the Instruction of the Biblical Commission "On the Historical Truth of the Gospels" have emphasized this service. Thus theology in the sense of a scholarly understanding of the faith is the foundation for both the pastoral and the liturgical activity of the Church. Theological thinking and spirituality are not in opposition, but help and even presuppose each other. Thought and prayer belong together. One supports the other, if each fully comprehends its own nature: each stimulates and enlightens the other.

Although the teaching office in the Church has the final decision on truth and error in interpreting Sacred Scripture, the entire Church is always a listening Church. This listening also involves readiness to take the assured results of scholarly theology into the sphere of proclamation. In this way a relationship of mutual confidence and exchange develops between the holders of the teaching office in the Church and the body of theologians.

As the theologian is not concerned with asserting himself in the Church but with contributing to the life of faith in responsible service, he is also willing to have misinterpretations corrected by the ecclesiastical teaching office. He, in his turn, endeavors to offer products of his study which are not only interesting in themselves but worthy of acceptance by the Church. Even where he must leave a question open, he can offer attempts at a solution. In this procedure the theologian (like the holder of the preaching office in the Church) must work with what are called "theologoumena"— that is, with statements which do not formally express a truth of revelation proclaimed by the Church, but emerge from the over-all context of the truths of revelation and result from linking up the faith with the general understanding of reality which prevails at the time. The theologoumena express, therefore, the underlying unity of human experience, including the union of faith with the experience of the world, and the perspectives of the concrete historical and intellectual landscape within which the faith must live. It is important for the theologian that he should try to take fully into account the perspectives within which he makes his statements; thus he will be able to distinguish between what is really revealed and the manner of its integration into the unified whole of human awareness.

The ecclesial orientation which is so necessary for theology shows that it is not appropriate to distinguish a scholarly from a proclamation theology (*wissenschaftliche* and *Verkündigungstheologie*). All genuine theology is theology for proclamation and is itself, in a certain sense, proclamation.

THEOLOGY AS A SCIENCE

This problem did not exist before the Aristotelian concept of science became familiar to the Christian world. Until then theology was carried on in the Platonic and neo-Platonic spirit without reflecting at any length on this aspect of it. Theology was certainly defined even in earlier centuries as knowledge in faith, as *intellectus fidei*. But this insight into the faith was gained more in meditative than in discursive thinking, although the latter was never entirely lacking. In the West the attempt was made most decisively by Augustine, who brought the entire philosophy and culture of his time into confrontation with the Christian faith and evaluated it for the understanding of the faith. According to him knowledge is meant to penetrate through the transitory reality of this world to what is truly lasting. The knowledge of the transitory Augustine called science; the understanding of what is permanent and enduring he designated as wisdom. The goal of science is wisdom. Science is concerned with the history of salvation, wisdom with eternity. The knowledge of the historical Jesus leads to the vision of his everlasting, divine nature, according to Augustine. He thus understands theology, at its highest level, as a science concerned with the essence of things, but he never separates this from science concerned with facts. The striving after true knowledge will be the more successful, the more man is liberated from attachment to this world. From the eleventh century on, *ratio*—discursive thinking—came to occupy a more prominent place, as compared with *meditatio,* meditation. The *quaestio* is the typical expression of this theological procedure. It attained its climax in Thomas Aquinas. Its medium and its main impulse were Aristotelian philosophy.

(It was only in the thirteenth century that the question of the science-character of theology began to have existential importance. This resulted from the general adoption of the Aristotelian concept of science at the medieval universities. The theologians of the time, if they wanted to respond to the needs of their age, were compelled to demonstrate that theology was a science in the new—that is, in the Aristotelian—sense, and therefore that it was entitled to its place in the university. They carried out this task with varying degrees of success. What they achieved was of value chiefly for systematic theology. But even exegesis and history could be fitted into their concept of theology.)

The question, then, is whether or not theology is a science in the Aristotelian sense. According to Aristotle, knowledge is insight into a matter of fact gained by logical or discursive proof. The proof is obtained by drawing a conclusion from given premises as principles. Science is the totality of the knowledge gained by sound deduction and arranged in an ordered fashion, or else the activity involved in obtaining it. The premises, the basis of the knowledge, are taken over in every case from a higher science. Thus physics owes its principles to mathematics. In this way a hierarchy of sciences arises. The highest of them is philosophy, because it does not receive its principles from a higher discipline. Its principles are axioms, which cannot be proved and, because they are self-evident, do not need to be proved.

According to this concept of science, theology is a science insofar as it has principles from which new knowledge can be gained through deduction. Its principles are the articles of faith—that is, formally revealed truths which are of significance for faith and the life of faith, and which the Church teaches.[4] Here a great difficulty arises. The axioms of philosophy, while they cannot be proved, are self-evident; but the principles of theology can neither be proved nor be made evident, they can only be affirmed in faith. Thomas Aquinas tries to escape this antinomy by declaring that the insight which God provides and the insight of the saints are proof for the principles of theology. In revelation God offers men a share in that insight which belongs to his wisdom. We have this in the articles of faith. In faith man enters into communion with God and hence into participation in the divine knowledge. Faith as participation in the life of God is thus the vision with which the theologian perceives, not the evidence of revealed truth in itself, but its evidence as guaranteed by the divine insight. The knowledge of revelation which belongs to faith as truth seen and guaranteed by God is therefore based on confidence in God, with whom faith binds men, not in identity of existence, but in a vital union. Faith has its origin in the consciousness of the believer. Likewise theology begins in the consciousness of the theologian. Let us refer again to the statements made earlier regarding "Thou" faith. Theology is a science subject to God's own knowledge. If we pose the question whether the human mind does not succumb to self-deception when it is convinced that it can lay hold of God's own knowledge in faith, it is possible to give those answers which are offered by the *analysis fidei*. Also, fundamental theology, as the discipline which lays the foundation for the rest of theology, can demonstrate that the articles of faith are indeed principles for theology, not insofar as they are self-evident, but insofar as they can be shown to be guaranteed by God. In this way theology gains not direct but indirect insight into the validity of its premises.

Even if we agree with Thomas that the Aristotelian concept of science applies to theology, theology does not thereby become a mere science of conclusions. For regarded from that standpoint with which we have become familiar owing to Thomas, it can nevertheless fulfill its task only if it investigates the articles of faith in their differing historical development and form, and if it reveals by rational processes of thought how the individual elements of revelation are interconnected. But this task can only be fulfilled by the explication of what is implied in Sacred Scripture. Besides, a deduction from premises need not lead to new truths beyond the domain of revelation. It can lead, and with Thomas almost always does lead, to other truths of revelation. Thus the conclusions serve to reveal the unity of the individual truths with one another in the whole of revelation. It would certainly be a symptom of decline if the theologian wanted to derive from the articles of faith, by a purely abstract and logical deduction, all kinds of results, however remote they might be from the faith. This game, foreign to true theology, was played by some theologians during the era of late scholasticism in the fourteenth and fifteenth centuries. The conception of theology developed by Thomas, with all its conclusions, remains in the sphere of faith. It is concrete and realistic, always centering on sacred doctrine. Therefore, in principle, exegesis and history also belong in it, although they may have remained underdeveloped in the Middle Ages.

Against the application to theology of the Aristotelian concept of science, it would be possible to raise the objection that a presupposition is made in theology which cannot strictly be tested, and that therefore the entire theological procedure is unscientific. But the reply to this is that every science has its presuppositions, a science without presuppositions is simply impossible. To preserve the character of science in spite of the presuppositions, which are unavoidable, what is principally necessary is that the scholar should reflect on his presuppositions and keep them constantly in mind; he must not introduce them into the inner movement of his thought to make up for knowledge which is lacking. Theology approaches its task in a strictly methodical procedure which is not formally different from that of the philologist, the historian, or the philosopher. The difference lies in the fact that the theologian regards the historical, philological, and philosophical results which he obtains in his studies as instruments for grasping the divine reality present in and shining through them.

Today, however, we must view theology from the standpoint of the modern concept of science. That theology can be called a science if it is understood in the sense of history of religion is obvious enough to need no further discussion. But theology in its intention is more than scientific study of religion or philology. The question is whether we can speak of theology as the science of faith if we understand the word "science" in its modern sense. If only one method is allowed to be valid for science—for example, the method of the natural sciences—then it must be denied that theology is a science. However, this would be to set up a methodological dictatorship, which would be quite unfair to the plurality and variety of the sciences. Just as there are different sciences, so there are different methods: in each case the method is determined by the object under investigation.

At the present time it seems as if a rapproachement is taking place between the natural sciences and the others; e.g., the social sciences and the humanities approach each other in the process of understanding reality so that within the plurality a unity seems to be growing. Nevertheless there remains a great difference between the individual sciences.

If we understand by theology the methodical investigation of a significant phenomenon, and if we take into account the fact that the results are capable of general communication, then theology is a science, and in all its branches.

The fact that the theologian is personally involved in his science by reason of his faith does not injure its scientific character but guarantees it. For faith brings the subject matter of his science into focus and produces in him that ethos which leads him to use his intellectual powers to the utmost, and to apply all appropriate methods, in the investigation of his subject. The information which theology is able to give to the public is of the greatest significance, not only because Christianity is a widespread phenomenon in the world and determines the way of life of many people, but because it is the task of theology to give an answer to the most fundamental questions of human life, and it is these questions, and the answers given to them, which will largely decide how man shapes his future in the matters that affect him most closely.

The way in which man shapes his future is determined not by metaphysical super-subtleties but by the course of historical developments, which is to say that it depends very considerably on the relationships that exist between people. To treat of theology in this connection presupposes, to be sure, that theology is not simply concerned with the unchangeable and ahistorical essence of things, but above all with the absolute future of man proclaimed by the Church. In this case theology is capable of making a decisive contribution to man's understanding of himself (J. Metz).

There are two methods in particular by which theology endeavors to carry out its task. They are usually called the positive method and the speculative. Although they are of use primarily in systematic theology, they also apply to the nonsystematic branches with suitable variations, because theology is the science of faith in all its departments. Thus, for example, biblical exegesis, which analyzes the meaning of texts of Scripture, is never merely philology or history. In all its philological endeavors it is concerned with understanding the reality expressed in the words. The positive method corresponds to the *auditus fidei,* the speculative method corresponds to the *intellectus fidei.* The positive method consists in establishing historically the fact of revelation and its direct content. The speculative method consists in the intellectual penetration and more explicit comprehension of revelation. The two methods cannot be separated, but require one another. For God promised himself to men in a definitive and irrevocable way in a unique historical event, namely in Jesus Christ. And this divine gift of himself was definitively accepted by the man Jesus. The first question therefore concerns the existence, the life, the actions, the words of Jesus Christ. But then the question must also be posed: Who is the God who has revealed himself in Jesus Christ, and what is he like? The question of the nature of things is thus indispensable for the understanding of the historical phenomenon of Christ. The Christ-event, however, needs to be established by means of philology and history. Otherwise the question of the nature of things would not even arise. In investigating the Christ-event the questions of the fact and of its nature are closely intertwined. Yet we must say that while the question of its nature is contained in the question of the fact—that is, ontology is included in history—the reverse is not the case.

We can distinguish both questions, and put the stress sometimes on the one and sometimes on the other. Since in theology it is always a matter of the interpretation of the answer of faith to the divine self-revelation, the positive method works best if it starts with the belief and preaching of the Church of its time, and goes back from there, in a longitudinal section, as it were, through the various levels of faith to the beginning. Using this procedure, its task is to unveil the continuity between the original form and the present form. In order to do justice to this comprehensive and difficult task it must also make cross-sections through the changing forms which the faith took on at various periods in the course of its development. If it did not do this, it would run the risk of losing sight of the totality of the faith in favor of this or that particular element which happens to predominate at the moment. Through returning to the original form of the faith, theology contributes to the understanding of its present form. To fulfill this task it employs philology and history: history of culture, of religion, and of philosophy, archaeology, and the auxiliary disciplines of these fields. The complete fulfillment of this task requires such comprehensive knowledge in so many fields that an individual theologian cannot hope to accomplish it. The positive task of theology, therefore, demands the cooperation of many people who communicate the results of their research to each other, assist each other, and in that manner serve together the progress of theology. This work is furthered by theological journals, societies, symposia, libraries, institutes, and universities.

As regards the question concerning the nature of things, implicit in the historical events, the principal tools for gaining some light are philosophy and human experience. Without these two aids man would be blind to the true reality of what has happened in history. He would have to content himself with describing events and would be unable to penetrate to an understanding of them. Theology would be no more than phenomenology. Without philosophy, then, there can be no theology, just as there would be no theology if there were no history. The difficult problem arises here of what we are to understand by "philosophy." There are many and various types of philosophy, and the theologian must give full consideration to the question of what meaning he is going to give the term if the thing itself is really to be of assistance to him.

In this connection it should not be overlooked that even in the writings of the Old Testament there is a definite philosophical, even metaphysical, way of thinking to be found, not the ontological philosophy of Plato and Aristotle but an intersubjective understanding of reality, and it is within just such a horizon that history lies intellectually. Thus Christian proclamation, when it moved out into the Hellenistic world, did not encounter philosophy for the first time, but only a different and foreign philosophy (Claude Tresmontant).

In the history of theology it has been chiefly the philosophies of Plato and Aristotle which have been of assistance, at times the Platonic, at other times the Aristotelian. From the thirteenth century on, the latter was more influential than the former. Both philosophies have their advantages and their shortcomings. The philosophies of Plato and Plotinus, because of the sharp distinction they make between the world of ideas, which is true being, and the world of reality, which is a world of shadows, strongly emphasize God's transcendence. But this kind of thinking contains the risk that created being may come to lose its own separate reality and value, that God may be regarded not only as the being who most truly exists but as the only reality. A theology which is strongly influenced by Platonic philosophy has constantly to struggle against a pantheistic tendency to merge God and his creation and is liable to lose sight of the distinction between the natural and the supernatural.

Aristotelian philosophy offers clear and concise concepts to theology. Since it affirms the reality and value of the world of our experience, it is of great assistance to theology in maintaining the distinction between God and his creatures and between the natural and the supernatural. Its danger is rationalism. In the subsequent course of western history the concept of the world as a reality in its own right—legitimately stressed by Aristotle and, following him, by Thomas Aquinas—was developed to an extreme in the secularized philosophy of Karl Marx, while the pantheistic tendencies of neo-Platonic thought found a late and impressive expression in Hegel.

Contemporary philosophical trends can be of assistance to theology in many respects. The philosophy of existence can further the effort of theology to understand and to formulate God's revelation of himself in terms of its inner reference to man. Other philosophies can assist theology in various ways to appreciate and clarify the truth concerning the absolute future promised by God to men. These modern philosophies can thus help faith to reveal its own inner meaningfulness and dynamism. They do not add to the content of revelation, but they have the effect of unsealing and making available the riches it possesses. Of course it is possible to use any philosophy in a way that contradicts, and so perverts, theology.

Since the thought-forms of Platonic and Aristotelian philosophy have become largely unintelligible at the present time, while more existential thought-forms and expressions, for example, are intelligible and find ready acceptance, theology would be guilty of a serious omission if it simply passed over contemporary philosophy or took up a merely defensive attitude to it. Quite apart from any considerations of expediency, contemporary philosophy can, for one thing, assist theology to regain what, through the adoption of the ontological thought-forms of Greek philosophy, it lost sight of for so long—namely, the structures of the historical and the social (for example, the "I—Thou" category), which are so characteristic of the Old and New Testaments.

The modern era has frequently had to assert the concepts of

freedom, of the autonomy and secularity of the world, of history, and of intersubjectivity in the face of hostility from Christian theology, but in one of the many enigmatic twists of history this emphasis has served to make explicit values which belong to the heart of theology but which were lost to view for centuries, even if never entirely abandoned, through the dominance of Greek metaphysics. Augustine, Thomas, Bonaventure, Scotus, and many others were able to introduce, within the Greek horizon of their thought, biblical thought-forms, especially from the Old Testament. It is only at the present time, however, that these thought-forms are regaining the place due to them. The categories which have become and are becoming dominant in contemporary thought are native to the Bible, especially the Old Testament. On the other hand—to its own surprise as well as that of the nontheological world—theology is finding in contemporary thought-forms the explication of its own inmost being. Through the stimulus of intellectual movements which were and are hostile to it, it has been enabled to reach a deeper understanding of itself, and that not in a marginal way but at its vital center.

If theology today views the world as centered on man, and on the basis of this conviction has oriented itself fundamentally towards the future, so that it can be characterized as a "creative and militant eschatology" (J. Metz), this is evidence of a way of thinking which is common to both theology and much of philosophy, despite many differences in their particular convictions, and which may eventually serve as the point of departure for a dialogue regarding these convictions. This hope seems all the more justified in that much of contemporary philosophy has succumbed to scepticism and an aversion to metaphysics; the way out may indeed lead to atheism and nihilism, but it may equally lead to faith (H. R. Schlette, J. Metz). Ultimately every philosophy which has an understanding of its own truth opens the way of transcendence for the human mind towards the Absolute (K. Rahner).

Furthermore, the religious philosophies of the Far East are capable of fertilizing theology. If we fear that they might become dangerous to Christianity because of their pantheistic inclinations, let us remember that the situation of theology was no different in the thirteenth century, in the face of Aristotelian thought, or even in the fourteenth century. As the prohibitions issued against Aristotelian philosophy and theology by two bishops in 1277 show, the anxiety to keep the ancient faith pure in the face of Aristotelianism was considerable. It was not unfounded. Even Aristotle had first to be freed from the embrace of pantheism, so to speak, before he was fit to be an instrument for the explanation of revelation.

If we consider the abundance of its material and the immensity of its tasks, the question arises of the arrangement or structure which theology must adopt if it is not to become totally unmanageable. It would be possible to maintain that all the statements of theology should be grouped with reference to Christ. In this way it could establish a fixed center for itself. However, if it were content with this, without any further differentiation, it would run the risk of becoming static.

The centering of theology upon Christology must be linked with an evolutionary viewpoint. We do not need to add this viewpoint onto Christology from the outside; rather, it develops naturally out of the heart of Christology itself. For our understanding of the Christ-event hinges on his relationship to the past that preceded and prepared for him, and to the future which will bring his work to completion. The structural principle of theology must therefore consist in a Christological-eschatological view. In this case theology will be seen to be not a science concerned with supernatural essences but a science of the way; that is, a science concerning the way and a science itself still on the way—the way which is Christ—towards the future, which is God (1 Cor. 15,2).

UNITY AND STRUCTURE OF THEOLOGY

In spite of the variety of its statements theology is a unified discipline. In the Church of antiquity there was only one theological discipline, "Sacred Doctrine." In the Middle Ages a distinction was made between theology as biblical science and speculative or systematic theology. Precedence was given to the former. A further discipline was added by the fact that in the twelfth century Canon Law was separated as a science from Civil Law. At the time of the Reformation, with the development of philology and history as sciences, historical theology arose. It was out of this that the method of historical criticism was developed for the investigation of Scripture. Only with this did biblical exegesis become a science. At the same time polemical theology took shape in the struggles of the Reformation. During the period of the Enlightenment in the eighteenth century this developed into Apologetics, and in the nineteenth century into Fundamental Theology. The practical disciplines, those which make up Pastoral Theology, came into being in the eighteenth century as the result of the growing differentiation of the problems facing the Church. The unity of theology despite the variety of its disciplines is guaranteed by the fact that in all its forms it is the statement, explanation, presentation, and systematization of the word of God.

For the practical purpose of carrying on theology it has become customary to divide it into three groups of disciplines. The division is not entirely justified on the basis of subject matter. It is based more on language than on difference in content. According to this accepted usage, a distinction is made between the historical, systematic, and practical groups. Each of them is connected with each of the others. No one group can exist without the others. But it is possible to distinguish the groups from one another insofar as each one views revelation from a different aspect. The historical disciplines are divided further into Biblical Science and Church History. The former investigates the origin of the Canon (Biblical Introduction) and explains the text of the individual books of the Bible (Exegesis). The presentation of the doctrinal contents of Scripture is done in Biblical Theology or theologies. The worker in this field must know the languages in which the Scriptures were written and also their neighboring languages, since the milieu in which the Bible was written must be investigated. Church History is the study of the effect on the world of God's communication of himself in Christ.

The systematic group comprises Dogmatic Theology, Moral Theology, Ascetical and Mystical Theology, Christian Social Teaching, and Ecumenical Theology.

The third group includes Liturgy, Canon Law, Pastoral Theology in the strict sense, Homiletics, Catechetics, and Missionology.

Fundamental Theology (Apologetics) occupies a position introductory to the three groups. It has the task of demonstrating the credibility of the fact of revelation, and thereby of showing that faith in it is reasonable. Christian philosophy as a discipline is closely related to this.

The Second Vatican Council issued the following decree for the organization of theological studies in ecclesiastical educational institutions (Decree on Priestly Formation, #16):

Under the light of faith and with the guidance of the Church's teaching authority, theology should be taught in such a way that students will accurately draw Catholic doctrine from divine revelation, understand that doctrine profoundly, nourish their own spiritual lives with it, and be able to proclaim it, unfold it, and defend it in their priestly ministry.

In the study of sacred Scripture, which ought to be the soul of all theology, students should be trained with special diligence. After a suitable introduction to it, they should be accurately initiated into exegetical method, grasp the pre-eminent themes of divine revelation, and take inspiration and nourishment from reading and meditating on the sacred books day by day.

Dogmatic theology should be so arranged that the biblical themes are presented first. Students should be shown what the Fathers of the Eastern and Western Church contributed to the fruitful transmission and illumination of the individual truths of revelation, and also the later history of dogma and its relationship to the general history of the Church. Then, by way of making the mysteries of salvation known as thoroughly as they can be, students should learn to penetrate them more deeply with the help of speculative reason exercised under the tutelage of St. Thomas. Students should learn too how these mysteries are interconnected, and be taught to recognize their presence and activity in liturgical actions and in the whole life of the Church. Let them learn to search for solutions to human problems with the light of revelation, to apply eternal truths to the changing conditions of human affairs, and to communicate such truths in a manner suited to contemporary man.

Other theological disciplines should also be renewed by livelier contact with the mystery of Christ and the history of salvation. Special attention needs to be given to the development of moral theology. Its scientific exposition should be more thoroughly nourished by scriptural teaching. It should show the nobility of the Christian vocation of the faithful, and their obligation to bring forth fruit in charity for the life of the world. Again, in the explanation of canon law and Church history, the mystery of the Church should be kept in mind, as it was set forth in the Dogmatic Constitution on the Church, promulgated by this holy Synod. Sacred liturgy, which must be regarded as the primary and indispensable source of a truly Christian spirit, should be taught according to the prescriptions of Articles 15 and 16 of the Constitution on the Sacred Liturgy.

According to an opportune evaluation of the conditions of various regions, students should be led to a more adequate understanding of the Churches and ecclesial Communities separated from the Roman, Apostolic See. Thus the students can contribute to the restoration of unity among all Christians according to the directives of this sacred Synod.

They should also be introduced to a knowledge of the other religions which are more widely spread through individual areas. In this way, they can better understand the elements of goodness and truth which such religions possess by God's Providence, and will learn how to disprove the errors in them, and to share the full light of truth with those who lack it.

Notes

[1] In Joan. Tract 29, N. 6.
[2] Denz., 3016.
[3] *Loc. cit.*
[4] Denz., 3011.

◄ 14

Dogmatic Theology

ITS OBJECT: DOGMA AND CATHOLIC TRUTHS

The term "dogmatic theology" is found first in the seventeenth century, among the Lutherans, and later among the Catholics. The thing meant by the term, however, originated towards the end of the second century in the theology of Alexandria. We can call it the science of dogma if we understand by dogma the whole faith of the Church, and not only the truths of revelation formally defined as individual dogmas. It has the task of explaining the meaning of revelation, insofar as this has been given to man both in the form of doctrine and in a series of salvific events. The interpretation of the formally defined dogmas of the Church has, however, a special significance in this. Insofar as the function of dogmatic theology consists in interpretation, it has a twofold task. First, it has to explain the individual dogmas of the Church and of the whole Christian faith in such a way as to show their meaningfulness. For this purpose it has to investigate their historical development, since a dogma can only be explained as the result of an intellectual struggle for the faith in which certain elements were able to assert themselves successfully and others not. Secondly, once it has arrived at an understanding of the dogma it must translate it into a language intelligible to its own age.

In carrying out these tasks dogmatic theology has to avoid two extremes: on the one hand, that of interpreting dogma simply in its existential significance for man; on the other, that of focusing exclusively on the truth expressed. Both the truth expressed in the dogma and its salvific meaning for man must be brought out. Without doctrine, the existential element has no basis. Without its existential significance doctrine is sterile.

Within the sphere of the things dogmatic theology treats of lie what are called "Catholic truths." This is a technical term which is understood differently by different theologians. For the sake of completeness the problem involved must be mentioned here, if only briefly. We can distinguish between a stricter and a broader sense of the term. In the broader sense we can count among the "Catholic truths" the whole of revelation, whether this is taught by the Church in solemn decrees or in the course of its ordinary preaching. In the stricter sense the term refers to doctrines which the Church teaches infallibly but which cannot be considered to have been formally revealed: for example, truths of reason which are so closely linked with truths of revelation that to deny them would be to endanger revelation. A case in point would be the Church's rejection of total scepticism. Catholic truth understood in this sense is closely related to the phenomenon we have described above as a "theologoumenon."

Some theologians include among the "Catholic truths" what are called "dogmatic facts" (*facta dogmatica*). These again are divided into two groups. A dogmatic fact in the wider sense is a historical fact which has not been revealed but which is a necessary presupposition for the proclamation and defense of revelation—e.g., the validity of a papal election or of the convocation of a general council.

In the narrower sense the term refers to the Church's statements as to the meaning of writings it condemns. Most theologians consider that the Church is entitled not only to pass judgment on a particular writing concerning faith or morals—that is, to say whether it is correct or incorrect—but also to say what the objective meaning of the text itself is, in order to pass judgment on it. The fact that the Church states: This sentence means such-and-such (this is the dogmatic fact) does not say anything about the meaning the writer *intended* to convey, but only what he does actually convey.

The Church in this case simply points out the meaning which an ordinary reader would take from the text, one which might have an injurious effect on the faith of the community. Thus when the Church rejected certain sentences taken from the works of Meister Eckhardt, there was no question of condemning his own personal belief or attitude, but only the meaning which the sentences had "according to the words themselves." The problem connected with dogmatic facts in this sense did not receive explicit treatment until the Jansenist controversy (1653): the question arose whether Jansenius's work *Augustinus* could be condemned by the Church for its doctrinal content only, or also as representing the true mind of Jansenius. Here for the first time the idea was put forward that such judgments of the Church regarding "dogmatic facts" were binding only in "ecclesiastical faith," not in "divine faith."

ITS CONNECTION WITH OTHER THEOLOGICAL DISCIPLINES

The statements made earlier about theology in general all apply to dogmatic theology too. However, dogmatic theology represents its own type of theological science. Its significance derives from the importance which a correct understanding of the faith has for the Church. Whereas formerly it considered itself the center of the theological enterprise, and sometimes exercised a sort of censorship over the other branches of theology, more recently, as a result of general developments in theology and of the statements of the Second Vatican Council, it has come to see more clearly that it occupies one position within a totality.

In particular it has a close connection with biblical theology, and this not simply in the sense that biblical theology supplies proof texts for the theses which dogmatic theology has already formulated from its own tradition. Biblical theology is, on the contrary, the foundation on which dogmatic theology must be built. Calling the study of Sacred Scripture the "soul of all theology," the Second Vatican Council declares in the Decree on Priestly Formation (#16) that the teaching of dogmatic theology "should be so arranged that the biblical themes are presented first." The Dogmatic Constitution on Divine Revelation (#21) states:

The Church has always venerated the divine Scriptures just as she venerates the body of the Lord, since from the table of both the word of God and of the body of Christ she unceasingly receives and offers to the faithful the bread of life, especially in the sacred liturgy. She has always regarded the Scriptures together with sacred tradition as the supreme rule of faith, and will ever do so. For, inspired by God and committed once and for all to writing, they impart the word of God Himself without change, and make the voice of the Holy Spirit resound in the words of the prophets and apostles. Therefore, like the Christian religion itself, all the preaching of the Church must be nourished and ruled by sacred Scripture. For in the sacred books, the Father who is in heaven meets His children with great love and speaks with them; and the force and power in the word of God is so great that it remains the support and energy of the Church, the strength of faith for her sons, the food of the soul, the pure and perennial source of spiritual life.

Dogmatic theology must therefore return again and again to biblical theology, which is its source, if it is not to become sterile (Pius XII). It derives from Scripture and is bound to Scripture. On the other hand it is not required simply to take over the results of biblical theology blindly. It has a right and duty to subject these to critical and scientific judgment. This is all the more legitimate because, like the Old Testament, the texts of the New Testament are frequently capable of a variety of interpretations. Dogmatic theology can show which of these opens the way for the dogma of the Church.

Dogmatic theology goes beyond biblical theology, insofar as it deals with the development, through the preaching and teaching of the Church down through the centuries, of the revelation embodied in Scripture and interpreted by biblical theology. It is from the Church, which constitutes the proximate norm of faith (*regula proxima fidei*), that it receives the faith which it has to interpret. It has a special duty, then, to begin with what is at present being preached in the Church, and with the appropriate scientific methods trace the way back to the original form of the faith as found in Scripture, showing the continuity of the development. It is essentially therefore a science of tradition.

In doing this it must not restrict itself simply to describing phenomenologically changes which have taken place in forms of thought and expression. It has to show the agreement of the later with the earlier. And here the danger arises of wanting to prove more than can be proven. Therefore the dogmatic theologian must continually ask himself whether, through habits of thought or through the justified a priori conviction that the dogmas of the Church do have a basis in Scripture, he is not perhaps allowing himself to be misled into reading more into the texts than they can bear. In view of the difficulties of the situation, caution is to be recommended, such as that shown by L. Scheffczyk when he maintains on the one hand the living continuity between dogma and Scripture, but on the other hand endeavors to explain this in terms of "points of departure" (*Ansätze*) which Scripture offers for dogma. He states that dogmatic theology has the task of comparing the points of departure which Scripture offers with the developed dogma, in such a way as to show the possibility of a legitimate development of the one from the other. The points of departure, he says, can only be recognized as such if they are sought, not in individual passages, but in the total context of Scripture. As an example he gives Christology: one ought not to look to individual passages to provide a biblical proof for the divinity of Christ. All the Christological statements of the New Testament must be taken into account, for example the titles applied to Jesus, such as prophet, servant of God, Messiah, Son of Man, and *Kyrios*. If we look at all of these together, he says, we will see the development of a climax, pointing to a belief that Christ possesses a position of extraordinary closeness to God. Later, when the question of Christological heresies arose, this could be formally defined by the Church as the divinity of Christ. Scheffczyk rightly points out that the path of the development from Scripture to dogma must correspond to the path traced back from the dogma to its original form in Scripture.

It is, however, a serious question whether dogmatic theology should follow this direction not only in carrying out its research but also in presenting the results of the research. It seems reasonable to hold that it is more in keeping with the course of history, and with people's readiness to listen, if we begin with the beginnings of faith and show its development into its present form. If the theologian elects to do this, he will have to keep before his eyes, in the process, the present form of the Church's faith, since this is the goal to which he must direct his steps.

It is difficult to draw a sharp line between dogmatic and moral theology. It was not until the seventeenth century that a distinction was made and moral theology set up as a science in its own right. It is not as if dogmatic theology were concerned only with theoretical truths, and moral theology with the practical ones. Such a division is contrary to Scripture and impossible to carry out. In the epistles of St. Paul indicatives and imperatives are so interwoven that they both carry one another. It is precisely the task of dogmatic theology to show the salvific dynamism of revelation and its significance for life; yet moral theology must point out the basis in the Christan faith of the norms for living that it is concerned with. It is to be expected, then, that dogmatic and moral theology will overlap to a considerable extent. They are concerned with basically the same material, but they develop it in different directions. Dogmatic theology presents revelation from the point of view of its finalization in the absolute future. Moral theology endeavors to point out the values and norms for human living which arise from union with Christ and the community of the Church, and this not only in terms of general principles but also of the particular prescriptions demanded by the circumstances of the time.

ITS IMPORTANCE

Since dogmatic theology treats of the whole of divine revelation, even insofar as this has not yet become part of the conscious and explicit faith of the Church, and since the analyses which it offers serve to develop further the knowledge of revelation, it thus provides the whole Church with a deeper and more comprehensive understanding of revelation. In this way it serves the Church's preaching and prepares the way for official statements on doctrine.

ITS METHODS

In doing all this dogmatic theology has to make use of both the historical and the speculative methods which apply to theology as a whole, and it must use them with constant reference to the existential (*existential* and *existentiell*) significance of what is being said. This does not need further treatment here. But something must be said briefly about what is called the "history of dogma" (*Dogmengeschichte*). If it is a special task of dogmatic theology to investigate the continuity in discontinuity of the Church's preaching, insofar as later generations have believed, not something different, but the same thing in a different way from earlier ones, then the history of dogma is not a separate theological discipline alongside dogmatic theology but a constitutive element of it. Only for the sake of practical expediency in carrying out the work can it be separated from systematic theology and established as a discipline in its own right. In point of fact dogmatic theology as a systematic discipline also has constitutive force for the study of the history of dogma, since otherwise this would become merely a collection of facts. In investigating the historical development of the faith, dogmatic theology also has to point out the factors which influenced the various stages of its formulation—the linguistic peculiarities, the philosophical currents, the political divisions of power, the psychological limitations, the economic interests, the characteristics of the ethnological groups involved, and so on—in order to be able to distinguish more clearly between the forms of expression conditioned by the times and the unique and enduring revelation given by God.

ITS CRITICAL AND PROPHETIC
FUNCTION

In the field of its critical investigations dogmatic theology can also include so-called private revelations, not insofar as these may have brought new revelations, but insofar as they have on occasion had great influence on the manner in which elements implicit in the Christ-event were made explicit—for example, in deciding what received emphasis and what did not, or from what perspective the matter was viewed. The devotion to the Sacred Heart and some forms of devotion to Mary are outstanding examples. By its investigations of these, dogmatic theology can help ensure that a due balance is preserved in the totality of revelation by preventing an overemphasis on what is unimportant and a neglect of what is important. Furthermore, it has the duty of distinguishing the Christian faith from pious opinions, and of detecting any superstitious elements which may be introduced under the guise of genuine faith. In this connection it will have to avoid giving offense where it can be avoided, but it will not be afraid to create disturbance where it is called for. The Church herself has given an example at the present time of the fact that statements must be made which, in the context of long-established habits of devotion, could be "offensive to pious ears." Christ himself did not avoid such statements. The critical function of dogmatic theology will make a contribution to the salvation of our brothers and to a right form of living in the Church if it is exercised not out of a destructive joy at fault-finding, but out of concern and love for all those who are affected by God's revelation.

Dogmatic theology ought also to endeavor to make some estimate of the trends of the time, on the basis of its own scientific and theological viewpoint, so as to be able to pass judgment on whether or not they are compatible with the faith. And in this connection it must also ask itself to what extent a new attitude towards life, a new social milieu, or a new psychological situation which may be arising may require a new understanding of the faith. Its bond to tradition does not condemn it to sterility but provides it, so to speak, with a rearguard, so that it can advance with courage and openness on the path into the future.

From these considerations we see that dogmatic theology has a threefold function. It has a receptive or analytical character, insofar as it takes the faith which is the object of its endeavors from the Church and shows the continuity of that faith. It has an active or synthetic character in that it deepens and broadens the understanding of the faith which it has received from the Church, and so stands in the service of the kerygma. It has a prophetic or eschatological character, insofar as it has the task of passing judgment on the intellectual, cultural, and religious movements of its time in the light of the absolute future for which man is destined.

THE DOGMATIC SYSTEM

In carrying out its work dogmatic theology will necessarily attempt to construct a system. But because it must create a synthesis of essential and existential truth, it can never succeed in achieving a system along the lines of a philosophical system. It is true of theology as a whole, and it is true of dogmatic theology, that it can only aim at creating an understanding of the faith which will remain open as a totality, and it will achieve this insofar as it develops a basic and comprehensive viewpoint in the light of which it can make all its statements. As we have seen, this is to be found in the Christological-eschatological viewpoint.

Dogmatic theology will never complete its task. It will always have to begin again from the beginning. But though his task will always and essentially be incapable of fulfillment, the theologian has no need to adopt an attitude of passive resignation. What remains necessarily incomplete within the course of history will find completion when Christ returns in glory. Until then let us take to heart the words of the Second Vatican Council (Dogmatic Constitution on Divine Revelation, #26):

In this way, therefore, through the reading and study of the sacred books, let "the word of the Lord run and be glorified" (2 Th. 3:1) and let the treasure of revelation entrusted to the Church increasingly fill the hearts of men. Just as the life of the Church grows through persistent participation in the Eucharistic mystery, so we may hope for a new surge of spiritual vitality from intensified veneration for God's word, which "lasts forever" (Is.40:8; cf.1 Pet.1:23–25).

Bibliography

Theology

Barr, James. "Revelation through History in the Old Testament and in Modern Theology" in *New Theology No. 1,* edited by Martin E. Marty and Dean G. Peerman. New York, Macmillan, 1964. Pp. 60–74.

Bulst, Werner. *Revelation.* Translated by Bruce Vawter. New York, Sheed and Ward, 1965.

Burke, Patrick (ed.). *The Word in History.* New York, Sheed and Ward, 1966.

Chenu, M. D. *Is Theology a Science?* Translated by A. H. N. Green-Armytage. New York, Hawthorn Books, 1962.

Congar, Yves. *The Meaning of Tradition.* Translated by A. N. Woodrow. New York, Hawthorn Books, 1964.

———— *Power and Poverty in the Church.* Baltimore, Helicon, 1965.

———— *Tradition and Traditions in the Church.* New York, Macmillan, 1966.

Cullmann, Oscar. *Christ and Time.* Translated by Floyd Filson. Philadelphia, Westminster, 1950.

de Lubac, Henri. *The Discovery of God.* Translated by Alexander Dru. New York, P. J. Kenedy and Sons, 1960.

———— *The Drama of Atheist Humanism.* New York, Sheed and Ward, 1965.

Geiselmann, J. R. *The Meaning of Tradition.* New York, Herder and Herder, 1967.

Küng, Hans. *The Church*. New York, Sheed and Ward, 1968.

Latourelle, René. *Theology of Revelation*. New York, Alba, 1966.

Lepp, Ignace. *Atheism in Our Time*. New York, Macmillan, 1963.

Levie, G. *The Bible, Word of God in Words of Men*. Translated by
S. H. Treman. New York, P. J. Kenedy and Sons, 1961.

Moran, Gabriel. *Theology of Revelation*. New York, Herder and
Herder, 1966.

Rahner, Karl.   "The Prospects for Dogmatic Theology";
              "A Scheme for a Treatise of Dogmatic Theology";
              "The Development of Dogma";
              "Concerning the Relationship Between Nature and
                Grace";
              "Some Implications of the Scholastic Concept of Un-
                created Grace";
              in *Theological Investigations*, I. Baltimore, Helicon,
                1961.

————————   "Considerations on the Development of Dogma";
              "Nature and Grace";
              "Theological Principles Concerning the Hermeneutics
                of Eschatological Statements";
              in *Theological Investigations*, IV. Baltimore, Helicon,
                1967.

————————   "Thoughts on the Possibility of Belief Today";
              "What is a Dogmatic Statement?";
              "History of the World and Salvation-History";
              "Christianity and Non-Christian Religions";
              "Christianity and the 'New Man' ";
              "Christology Within an Evolutionary View of the
                World";
              in *Theological Investigations*, V. Baltimore, Helicon,
                1966.

———— *Inspiration in the Bible*. Translated by Charles Henkey. New
York, Herder and Herder, 1961.

Urs von Balthasar, Hans. *A Theological Anthropology*. New York,
Sheed and Ward, 1967.

———— *Word and Redemption*. Translated by A. V. Littledale with
Alexander Dru. New York, Herder and Herder, 1965.

———— *Word and Revelation*. Translated by A. V. Littledale with

Scripture

Alexander Dru. New York, Herder and Herder, 1964.

Eissfeldt, Otto. *The Old Testament: An Introduction.* New York, Harper, 1965.

Wikenhauser, A. *Introduction to the New Testament.* New York, Herder and Herder, 1958.

Index